ALGORITHMIC DESIRE

Series Editors

Slavoj Žižek

Adrian Johnston

Todd McGowan

diaeresis

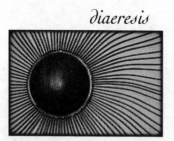

ALGORITHMIC DESIRE

Toward a New Structuralist Theory of Social Media

Matthew Flisfeder

Northwestern University Press
Evanston, Illinois

Northwestern University Press
www.nupress.northwestern.edu

Printed in the United States of America

10　9　8　7　6　5　4　3　2　1

Library of Congress Cataloging-in-Publication Data

Names: Flisfeder, Matthew, 1980– author.
Title: Algorithmic desire : toward a new structuralist theory of social
　media / Matthew Flisfeder.
Other titles: Diaeresis.
Description: Evanston, Illinois : Northwestern University Press, 2021. | Series:
　Diaeresis | Includes index.
Identifiers: LCCN 2020040286 | ISBN 9780810143333 (paperback) |
　ISBN 9780810143340 (cloth) | ISBN 9780810143357 (ebook)
Subjects: LCSH: Social media—Philosophy. | Online social networks—
　Philosophy. | Capitalism and mass media. | Structuralism.
Classification: LCC HM742 .F56 2021 | DDC 302.23/1 2 23—dc23
LC record available at https://lccn.loc.gov/2020040286

For Robyn—

The algorithm of *my* desire

The first thing that power imposes is a rhythm.
   —Roland Barthes

Everything moves to the rhythm of one and the same desire.
   —Gilles Deleuze and Félix Guattari

We're all chained to the rhythm.
   —Katy Perry

Contents

Acknowledgments

Mark Fisher writes, at the end of "Exiting the Vampire Castle," that "we need to learn, or re-learn how to build comradeship and solidarity instead of doing capital's work for it by condemning and abusing each other. . . . We need to think strategically about how to use social media." I have been very lucky to have built strong bonds, friendships, and a feeling of comradery with many fellow travellers who have inspired me, and who have generously supported my work in recent years. I have maintained correspondence with many of my friends, have debated, and have been able to use social media to better develop the emancipatory goals that I hope to have expressed in this book. Just as the working class develops a proletarian class consciousness on the shop floor, in the spaces controlled by the ruling class, so too can we produce an allied emancipatory consciousness in digital spaces that might otherwise aspire toward our "digitization," that is, our separation and our individualization. We can and must use digital spaces to fight this kind of digitization, and build a collective agency that makes our media social—as I say in the conclusion of this book, we must accelerate the social media metaphor.

First off, I want to thank the LACK community for their ongoing support, friendship, and collaboration. Sheila Kunkle, thank you for enhancing this book by reading the earlier draft of chapter 6 and giving me very helpful comments and feedback. Clint Burnham and Louis-Paul Willis, the other two thirds of the "Canadian Troika," thank you for the ongoing dialogue and constructive criticism about my ideas and projects. Russell Sbriglia, you are a true comrade. Todd McGowan and Anna Kornbluh, thank you for your important advice and support. Finally, Slavoj Žižek, you continue to be an inspiration to me, and I want to thank you for your ongoing support and for giving me the opportunity of a lifetime to organize the "debate of the century."

At The University of Winnipeg, I have been fortunate to become part of a welcoming community of scholars. I am grateful to my dear friends and departmental colleagues, Jason Hannan and Jaqueline McLeod Rogers, who have gone above and beyond for me, and who never cease to be supportive and encouraging. I also want to thank many of my colleagues throughout the university, with whom I have had very productive and interesting conversations while working together: Adina Balint, Jane Barter, Andrew Burke, Brandon Christopher, James Currie, Rory Dickson, Michael Dudley, Angela Failler, Fiona Green, Peter Ives, Serena Keshavjee, Paul Lawrie, Helen Lepp-Friesen, Helmut-Harry Loewen, Andrew McGillivray, Allen Mills, Heather Milne, Rose Moretti-Lawrie, Glenn Moulaison, Tari Muvingi, Kathryn Ready, Ray Silvius, Heather Snell, Catherine Taylor, Kevin Walby, and Doris Wolf.

Thank you to my amazing undergraduate Research Assistants, Luc Moulaison and Thomas Dickson, my Graduate Research Assistants, Dylan Armitage and Allison Norris, and to the wonderful students in my courses on Critical Studies of Social Media, for allowing me to work out some of these ideas in my teaching.

Thank you to my editors, Trevor Perri and Anne E. Gendler, and to the team at Northwestern University Press. I am also grateful to the very helpful comments and feedback on earlier drafts of the manuscript from the anonymous peer reviewers.

To Colin Mooers, thank you for continuing to be a most cherished mentor. Thanks also to Andy Mlinarski and Joanne Silver, Marnie Fleming, Tanner Mirrlees, Imre Szeman, and Stuart Murray, and to all of my loving friends and family back home in Toronto and Thornhill.

Thank you to all of my wonderful Winnipeg friends for being a truly IRL (in real life) community! Thank you to my mother-in-law, Rochelle Freedland, and to my parents, Janice and Avrum Flisfeder. Your love and support mean the world to me.

Lilah and Zane, in my role as your father, I have grown in ways I never thought possible, and I have gained so much perspective. Not only are you the sweetest and most authentic human beings I have ever known, but also you always amaze me with your brilliance and creativity, and you manage to inspire me on a daily basis. I hope to help to make a better world so that both of you have bright futures ahead.

Robyn—you are my world! I cherish all of our time together, as it is always meaningful and special. Through our daily conversations (do we ever stop talking?), you have helped me to hone many of the ideas contained in this book. Thank you for doing the hard work of challenging me, even when I may not be prepared for it. I appreciate everything you do for me and I would be lost without you.

This book is the sum of my writing since roughly 2013. I have been able to present some of the material in this book at a series of academic conferences and invited talks. Thank you to Tanner Mirrlees for inviting me to speak at *The Capitalism Workshop* series in Toronto in July, 2018. Thank you to Scott Kryzch for inviting me to give a talk in the Department of Film and Media Studies at Colorado College, Colorado Springs, in November 2019. I was invited to speak at the West Awake conference at the University of Winnipeg in September 2018; thank you to Jaqueline McLeod Rogers for inviting me to participate in this event. I also spoke on some topics related to this book as a speaker for the Skywalk Lecture Series at the Millennium Library in Winnipeg—thank you to the organizers of this series for inviting me to present my research. I was able to present an early version of some material from chapter 1 at the Union for Democratic Communication conference in Toronto in May 2015. An early version of chapter 5 was presented at the *Labour Pains, Labour Gains* conference in Toronto in May 2015 and at the *Social Media and Society Conference* in Toronto in July 2015.

An earlier version of chapter 2 appeared in Matthew Flisfeder and Louis-Paul Willis, eds, *Žižek and Media Studies: A Reader* (New York: Palgrave Macmillan, 2018); chapter 3 appeared as "The Ideological Algorithmic Apparatus: Subjection before Enslavement," in *Theory and Event* 21, no. 2: 457–84, copyright © 2018 John Hopkins University Press; and an earlier version of chapter 5 was originally published as "The Entrepreneurial Subject and the Objectivization of the Self in Social Media," in *South Atlantic Quarterly* 114, no. 3: 553–70, copyright © 2015 Duke University Press. All republished with permission.

ALGORITHMIC DESIRE

Metaphor as Totality, or, Social Media as Our Metaphor

For many, the concept of social media is itself contradictory—what is so "social" about "social media," after all?—doesn't it disrupt democracy through surveillance?—doesn't it displace enjoyment with domination? Despite such protestations, the overarching ethic of *Algorithmic Desire* is not to abandon the metaphor ("social media"), but to push it forward. Social media remains the correct concept for reconciling ourselves with the structural contradictions of our media, our culture, and our society. Here, we need to adapt the Lacanian motto: do not abandon *the algorithm* of your desire. Do not give up on the social media metaphor.

The difficulty, today, is that too often our media are blamed for the antisocial dimensions of our culture. Instead, what we should say is just this: social media does not make us antisocial; capitalism does! To realize a truly social media, we must use the concept to bring to the surface the lack in the realm of the social itself. This means that "social media," as a concept—as a metaphor—must not be abandoned. We must continue to refer to the social media metaphor as a measuring stick against which we can assess the antisocial dimensions of our media in twenty-first-century capitalism. My (modest) proposal is that we should strive and continue to aspire toward and build an authentically *social* media. This is the political goal of *Algorithmic Desire*. Its analytical goal is to use the social media metaphor to read the form and structure of the reigning ideology and consciousness, and the reigning forms of enjoyment, their contexts, and their settings within the culture of twenty-first-century capitalism. So, to begin, let's turn toward a bit of periodization through popular culture.

Algorithmic Desire

Tom Hooper's *The King's Speech* (2010) is a story about power, ideology, . . . and new media—not, of course, on the surface! The film, however, does make clear—at least from the perspective of a sympathetic gaze—the significant ties between political communication and the rise of new media. The story centers on King George VI ("Bertie") who has a terrible stutter, making it increasingly difficult for him to lead a life in public. Near the beginning of the film, Bertie's father, King George V, makes his wireless Christmas address and explains to Bertie, that the machine will have a tremendous impact upon the future perception of the Royal Family, allowing them to come right into the homes of the people and to speak to them directly. However, his ongoing failure to correct his speech impediment leads Bertie (played by Colin Firth) to seek the expertise of Australian speech pathologist, Lionel Logue (played by Geoffrey Rush). In the course of his treatment, it becomes somewhat clear that Lionel is more than just a speech therapist. In many ways, he ends up acting much more like a Freudian analyst, identifying Bertie's speech problem as a symptom of some of his deeper repressed and unconscious feelings and memories. He eventually comes to terms with his inner turmoil and becomes capable of making use of the new radio medium to address the people with his war declaration in 1939, announcing Britain's entry into war with Germany. Lionel accompanies Bertie into the broadcasting booth while he makes his speech, providing instruction as Bertie speaks. But by the end, we see that Bertie is fully capable of conducting his speech on his own. Afterward, Lionel quips that Bertie still had trouble pronouncing his "w" sounds. Bertie replies by saying: "I had to throw in a few extra ones so they knew it was me."

The King's Speech portrays a few different themes that are relevant to the discussion that follows about social media and ideology today. In fact, the film depicts what is central to any lasting form of ideological hegemony: a strong media presence. Political rhetoric must constantly and consistently be updated to conform to the specifications of ever changing new and emergent media. This, of course, has been true for millennia, as we see in the work of Harold Innis, for example, whose "bias of communication" suggests that any lasting political power must bear an alignment with the dominant medium of the era.[1] According to him, it is only when new media emerge that we begin to witness shifts in the political order.

A second point to note about the film is the way it depicts the therapeutic relationship between Bertie and Lionel. The film intriguingly portrays Bertie's speech therapy as an exercise in psychoanalysis. What troubles his speech, mostly, is the awkward relationship he holds toward his own repressed trauma, and the fantasy coordinates around which he stages his desire. The film therefore expresses a parallel between our ability to communicate through new media and our own personal relationship to our desire and enjoyment.

Finally, with the closing line of the film, Bertie expresses what is particularly important about the relationship of new media, its form, and ideology. While it is essential for political rhetoric to conform to the formal criteria of every new dominant medium, the speaker must also maintain some distance from this; there must still be a tie back to the residual to soften the blow of the new and emergent. Dominant media therefore suture the relationship between the old and the new; between the residual and the emergent, to use Raymond Williams's historical paradigm.[2] By slurring his speech, Bertie recognizes the fact that being convincing—even ideologically convincing and persuasive—means still identifying and manipulating some of the existing flaws of the speaker that might condition the relationship between the speaker and the medium. In other words, if his address were perfectly clear and adequate for the medium, conforming to its finest elements (if it came through in "high definition," let's say), then the audience might be less inclined to take it as authentic. Every representation must therefore maintain some distance from itself as part of its interpellative strategy—that is, as part of its invocatory and scopic dimensions. Every successful and persuasive form of communication must, in other words, take into consideration the form in which the medium organizes and structures our desire. If it is too direct then it misses its mark. The only way for it to succeed is by anamorphically curbing the space through which we are lured by our desire. It must activate our desire so that we come to search out its object ourselves. In other words, every medium of communication bears witness to the "algorithm" of our desire: this is the claim that I defend here by examining the form of social media.

The medium is thus, in this sense, too, the message—this is true. But what the medium indicates also concerns the feedback of our relationship to our desire and to our enjoyment . . . and isn't this point demonstrated most poignantly in the case of President Donald Trump? Isn't Trump's direct contact with the people via social media not unlike the way that Bertie used the radio to bring the Royal Family directly into the home? Trump, not Obama, we might say, is the first "social media president." When liberal critics gaze with wonder and amazement at the effectiveness of Trump's blatant disregard for truth and rectitude, they miss something essential about his rhetorical clout.[3] Social media, Twitter in particular—Trump's preferred platform for communicating directly with his audience—caught as it is within the matrix of contemporary neoliberal capitalism, is first and foremost a "selfie machine." It exacerbates the neoliberal ethic of the individual, in which everyone is allowed their voice (and nothing more), but nowhere do we find anything resembling democratic consensus. Far from the digital public sphere that we were promised, it is a platform that works better as a swarm magnet. It has become what the CCRU (Cybernetic Culture Research Unit) describes as "schizophrenic capitalism:" a culture without society, "a mutant topology of unanticipated connections." It has become defined by the "space-time of hypercommoditisation;" it is a "nomoid zone of made clusters where the polis disintegrates into unintelligible webs of swarmachinery."[4] However, the latter, envisioned as a kind of emerging situationist and schizo-analytic practice of resistance, now has come much closer to the dominant ideology. What matters on the side of the mainstream, on the one hand, is the "like" or the "follow" or the "share and retweet;" on the side of schizoanalytic subversion, it is all done for "lulz"—more so than the accuracy or "truthiness" of the statement, or the decorum that one is supposed to show. The louder the better. Like Bertie, Trump shows that identification with the algorithmic logic of the medium—the algorithm of our desire—is the only and the best way to use it; it is the only way to allow the medium to capture the desire of the Other. In this sense, the medium truly is the message (or massage).

Some of these insights have been developed in another way, of course, in the work of Marshall McLuhan in his distinction, for instance, between hot and cool media. McLuhan, we know, was particularly interested in the way that audiences participate with new media corporeally and aesthetically through the sensorium. His distinction between hot and cool media was designed to show the degree to which the formal features or criteria of a medium speak to the range of sensory participation on the part of the audience. A hot medium, he says, "extends one single sense in 'high definition'."[5] By high definition he means "the state of being well filled with data"—or, the state in which the audience is less required to fill in the bits of less data. The telephone, he says, is a cool medium because it transmits less information, requiring the listener to participate more in filling out the gaps that are not fully present. Cool media are thus higher in participation. This is how McLuhan then famously read the differences between the televised and radio broadcasts of the 1960 Presidential Debate between John F. Kennedy and Richard Nixon. Research on the debate has shown that television viewers found Kennedy to be the winner of the debate; however, radio listeners claimed the opposite, that Nixon won the debate. According to McLuhan, the difference has to do with the different ways that the candidates, Kennedy and Nixon, are themselves amenable to the different forms of radio and TV. Kennedy—his appearance, manners of expression—was much cooler and therefore more articulate through the medium of television. Nixon, however, was much hotter and therefore more suitable to radio. It is perhaps no accident, if we think of the debate and the election in these terms, that Kennedy would go forward to win the election. It is perhaps an indication at this moment of the rising centrality of the television algorithm over that of radio as the dominant medium of the period.

The hegemony of the TV lasted for several more decades, through the Reagan period in the 1980s. The latter is pronounced most vocally by the humorous line from Robert Zemeckis's *Back to the Future*, in which Doc Brown (played by Christopher Lloyd) exclaims to Marty (Michael J. Fox): "No wonder your president has to be an actor, he's got to look good on television!" Doc Brown had earlier asked Marty who the President of the United States would be in 1985, as Marty had travelled back in time thirty years to 1955, just a few years prior to the 1960 debate between Kennedy and Nixon. At one point in the film, Marty even asks his future grandfather for directions, and upon receiving them he remarks that the name of the street he knows is John F. Kennedy Drive—after which his grandfather asks: "Who the hell is John F. Kennedy?" The scene is made all the more relevant in that in this scenario the family is sitting down to have dinner for the first time watching their very first television set. Later, when Doc asks Marty who is the President in 1985, Marty responds that it is Reagan, who was a B-rate movie actor in the 1950s. Doc is surprised, yelling: "Ronald Reagan? The actor?!" But of course, the fact that Reagan's prior career was in acting almost makes sense when we consider the influence that new media have in maintaining ideological hegemony. Just like Trump—a reality television star before he became President— Reagan was a persona appropriate to the dominant medium of the time, which bears upon the dominant form of discourse marking a historical period. This is one of the main theses of Neil Postman's canonical book, *Amusing Ourselves to Death*.[6]

Postman's argument in *Amusing* is that television, as the dominant medium at the time, is largely responsible for organizing the form of the various other discourses that regulate society, from political and religious discourse, to news, advertising, and even children's programming. Television, he says, is in its essence geared toward entertainment and amusement. While disagreeing somewhat with this claim and approach, I find his conclusion nonetheless quite compelling. Drawing on McLuhan's well-known aphorism, that "the medium is the message," Postman claims instead that the medium is rather the *metaphor*. The dominant communications medium in any period, he says, relates to and opens up an avenue for understanding a great many aspects of the broader culture and society. This is a claim that I wish to explore. However, my disagreement with Postman relates to the following: although I don't find anything disagreeable with the argument that entertainment and amusement color much of our public discourse today, I would argue instead that this is so, not because of something inherent to the dominant medium, but rather because of the way in which the medium is caught up within the already existing relations of power, domination, and exploitation within culture and the broader society. The impact of the medium, in other words, bears less upon its own inherent devices or "affordances" and more so on the way that it is used or deployed within the existing culture, which is bound to the existing relations of power and resistance—or, to use the Marxist perspective, how it is implicated within the class struggle. Therefore, the medium, I agree, is the metaphor; however, my argument here is that the medium stands as metaphor for the existing *form* that ideology takes in the context of the present relations of production. That is, it helps to represent the dominant form of *consciousness*. The dominant medium of a particular historical period thus opens up for us a window to understand and examine the form taken by *ideology*.

The Medium Is Our Metaphor

How might the medium become a metaphor for ideology? Technology writer James Bridle addresses the way that we use metaphors to make sense of new media.[7] "Cloud" for instance is one of the primary metaphors we use today to make the internet more comprehensible. But the internet is anything but a soft or light cloud. It is, in fact, "a physical infrastructure consisting of phone lines, fibre optics, satellites, cables on the ocean floor, and vast warehouses filled with computers, which consume huge amounts of water and energy and reside within national and legal jurisdictions."[8] Such physical details are, however, obscured by the metaphor of the cloud. Nevertheless, the cloud metaphor creates a practical model for shaping our relationships to the internet as a technology that is both everywhere and nowhere at the same time (not unlike Foucault's understanding of power).

"Cloud" has today replaced the older internet metaphor of the network or the web.[9] But these are terms that Bridle also uses to look at the internet with regard to what Timothy Morton calls a "hyperobject."[10] Morton uses the concept of the hyperobject to explain the phenomena of global warming and climate change. A hyperobject is a thing that bears an influence on the action or behavior of another thing, but is itself not necessarily tangible. We feel its effects, but it exists nowhere for us to point to. As Bridle explains, because hyperobjects "are so close and yet so hard to see, they defy our ability to describe them rationally, and to master or overcome them in any traditional sense."[11] We can perceive hyperobjects through their impact or imprints on other things, and because of this we are able at the very least to model and to map them. Just like climate change, the internet or the network is according to Bridle a hyperobject.

The internet weaves together our ways of living and being in the world at the same time that it organizes our ways of thinking about and contemplating the world. The "network," for Bridle, "is an emergent cultural form, generated from our conscious and unconscious desires in dialogue with mathematics and electrons and silicon and glass fibre."[12] The network is a metaphor for the physicality of the technology, but it is also a metaphor for our current understanding, conceptualization, and representation of reality.

Wendy Hui Kyong Chun similarly writes that "software has become a metaphor for the mind, for culture, for ideology, for biology, and for the economy."[13] Both software and computers, like all media, she argues, are "metaphor machines: they both depend on and perpetuate metaphors."[14] Chun, like Bridle, proposes the network as the metaphor that ideally represents the present reality.[15] She introduces this claim by drawing on Fredric Jameson's postmodern Marxist conception of "cognitive mapping," wherein he proposes that technological metaphors enable a "privileged representational shorthand for grasping a network of power and control even more difficult for our minds and imaginations to grasp—namely the whole new decentered global network of the third stage of capital itself."[16] Viewed from this perspective, networks, software, the computer—all operate like hyperobjects . . . but we should pause here. Upon further reflection I'm motivated to ask if we might conceptualize this relationship differently, in a way that is somewhat familiar: Isn't what Morton calls a "hyperobject"—what Bridle, Chun, and even Postman refer to in terms of metaphor—isn't this reminiscent of what an older Hegelian-Marxist discourse conceived as the totality?

From Metaphor to Totality, and Back

Recently, Slavoj Žižek has compared the older Marxist notion of totality to another contemporary metaphor used to address the human-nonhuman relationship—relationships that tie the human both to nature and to technology: the assemblage.[17] Assemblage, like the network, is a metaphor commonly in use today to reflect upon the horizontal relationships between human and nonhuman actors. Some theorists today, according to the Deleuze scholar, Andrew Culp, see the world as made up entirely of assemblages, which are also conceived as subjects: "In no time, people, hurricanes, and battles all get addressed in the same register (all sub-jects should be afforded proper names)!"[18] Such assemblage thinking, he writes, misses the mark by reducing subjectivity "to the name we use to pin down the sum of a body's capacities." Instead, he says, we need to recognize that assemblage thinking is the product of a world where capi-talism produces subjectivities in humans in the way that it produces other branded commodities, so that by subjectivizing the nonhuman, we end up objectifying ourselves—this, of course, is not too distant from neo-liberal rhetorics of entrepreneurialism wherein we must "invest" in our "human capital."

The aim of the assemblage metaphor, it seems, is to evade an older hierarchical language that deems humans as exceptional, as in some ways dominant over the nonhuman. Assemblage theory, instead, sees human actors as something like the conscious operators of machines, who also in their own way bear upon the impact or flow of outcomes. Both human and nonhuman components apply their own inputs to the overall system, in which neither of them, from this perspective, is more or less superior than the other. The same applies to nature. What we get instead of the hierarchical relationship between human and nonhuman is a kind of "flat ontology" that aims to democratize in the name of an equality of objects—if objects are subjects, then subjects are objects, and we are all one and the same (or nothing at all). No hierarchy and no exploita-tion . . . but is this in fact the case?

Assemblage theory is often tied to contemporary New Materialism, which, according to Žižek, takes aim less (or not only) at transcendental humanism than at the "specter of Marxism."[19] It is with this in mind that he compares Assemblage theory to the Marxist category of the totality. To-tality is distinguished from assemblage, not due to some kind of "higher organic unity of the assembled elements" in the latter, but because of "the antagonism that cuts across every assemblage."[20] An assemblage is "totalized," according to Žižek, not because of some "all-encompassing universality," but because of the fact that every assemblage "is traversed by the same antagonism," which for him (and for me as well) consists of the class struggle.[21] Class struggle, as he puts it elsewhere, "is ultimately the struggle for the meaning of society 'as such', the struggle for which of the two classes will impose itself as the stand-in for society 'as such', thereby degrading its other into the stand-in for the non-Social (the de-struction of, the threat to, society)."[22] Totality, then, is precisely what the ruling class is unable to bear: it is a view of society that includes what re-mains excluded from its own self-understanding.

Totality, as Georg Lukács has explained, *is* a way of knowing about the world. "From systemic doubt and the *Cogito ergo sum* of Descartes, to

Hobbes, Spinoza and Leibniz there is a direct line of development whose central strand, rich in variations, is the idea that the object of cognition can be known by us for the reason that, and to the degree in which, it has been created by ourselves. And with this, the methods of mathematics and geometry . . . and, later, the methods of mathematical physics become the guide and the touchstone of philosophy, the knowledge of the world as a totality."[23] This way of thinking the totality is also not unlike what Jameson meant when he described "cognitive mapping" as a return to the Symbolic, missing in the Althusserian formula of ideology as "an imaginary relationship of the subject to its real conditions of existence."[24]

The Althusserian formula, as Jameson points out, contains only a reference to the Lacanian dimensions of the Imaginary and the Real, missing entirely the Symbolic. The Symbolic, we can read in its deployment by Jameson, functions like the Marxist category of the totality, or of "class consciousness," which Jameson later on admitted to being very close to what he has in mind with his conception of cognitive mapping.[25] The Symbolic in this sense, rather than referring to the Lacanian big Other, has a function in the analytic discourse—cognitive mapping is the practice of intervening in the Real. As Žižek puts it, historical materialism and psychoanalysis are similar in the way that their interpretive strategies "constitute a direct intervention of the Symbolic in the Real" of how "the word can affect the Real of the symptom."[26]

Conceiving the world as a totality requires thinking it in its associated relationships—not only the social, but also the actual, the natural, and the technological, all of which still are impacted by the social and the human ethical relationship to the nonhuman. But thinking in terms of totality also means that we take into consideration the complete picture of existing antagonisms. As Lukács describes, we tend to view the world primarily according to the formal terms of the ruling class. Its practice of rational thought is one that tends to support, not necessarily the direct interests of individuals or the ruling class itself, as much as it supports the *preconditions* for the dominance of the ruling class. As Jameson puts it, "in the realm of thought, he [the individual] is willing to venture only to the point at which those preconditions begin to be called into question."[27] Dialectical thought, in contrast, is "in its very structure self-consciousness;" it is the process of reckoning with "the position of the observer into the experiment itself."[28] Rational thought, in other words, posits the presuppositions of the ruling class and the ruling ideology; and, that which tends to contradict the dominant form of the rational cannot but appear as irrational. Therefore, a totality, as Žižek puts it, is not merely a whole. It is a whole plus its surpluses that distort it.[29] A totality is like a hyperobject in the sense that it allows us to contemplate the entire scenario of the present, but insofar as it is split and traversed by human social antagonisms. Again, as Lukács explains, objective reality is in its immediacy the same for both the proletariat and the bourgeoisie; however, objective reality remains split by the antagonism that gives rise to their diverging consciousness and experiences.[30] "Class struggle" is the name for this political split in objective reality, and the materialist dialectic allows the thinker to gain awareness of the fact that consciousness is limited by the subject's position in society and history. But to make a totality comprehensible it requires formalization through the Symbolic, through metaphor. It is through metaphor that it comes to *make* sense.

We must recall that metaphor, according to Jacques Lacan, is the effect of substituting one signifier for another within the signifying chain.[31] Metaphor, like the Lacanian Master-Signifier, even allows us to mark the presence of an absence, to include the non-entity that over-determines the whole to become concrete. The Lacanian metaphor in the form of the Master-Signifier is a hyperobject *avant la lettre*. It helps to solidify and to make sense of a number of related phenomena that, without the metaphor, lack body and contextualization. The metaphor helps to formalize the totality, to make it comprehensible. In doing so, it provides a platform upon which we may act within the coordinates of the dominant consciousness.

My claim in *Algorithmic Desire* is that social media, the digital platform, and its algorithmic logic, serve as central metaphors for the present totality. That's not to say that they are the only metaphors we have for coming to understand our present conditions of existence and possibility. But just as Postman claims that the dominant medium of any historical period allows us to conceptualize the dominant form of discourse, I argue that social media teaches us about the dominant form of *ideology* (and thus the dominant consciousness) in contemporary, twenty-first-century neoliberal capitalism. Social media is our metaphor—it *is* our ideology. Although I make no claim to speak in totality to the various ways that social media operate our totality, the chapters that follow attempt to create and build insights into some of the ways that forms of social media have served as metaphors for the present. I here look at the way that social media figures our understandings of such rudimentary concepts as democracy and enjoyment, but also at the way that social media enacts instrumental forms of consciousness as in the turn toward algorithmic logic. I examine the ways that forms of social media incorporate and build upon neoliberal rhetorics of entrepreneurialism and curation as the economic and aesthetic modes of subjecthood. But what truly interests me is the way that social media as ideology—as the form of ideology—treats our relationship to our desire and our enjoyment.

How, in other words, are we chained to the (algo)rithm (algo-rhythm) of social media desire? To begin to answer this question, I want to return to Postman's thesis about amusement and entertainment in order to give it a kind of *détournement* for the post-Fordist age.

Our Brave New (Digital) World (of Enjoyment)

Desire and enjoyment are of particular interest in my own Lacanian-Marxist reading or rendering of the social media ideology, as I will call it. Postman, too, was interested in enjoyment—or more appropriately amusement and entertainment, in his book. He begins *Amusing Ourselves to Death* by comparing the two dystopian narratives of George Orwell's *1984* and Aldous Huxley's *Brave New World*. Both novels approach the possibility of a future dystopian society; however, they do so from two opposed perspectives. While the future world depicted in *1984* shows mass surveillance as the chief mechanism for maintaining order, obedience, and control—through the figure of Big Brother, who is always watching—*Brave New World*, instead, shows that order can be kept, not through the fear and paranoia of constant surveillance, but through constant, never-ending entertainment. Through an order, that is, in which no one can, or is allowed, to do anything *but* enjoy. As the character, Mustapha Mond, puts it in *Brave New World*: "The world's stable now. People are happy; they get what they want, and they never want what they can't get. They're well off; they're safe; they're never ill; they're not afraid of death; they're blissfully ignorant of passion and old age; they're plagued with no mothers or fathers; they've got no wives, or children, or lovers to feel strongly about; they're so conditioned that they practically can't help behaving as they ought to behave. And if anything should go wrong, there's *soma*."[32]

Brave New World is a story that is largely based on Huxley's rendering of the Fordist consumer society, and as such it is a depiction that reflects much of the postwar mass culture. According to Postman, it is Huxley's book, more than Orwell's, that had in the mid-1980s come to fruition. For him, television (or electronic media more generally) is inherently a technology of entertainment, in contrast to the contemplative dimensions of print media. The logic and the sequential dimensions of print allow for a more reflective practice of reading, according to Postman, and thus a more rational form of consciousness. Electronic media are, however, much more holistic, and do not fracture the human sensory, compartmentalizing it into distinguished sensations. Print privileges the visual; electronic media aims to recombine the sensorium, and in doing so, according to Postman, to make amusement the primary force of the medium. This, he says, then translates into the other various discourses that make up society: from news and politics, to religion and education— everything must be inscribed with entertainment value in order to be effective. This is still a convincing account of our postmodern society of the spectacle. But what I find missing in Postman's account is a deeper reflection on the relationship between the medium and its political-economic context, caught as it is both in tension with the capitalist relations of production and in the class struggle.

There are (at least) two ways to approach this context. We might look at the political economy of the media to understand how it is that structures of ownership, and interests from advertisers, for instance, inform the type of content that we see across our media. There have been some very important studies from this perspective, most notably books like Edward S. Herman and Noam Chomsky's *Manufacturing Consent,* and Robert McChesney's *Rich Media/Poor Democracy.*[33] In addition, there is a tremendous amount of research about social media that is being conducted in this tradition.[34] As much as I value this approach, I find it in some ways still limited—for it simply views the content of a medium as directly tied to the interests of its producers. This is suggestive of mechanistic determinism. This analysis is truthful, of course, in the sense that organizational structures of ownership do tend to filter out information that contradicts the preconditional interests of the ruling class. But this, view, I believe, is too limiting. Something still seems to be missing.

Another way to approach this context stems from what I have already proposed, in concert with Postman, that we can read our media formally as a metaphor for the existing structure of society, or at least as the structure of the dominant consciousness. But unlike Postman, for me this means reading social media as a metaphor for the form of ideology. If we understand media as *ideological* metaphors, we can see just how much the consciousness they represent is a product of the overall structure and form of society. Read in this way, we can also see a kind of determinism present in Postman's own reading of the inherent qualities of media that differs from the political economic account. Amusing consumer content, on the political-economic account, is a result of the structures of ownership and the interests of advertising and consumerism; on Postman's account, it is the result of something inherent in the medium. My position, in contrast, suggests that the medium reflects the dominant form of consciousness in society. That is to say that, as a metaphor for the form of ideology, it is less a result of something inherent in the medium, or it is (only) the product of the interests of those who have created it.

Certainly, every medium has an inherent bias, since it is limited by its technological components as well as by its conditions of having been produced by people with a particular set of interests and goals. But it is also a manner of coming to terms with the way that a society thinks overall. If we begin, neither from the position of the technology, nor from that of the political economy, but from the position of ideology, then we can detect in what sense both the uses of technology and the structure of the political economy—including the existing dominant relations of production and inequality—are themselves justified and legitimized. By looking at social media as a metaphor of ideology—that is, of the dominant form of consciousness or the total worldview of the existing dominant form of culture—then we can, I claim, come to understand, firstly, how the existing society self-legitimizes or self-authorizes, and secondly, how it reflects and reproduces itself materially. However, as a metaphor for ideology, we need to understand, as well, in what sense contesting points of view are expressed in its terms—in terms of the dominant ideology and the dominant medium—and how the new arises as a result of the contradictions in the existing consciousness. For this reason, unlike Postman, I prefer to examine social media, not at the level of mere amusement or entertainment, but at the level of *jouissance*, or enjoyment. This, we will see, is a feature of our ideology that comes to fruition in the context of the post-Fordist culture.

Fordism, the basis for Huxley's dystopian depiction of the future, describes a culture learning about and coming to terms with the rising consumer society. It is tied to the Keynesian welfare state model and to a later industrial capitalism, where workers are paid enough to afford to buy the mass, assembly-line produced goods that they participate in producing. Fordism and the welfare state, while helping to grow the size and quality of life for the middle classes, were also codified in Eurocentric and patriarchal values of the "father-knows-best" variety—that is, the metaphor of the Father or the paternal metaphor (as it is dubbed by Lacan). The twin phenomena of the later postwar period of the 1960s, of the shifting technological basis of capitalism from Fordism to post-Fordism and the rise in New (non-class-based) Social Movements, help us to make sense of the culture that now dominates. With post-Fordism, we see a shift away from industrial production in the developed world as dominant, and a movement toward the electronic and the digital. This also signals a movement toward new managerial prescriptions, away from the idea of the full-time job for life (until retirement) and toward lean production models of increased precarity, part-time and contract labor, just-in-time production instead of the stockpiling of goods, and with the arrival of neoliberalism, new regimes of austerity that shift the burden of welfare onto the family and the individual. Post-Fordism coincides with the "new spirit of capitalism" that sees horizontal and rhizomatic management, sparked by the spirit of '68 culture, that enables the dispersion of managerial authority.[35] If *Brave New World* was a dystopian picture appropriate to the Fordist society, then more recent representations that hit much closer to home for the post-Fordist culture include postmodern gems like *Blade Runner* and *Blade Runner 2049, The Matrix* trilogy, and the television series *Black Mirror* and *Mr. Robot.* These dystopian depictions of the future show a society and a culture of precarious life, combined human and nonhuman assemblages, structures and inevitabilities of the digital and cyber economy, cyberwar, and artificial intelligence, that blur the lines between human and nonhuman identity and subjectivity, and show a deeper integration of new mechanisms of control through the intensification of living and uninhibited *jouissance.*

In fact, one way that we can distinguish between the earlier Fordist culture and the post-Fordist one centers on the different relationships to enjoyment prescribed by each. If the phallocentrism and patriarchal family structure were dominant in the Fordist culture, then the post-Fordist or postmodern culture is one in which the power and authority of the phallus and the *paternal metaphor* are (if not destroyed, then at least) troubled and questioned. In a sense, we see in post-Fordist and post-modern culture a contradiction between the cultural decline of phallocentrism and patriarchy, and an institutional and political arrangement and structure that still favors the masculine. At the same time, the declining authority of the paternal metaphor and phallocentrism signal a shift in the postmodern consumer culture with regard to our structures of enjoyment. If modernism organized our relationship to enjoyment based around its prohibitions, then postmodern culture—the culture of post-Fordism and the declining agency of the Father—represents one based on the constant *obligation* to enjoy, so much so that we are made to feel guilty when we are not enjoying. This is a condition that Mark Fisher has described as "depressive hedonia."[36] Depression is typically conceived as a state of *an*hedonia, in which we are unable to obtain pleasure or enjoyment or satisfaction. In depressive hedonia, according to Fisher, we become depressed from the constant and unending injunction and obligation to enjoy. The culture is signalled by constant enjoinders to enjoy and consume, but our consumption is never satisfying. There always seems to be a new product, gizmo, or gadget (what Lacan called *lathouses*) to replace the previous one that is now well past its due date.

One of the problems with this model, as I see it, is that *un*limited enjoyment and consumption begins to call forth and demand a limit. I mean this in two different ways.

On the one hand, we demand a limit because enjoyment only seems possible when it is prohibited. An object of desire only becomes such when we find that it is somehow prohibited or unobtainable. When the limit disappears, it does not change our orientation toward it with regard to our enjoyment, and the result is a combination of depressive hedonia and increased control. Here, I am using control in the sense described by Gilles Deleuze in his short essay on the societies of control, where he describes how we become tethered to the (digital) machinations of control through its combination of surveillance and enjoyment.[37] In other words, Deleuze marks a scenario that combines both the unceasing enjoyment of *Brave New World* and the constant surveillance of *1984*. The end of the prohibiting agency, then, appears not to have brought about more freedom, but rather a constant nightmarish schizoid-paranoia of debt and addiction.

On the other hand, we have witnessed in the post–Cold War era, and especially in the post-2008 crisis period, a demand for new forms of hierarchical authority and paternal metaphors, a Fascism 2.0, that demands a return to older chauvinisms (which produce an artificial limit to enjoyment by claiming its theft by figures such as feminists, "Islamicists," and other examples of racialized Others), materialized in a wave of international political phenomena, that features the rise of new extremist fundamentalisms, including the so-called Alt-Right movement, the Brexit vote in the UK, and the election of Donald Trump as President of the United States. We might see these demands as coming from popular despair with regard to the *un*limited societies of control. In conditions such as these, it is difficult to imagine a dystopian fiction that departs from the present reality, which is itself already coming close to early postmodern depictions of the twenty-first century in the cyberpunk fiction of the 1980s and 1990s. In fact, combined with emerging technologies based on algorithmic logic, like social media and digital automation, these end-of-the-world scenarios, resulting from climate change, form the front and back of the two predominant fantasies giving content to the dystopian visions of "the end." If, as Fredric Jameson claims, every ideology must have a utopian dimension, we might also add that each one, too, is set against the background of its dystopian fantasy, which I mean in the Lacanian sense.[38] Fantasy is a structure that narrativizes our relationship to our desire. On the Left now, we find two versions of this scenario that seem to offer emancipatory cognitive mapping. These are New Materialism and

Accelerationism. But as I claim, they miss the mark: both are now embedded in the dominant ideology. They are, more or less, cynical versions of what I will refer to as a "do less" ethics.[39]

Looking Back at Nature, Looking Forward to Technology

In his book, *Four Futures*, Peter Frase suggests that today there are two "specters" haunting the twenty-first century: climate change and automation.[40] For Frase, climate change and automated production signal two looming, yet contradictory threats—a threat of scarcity and a threat of abundance. Noting that the mitigation of these threats is at its core political, along the lines of the class struggle—the struggle for equality, or the struggle against it—he devises four potential postcapitalist forms of society. Communism, he says, would be a society of equality and abundance, whereas Socialism would be a society of equality and scarcity; a society of inequality and abundance he calls Rentism, and one of inequality and scarcity would fall into Exterminism. Frase's permutations of postcapitalism pose an interesting thought experiment of how we might imagine the movement beyond the present. They are visions of where we are currently heading, and they are the potential directions that the world can take depending on the way that political forces are mobilized and how we might respond collectively to existing contradictions. What I find equally intriguing, though, about Frase's matrix and his proposition regarding the twin specters of the twenty-first century is how similarly these haunt contemporary theory. In fact, the specters of climate change and ecological catastrophe, in addition to that of automation, inform two relevant critical theories that are growing in popularity: the so-called New Materialisms and Accelerationism.

The basic premise of New Materialisms (including Object-Oriented Ontology—OOO, Speculative Realism—SR, Vitalist Materialism—VR, Actor-Network Theory—ANT, and some versions of Assemblage theory) is the need to dissolve the hierarchical relationship between human and nonhuman agents. New Materialism is thus a school of posthumanist theory whose aim is the study of nonhuman ontology and agency. It is this latter point that distinguishes New Materialism from Old Materialism (that is, historical and dialectical materialism): it assigns agency to matter. The view is thus that "agency has been wrongly conceived as the prerogative of humans and must now promptly be recognized in the things themselves."[41] Given the deleterious impact of human agents upon the nonhuman, a strategic anthropomorphism of the nonhuman is deemed to be necessary in order to avoid too much anthropocentrism.[42] The way to encourage human agents, so it is deemed, is to decenter the human subject within the field of all actors, in order to create a "democracy of objects," so to speak. Rather than a vertical relationship between the human and the nonhuman, New Materialisms endeavour to make progress toward a horizontal relationship with nonhuman actors, creating a "flat ontology." This kind of posthumanist moralism is certainly understandable given the naïve and perhaps ignorant fashion with which humans have acted upon the nonhuman, which includes nature, the environment, and nonhuman animals. But going forward, I would add to this list machines, technologies, and new media, which also occupy positions of the nonhuman. This, we might imagine, becomes pertinent, not necessarily for conceiving the agency of machines and robots. Instead, when we begin to consider the agency of nonhuman actors, this should give us pause and help us to reconceive how, in fact, we might define the *human* subject.

Rising concerns about climate change do, indeed, give us reason to think about some of the ways that human civilization has mistreated and abused the nonhuman, so much so that it now bears upon our own *species* survival (or perhaps even our "species-being," to put this in Marxist terms). However, in contrast to theorists like Steven Shaviro, who advocates an ethics of anthropomorphism as a means of overcoming anthropocentrism, I would argue instead for the reverse. What is needed is still an anthropocentrism as a way of centering human survival and human epistemology as an ethical strategy for taking care of the nonhuman. In other words, what matters to me is not merely our moral awareness of how human agency and culture have harmed the nonhuman. What matters is how our treatment of the nonhuman ultimately comes to bite *us* back in the ass.

As Jodi Dean puts it, "Climate change tethers us to a perspective that oscillates between the impossible and the inevitable, already and not yet, everywhere but not here, not quite."[43] This is a state not so unlike that of *jouissance* in the Lacanian sense: both too much and too little enjoyment. Once we get what we want, we start to feel as though it wasn't really what we wanted in the first place. Some on the Left, according to Dean, see climate change as a vehicle for this kind of *jouissance*: a vehicle for enjoying punishment, destruction, and knowing. Posthumanist theorists of the Anthropocene, she writes, "embrace extinction, focus on deep time, and displace a politics of the people onto the agency of things."[44] For her, the knowing moralism of this current of the Left is a form of disavowal: it lets us off the hook. It is, in a sense, an *ethics of "do less."* It is, if I can put it this way, a view of human agency that is somewhat backward-looking. Human agents are interpreted as those who became overly anthropocentric. Anthropocentrism is interpreted as the cause of environmental degradation; human impact as the detrimental source of the crisis. Even the very term, "Anthropocene," according to Dean, provides a kind of compensatory charge. So often, she notes, in contemporary discussions of the Anthropocene, "the organization of people—our institutions, systems, and arrangements of power, production, and reproduction—appears only as a distortion. Everything is active except for us, with no role other than that of observers, victims, or lone survivors."[45] I cannot help but agree, then, with Dean when she writes that the goal of the Left shouldn't be to "undermine collective political power in the name of a moralistic horizontalism of humans and nonhumans."[46] By this, I do not mean to suggest that we should eschew the suggestion that nonhuman matter possesses agency. Rather, the perspective I insist upon here is still one of (to reverse the trajectory employed by Shaviro) strategic anthropocentrism that may still include a degree of anthropomorphism. It is a view that is oriented toward building an ethics of postcapitalism and of universal emancipation.

Prioritizing the centrality of human agency, for me, only makes good sense when it comes to questions of ethics. In noting the historical impact of humanity upon the world, I still find that a forward-looking ethical dimension (in the sense of "what is to be done?") is currently lacking in some contemporary New Materialisms, the result of which is a kind of cynicism, not unlike the reigning forms of capitalist realism, that ends up ultimately resigning into frantic and subtractive despair. As Andreas Malm puts it, the only way forward, ethically, is "to put a stop to the extension of agency. In this warming world, that honour belongs *exclusively* to those humans who extract, buy, sell and combust fossil fuels, and to those who uphold this circuit, and to those who have committed acts over the past two centuries: causing the climate system to spin out of control, they and they alone instigate the paradox of historicised nature."[47] Our point here must be against flat horizontalism and in favor of a return to the exceptionality of humanity—not because humanity is in any way greater than or more important than the nonhuman; here I imagine an *equity* of objects rather than an equality of objects that recognizes the differences among actors—but because the only ethics we can deploy—that we are capable of deploying—is a *human* ethics, caught as it is within the realm of the social, the political, and the cultural. This means that bearing in mind human responsibility or accountability for the impact we have had upon the nonhuman, moving forward we need to take responsibility to act according to an ethics that insists upon our mutual and sustainable

future. But, again, as Malm reminds us, "*any* call for a more environmen-
tally beneficial practice by necessity puts humans front and centre."[48]
What now bears upon a strictly human ethics, though, with hindsight,
accountability, and responsibility, and with New Materialist critical theory
in mind, is the question of what precisely *is* the human?

To begin to answer this question, it is worth considering the historicity of
New Materialism and questioning why, along with the looming threat of
ecological catastrophe brought on by climate change, does posthumanism and the nonhuman factor so heavily in contemporary critical theory.
We might consider, in other words, the rising interest in posthumanism
and nonhumanism as symptomatic of neoliberal dehumanization. Writing critically about posthumanism, New Materialism, and the representation of Indigenous populations, W. Oliver Baker suggests that these
theories should be read "as an ideological response to the perceived erosion of the liberal social contract in the era of late capitalist and deindus-
trialization when more and more groups of people experience structural
exclusion from wage labor as well as fall victim to neoliberal forms of what
David Harvey calls 'accumulation by dispossession'."[49] We might read this
to indicate that the increasing forms of precarity through austerity, deregulation, structural adjustment, financialization, and entrepreneurialism have impacted our very sense of self in relation to the nonhuman. In
other words, the more that the traditional middle classes are feeling the
stress of the deeper commodification of all of life—in a sense, what Foucault refers to as biopolitics, or the work on the Self—so much so that our
lives are transformed away from *subject*hood and into *object*hood, the more
that only now do we begin to show signs of real care for the nonhuman.
That is to say that concern for the object world—object-oriented ontologies, for instance—enters the field the more that the middle classes experience their own degradation into objecthood, into reification. As Baker
points out, those who have "historically enjoyed protections from such
forms of exclusion and dispossession, but who today [have] come to experience late capitalism as a process that erodes the liberal social contract,
[are] the working- and middle- class white settler."[50] The category of the
"human," in other words, has historically been reserved for the subject of
the white settler. The colonized other was not even considered human.
Feeling the dehumanizing effects of neoliberalism now has positioned
the dominating culture to give more sympathies to that which has historically been excluded from the category of the human. Neoliberalism and
the class struggle, along with climate change, therefore factor as means of
coming to terms with the rising interest in the nonhuman. But as I have

alluded to already, another factor that is shifting the gears of our sense of human subjecthood is the rapidly increasing degree of technologization, from digital automation and new urban infrastructures, to the growth in algorithmic logic, deep learning, and artificial intelligence.

New Materialisms, as Diana Coole and Samantha Frost explain, explore a range of very contemporary complex issues that include climate change, global capital, and population flows, in addition to biotechnology and the bioengineering of genetically modified organisms; but these theories also touch upon "the saturation of our intimate and physical lives by digital, wireless, and virtual technologies."[51] Perhaps the most common metaphor used in responding to these new saturations of digital technologies into our everyday lives is that of the assemblage. Aside from the New Materialist reading of the human and nonhuman relationship to nature, we can also interrogate the assemblage of humans and machines from the opposite end, on the side of Accelerationism.

There have been, according to Benjamin Noys, two central tendencies in all post-Kantian philosophy, of which Accelerationism seems to follow one: that of immanence and that of transcendence.[52] Noys dubs Deleuze and Guattari's immanentist position "affirmationist." As both carry an influence from Deleuze, New Materialism and Accelerationism each falls into the camp of immanentist and affirmationist thought, itself a response to the events of May 1968. As Noys notes, texts that followed this line of thought, particularly *Anti-Oedipus*, respond somewhat to Marx's assertion that the limit to capital is capital itself. In arguing that it is necessary to "crash through the barrier by turning capitalism against itself," these texts represent a politics of "*ou pire*" (or worse): "If capitalism generates its own forces of dissolution then the necessity is to radicalize capitalism itself: the worse the better."[53] This tendency is what Noys has dubbed "Accelerationism."

Shaviro describes Accelerationism as a political, aesthetic, and philosophical movement that proposes pushing capitalism to its limits as the only way through capitalism. The hope of Accelerationists, he writes, "is that, by exacerbating our current conditions of existence, we will finally be able to make them explode, and thereby move beyond them."[54] Accelerationism is rooted in a particular version of classical Marxism that sees the forces of production outgrowing the relations of production: "Marx argues that capitalism tends toward a point where its very form— the property form—becomes an obstacle to the further development of the productive forces that it has unleashed."[55] One of the chief figures of the Accelerationist movement is Nick Land, whose neoreactionary writing has sparked a movement called the Dark Enlightenment, which advocates a mixture of "cognitive elitism, racist social Darwinism, and autocratic Austrian economics."[56] Land draws on Deleuze and Guattari's insistence in *Anti-Oedipus* to "accelerate the process" of capitalist deterritorialization as a modicum of revolution. As Shaviro puts it, Accelerationists like Land celebrate "absolute deterritorialization as liberation— even (or above all) to the point of total disintegration and death."[57] With a view toward total deterritorialization brought about by capitalism's own inherent limits, Land "extols capitalism precisely for its inhuman, violent, and destructive power."[58]

The problem with Accelerationism, Shaviro notes, is that, "like it or not—we are all Accelerationists now. It has become increasingly clear that crises and contradictions do not lead to the demise of capitalism. Rather, they actually work to promote and advance capitalism, by providing it with its fuel."[59] Accelerationism, then, "is a new response to the specific conditions of today's neoliberal, globalized and networked capitalism."[60] But as capitalism works to break down cultural barriers in order to overcome the limits of production for profit, it also acts upon its subjects, demystifying and disenchanting us in a way that distances us from our older worldviews. In this way, it unhinges the paternal metaphor, leaving open a space for revolution—or else, it creates a space for its much more violent and unrelenting imposition of new forms of Authority.

One of the inherent limits to exponential growth in capitalism is its constant and continued movement toward contradiction and crisis; or, as seen from the immanentist position of the Accelerationists, there is a need to *create* and *erect* barriers—new limits—that it can overcome to thrust it into new areas of profit creation. As most political economists will tell us, crises of capitalism always result from overproduction or overaccumulation. This is why, when faced with abundance, "capitalism needs to generate an imposed scarcity, simply in order to keep itself going."[61] This is perhaps why Deleuze and Guattari claim, against Lacan (for instance), that in capitalism, lack is something imposed, it is something created. Lack, they write, "is created, planned, and organized in and through social production. It is counterproduced as a result of the pressure of antiproduction."[62] Lack, in other words, is, according to them, an artificial attribute of capitalism. This, at least, is according to Deleuze and Guattari's immanentist reading.

Apart from Land, though, there is another Accelerationist tendency worth addressing—the tendency that is put forth by Nick Srnicek and Alex Williams, both in their Manifesto for an Accelerationist Politics (MAP) and in their book, *Inventing the Future*.[63] Whereas the Landian project of Accelerationism is one of heightening the contradictions of capitalism to its very limit, Srnicek and Williams imagine a postcapitalist future brought on by the deeper integration of technology into society. As Noys puts it, Accelerationists like Srnicek and Williams attempt to solve the suffering of labor by further integrating it into the machine.[64] Again, going back to Marx, one of the problems we find in its own inherent contradictions is that capital "depends on labor-power to generate surplus value, but on the other hand, it constantly tends to replace labor power with machinery" leading to crisis.[65] Srnicek and Williams argue, therefore, for an acceleration of the process of further integrating humans and machines; or, more specifically, they argue in favor of a society built around full automation, solving the fundamentals of our needs in the face of neoliberalism and climate change, and building-in, therefore, a system of basic income that would allow us to continue to live in a world *without* work. "The Left," they write in the MAP, "must develop sociotechnical hegemony."[66] Platforms, they correctly acknowledge, already form the basic technological infrastructure of global society: "They establish the basic parameters of what is possible, both behaviorally and ideologically. In this sense, they embody the material transcendental basis of society: they are what make possible particular sets of actions, relationships, and powers."[67] Although, they say, "much of the current global platform is biased towards capitalist social relations, this is not an inevitable necessity. These material platforms of production, finance, logistics, and consumption can and will be reprogrammed and reformatted towards post-capitalist ends."[68] It is with regard to the latter claim and perspective that their Accelerationism differs from that of Land. Theirs is a vision of an emancipatory egalitarianism, contrary to the Landian neoreactionary Dark Enlightenment.

However, in the current context of neoliberal capitalism, "the relief that technology was supposed to bring from labor merely leaves less labor doing more work. No longer, as in Marx's day, are we all chained to factory machines, but now some of us carry our chains around with us, in the form of laptops and phones."[69] As Noys puts the matter, "the fact that history advances by the bad side does not mean that we should celebrate the 'bad side' [as Land does], but rather recognize this is the ground on which we struggle, which must be negated to constitute a new and just social order."[70] Noys is one, however, who emphasizes the persistence of the negative. Negativity, he claims, is "the condition for re-articulating a thinking of agency."[71] In contrast to the claim of the thinkers of *Anti-Oedipus*, in which the lack or the negative is something imposed artificially, negativity is in fact the basic condition of all reality. Reality is incomplete, marked by a lack or a gap. Reality is contradictory. The latter claim is the one that I defend against the New Materialists and the Accelerationists, by now turning toward what Noys calls the "transcendental" position implicit in what I call a "New Structuralism." My conception of New Structuralism is inspired primarily by Lacanian scholars, like Slavoj Žižek, Alenka Zupančič, Mladen Dolar, Todd McGowan, Jodi Dean, Anna Kornbluh, the later work of Mark Fisher, and others currently writing in this area, whose work, although influential in several other key areas of humanities scholarship, has not yet attained the kind of profile it deserves in communications and media studies, and in social media studies in particular. New Structuralism is how I prefer to figure the totality of the social media metaphor in *Algorithmic Desire*.

Toward a New Structuralism?

My starting point for conceptualizing a "New Structuralism" bears upon what I believe to be the most significant point for the Marxist critique of capitalism—a point that shows where the Marxist critique departs from radical or social liberal critiques that tend to dissolve into moralistic signals of virtue. What matters most significantly about the Marxist critique is its identification of the structural limits, the inherent (material) contradictions of capitalism. Marxism is not merely a moral criticism of capitalism. Its clout rests primarily in its ability to show what is structurally contradictory about the capitalist mode of production, and its constant and consistent tendency toward crisis. Wolfgang Streeck provides an apt description of what I have in mind here:

> While labour has gradually been replaced by technology for the past two hundred years, with the rise of information technology and, in the very near future, artificial intelligence, that process is currently reaching its apogee, in at least two respects: first, it has vastly accelerated, and second, having in the second half of the twentieth century destroyed the manual working class, it is now attacking and about to destroy the middle class as well—in other words, the new petty bourgeoisie that is the very carrier of the neocapitalist and neoliberal lifestyle of 'hard work and hard play', of careerism-cum-consumerism, which . . . may indeed be considered the indispensable cultural foundation of contemporary capitalism's society.[72]

What this new shift from human to artificial labor indicates is the eventual replacement of humans with machinery. Electronization, according to Streeck, "will do to the middle class what mechanization has done to the working class, and it will do it much faster."[73] While this potentially poses a moral dilemma in that it will lead to vast unemployment, not only of the working class, but also (and more so) for the middle classes, it is the structural impact of this employment that needs to be considered as well. As human labor is replaced with machinery and automation, the result is of course a rising deficit in effective consumer demand. If people do not earn enough in wages, then it makes no difference whether humans or robots are producing our goods. If no one can pay for them, then no profits can result, and we fall back into crisis. Without diving into suggestions about Universal Basic Income, as Srnicek and Williams have done, I want to build from this structural understanding—that is of the structural limits to capitalism, crisis and contradiction as its normal state of affairs—in order to move beyond the New Materialist and Accelerationist positions. Instead of the immanent flow, what interests me is the position of the subject within the terrain of the structural limit—of the negative that grounds subjectivity: from the (Deleuzian) flux, as Žižek puts it, to the (Hegelian-Lacanian) gap.[74] In contrast to an older Althusserian structural Marxism, the latter is best expressed in terms of what Bruno Bosteels has called "the new doctrine of structural causality."[75]

Dialectical materialism, according to Bosteels, can be understood as a theory of "contradictory breaks." Applied, then, to historical phenomena, such as the material transition from one mode of production to the next arising out of contradictions in each previous one, historical materialism helps to define the object of dialectical materialist investigation, that is, through the production and deployment of a series of analytical concepts. Two of the concepts central to the Althusserian project are "structural causality" and its "absent cause." Structural causality, as Bosteels explains, rests on the fact that "a society always possesses the complex unity of a structure dominated by one of its instances, or articulated practices. Depending on the conjuncture at a given moment in the history of society, the dominant can be economical, political, scientific, religious, and so on."[76] Depending, then, upon the historical conjuncture, a certain tendency will have dominance upon the characterization of the social totality.

Tangentially, we can perhaps come to understand this through the prism of Raymond Williams's distinctions between dominant, emergent, and residual elements of a culture. Whereas it is difficult to claim that any one particular cultural formation totalizes the entire field, it is more so the case that the dominant tendency sutures the entire field of the social, while still running in parallel with new emergent cultural elements, as well as residual elements from older or more traditional culture. Similarly, although we might talk about the dominance, today, of finance capital, it is not as though we have witnessed the disappearance of agrarian capital, or industrial capital, or merchant capital. The dominance of finance capital speaks merely to its historically contingent position in organizing the entirety of the system within this particular stage or moment of the class struggle. Likewise, as Jameson argues, postmodernism is not the only cultural force—it is merely the "cultural logic of late capitalism," which is to say that it is the culture that dominates alongside residual elements of traditional, national or ethnic culture, modern culture, as well as likely emergent elements of a wholly new and not yet fully formed culture, perhaps reflective of the ideological tendency that Mark Fisher has called "capitalist realism," or of what Streeck now refers to as the "interregnum." This way of reading the relationship between the dominant, residual, and emergent is what makes the logic of the signifier or the metaphor, as a point of meaningful fixation, culturally and ideologically significant. It does not totalize in the way that Foucault, or Deleuze, or even Laclau and Mouffe describe; but it does articulate a point of closure that is not disconnected from the historical state of power and the class struggle.

What then gives cause to the structural emplacement of this or that dominant and overdetermining force is what Althusser, drawing on Spinoza, calls the "absent cause," or the ultimately determining instance of the mode of production. As Jameson explains in *The Political Unconscious*, Althusser identifies the entirety of the structure itself with the mode of production.[77] Therefore, he writes, if we wish to characterize Althusser's as a *structural* Marxism, "one must complete the characterization with the essential proviso that it is a structuralism for which only *one* structure exists: namely the mode of production itself, or the synchronic system of social relations as a whole."[78] For Jameson, this is the sense "in which this 'structure' is an absent cause, since it is nowhere empirically present as an element, it is not part of the whole or one of the [topographical] levels, but rather the entire system of *relationships* among those levels."[79] (We should note how closely this description resembles that of the hyperobject.) This means, then, according to Jameson, that history figures as the very absent cause of the entire structure—history, that is, as the movement from one mode of production to the next and the class struggle as the antagonistic relationship that colors the dominant cultural and social character of the historical conjuncture; but also, history figures as the sets of relationships between subject positions differently articulated according to the topography: base and superstructure. For what is the base if not the expression of a particular social relationship between agents, that is, the relations of production, which in the case of the capitalist mode of production is a relationship of exploitation? The superstructure similarly articulates the social relationship between agents, but it does so according to a different set of practices that are not unrelated to those of production.

Jameson writes, "history is *not* a text, not a narrative, master or otherwise, but that, as an absent cause, it is inaccessible to us except in textual form, and that our approach to it and to the [Lacanian] Real itself [as that which resists symbolization] necessarily passes through its prior textualization, its narrativization in the political unconscious."[80] Jameson's claim provides an important rejoinder to the Foucauldian critique of the apparent search for historical origins in Marxism, since historical materialism shows, according to Jameson's reading of structural causality and its absent cause, that each new expression of the class struggle in the present—each new historical conjuncture, marked by the ever changing conditions of the class struggle—retroactively determines the subjective reading of the historical. Marxism and historical materialism, upon this reading, are truly a "history of the present"—it is the signifier or the metaphor that gives history its dominant retroactive figurability. We can then read the development of what Bosteels calls the "new doctrine of structural causality" in the following manner.

Beginning with Ernesto Laclau and Chantal Mouffe, Bosteels identifies three points that can be made regarding the relationship between the Lacanian Real, the subject, and ideology. First, as Laclau and Mouffe point out in *Hegemony and Socialist Strategy*, the social field, just like the Lacanian Symbolic order (the field of the big Other), is "structured around the traumatic kernel of the real."[81] The traumatic kernel of the social field is identified by Laclau and Mouffe as (political) antagonism. In Lacanian terms, we could say that the social field is not-all, and in order for it to have some ultimate fixity, it requires the addition of the Master-Signifier—that is, of a structuring metaphor. For Laclau and Mouffe, as Bosteels explains, politics only emerges because society is lacking—it does not exist as a unified whole. There is, in other words, a gap or void in the structure, which they identify with the Lacanian Real, and which Jameson identifies with the absent cause of history.

But in a second move that veers toward Žižek and other so-called neo-Lacanians, such as Mladen Dolar and Alenka Zupančič, Bosteels notes that for them the subject, in fact, is this gap in the structure. If the Real is signalled by the very limits of the Symbolic, if antagonism posits the impossibility of society, then the subject is what overlaps with this very position; or, as Žižek puts it, just as the Real emerges as the limit of society, "the subject is strictly correlative to its own impossibility; its limit is its positive position."[82] The subject, in other words, "is *nothing but* the impossibility of its own signifying representation—the empty place opened

up in the big Other by the failure of this representation."[83] Better still,
as Dolar explains the difference between the truly Lacanian category of
the subject and the Althusserian one, is that for Althusser "the subject is
what makes ideology work; for [Lacanian] psychoanalysis, the subject
emerges where ideology fails."[84] Subject—the political or revolutionary
subject, the "proletariat"—is correlative with the impossibility of society.
Not some positive or affirmative character of society—not yet, anyway—
but the symptomatic point at which the deadlocks of the social emerge.
This is one reason why, for Žižek, the antagonism identified by Laclau and
Mouffe that forever prevents the full closure of the social has a precise
name: class struggle.[85]

Class struggle, for Žižek, names the social Real—the antagonism
at the heart of the social, its limit point—at the same time that it posits
the emergence of the subject of psychoanalysis: the hysteric. The hysteric
comes to figure and overlap with history as an absent cause in the way
that Jameson describes history as the absent cause of the structure. History, according to Žižek, is "nothing but a succession of failed attempts to
grasp, conceive, specify this strange kernel [of the Real]."[86] It is this point
that allows us, he writes, to reject the common reproach that psychoanalysis is nonhistorical and to transform it from a critique into a positive identification of the historical. Put differently, in his own defense of
the Hegelian dialectic (this is a point that asserts his own commitment to
dialectical materialism), Žižek argues that dialectics offers the most cogent articulation of what Laclau and Mouffe conceive as antagonism: "far
from being a story of progressive overcoming, dialectics is for Hegel a systemic notation of the failure of all such attempts—'absolute knowledge'
denotes a subjective position which finally accepts 'contradiction' as an
internal condition of every identity."[87] The Lacanian subject therefore
exists, according to Žižek, on two levels: both as the neurotic or hysterical subject and as the subject who emerges at the ends of analysis, when
the subject has traversed the fantasy and has gone beyond the deadlock
of subjective destitution—that is, when the subject herself occupies the
position of the analyst—this subject is for him the subject of history:
"hysteria is the subject's way of resisting the prevailing, historically specified form of interpellation or symbolic identification. . . . Hysteria means
failed interpellation."[88]

But, now, there is a third movement in Bosteels's description of
the new doctrine that moves us back from the revolutionary character
of the subject and into the subject caught in ideology; this movement is
where finally we can claim the originality of Žižek's theory of ideology,
which departs from the Althusserian one, but also which allows us to
understand more fully what remains ideological within the historical

context of the postmodern culture and society. That is to say, when we have reached the limits of the social, when we have reached the limits of the Symbolic—or, when we have begun to acknowledge first-hand the nonexistence of the big Other—what is there left to keep us within the terrain of the ideological? Žižek's response, of course, is *jouissance*: enjoyment! We can finally see in what sense Postman was wrong: rather than "amusing ourselves to death," we are instead "*enjoying* our media."

Enjoyment as a Political Factor

Žižek posits the problem of enjoyment at the beginning of *For They Know Not What They Do*; and, here, we should note the specific historicization and periodization of his writing, which took place precisely at the moment of the Fukuyamist pronouncement of the "end of History," at the moment of the apparent triumph of liberal democracy and of what it truly stands for within the coordinates of capitalism: the equation of consumerism with freedom. He poses the question: "How do we account for this paradox that the absence of Law universalizes Prohibition?" The answer, he says, is that "*enjoyment itself, which we experience as 'transgression', is in its innermost status something imposed, ordered*—when we enjoy, we never do it 'spontaneously', we always follow a certain injunction. The psychoanalytic name for this obscene injunction, for this obscene call, 'Enjoy!', is superego."[89] To understand this claim we need to return to the problem of the signifier—of the metaphor—and what it stands for, both as a marker of the postmodern, but also as a marker of prohibiting agency or authority.

What makes Deleuze and Guattari's reading of capitalism so intriguing is that they consider the relationship between capitalism, the structure of the modern family, and the impact upon each as they are reflected in the formation of the subject. As Marx states in volume three of *Capital*: "Capitalist production constantly strives to overcome [its own] immanent barriers, but it overcomes them only by means that set up the barriers afresh and on a more powerful scale."[90] In other words, as Deleuze and Guattari put it, capitalism constantly enforces processes of "deterritorialization," which implies that to overcome its own self-imposed barriers to accumulation, capital must become unhinged from its own processes and seek new ones as a means of survival. Such a practice implies, for them, the waning of the signifier that assigns meaning to the subjective dimensions of experience. The neurotic subject, for them, appears in the form of the bourgeois subject who is troubled by the changing conditions enforced by capital flight. However, rather than applying—as they see it—the re-Oedipalization of the subject (back into the mommy-daddy-me triad), they prefer an anti-interpretivist practice that seeks to maintain the barring of the signifier, restricting its (re)territorialization, keeping open the range of freedom for the subject to accelerate the decline of the capitalist mode of production. This is why the schizo figures as their ideal hero: he is the one who forecloses the (tyranny of) the signifier. But there is a problem here that Žižek rightly identifies, and it addresses precisely what is problematic about both the Deleuzian and the Foucauldian approaches.

On the one hand, the Deleuzian-Guattarian approach seems correct in demonstrating that internal revolutions to the capitalist mode of production end up producing new forms of subjectivity. But it is by positing desire as a positive, rather than a negative force—that is, a lack—that they miss the ideological dimensions of postmodern (consumer) capitalism. The dilemma, in other words, is not one with neurosis or Oedipalization, but with generalized *perversion* in the strictest Lacanian sense. Žižek points out at the end of *The Ticklish Subject* the historical waning of the Oedipus complex, which he says is somewhat tied to the postmodern fading of authority—more precisely for my purposes, the waning of the signifier, of the metaphor. But if the modern authority is on the wane, this creates a strange scenario for the subject. If, as Bruce Fink puts it, "neurosis can be understood as a set of strategies by which people protest against a 'definitive' sacrifice of jouissance—castration—imposed upon them by their parents . . . and come to desire in relation to the law, *perversion involves the attempt to prop up the law so that limits can be set to jouissance.*"[91] In perversion, the subject wishes to bring the law into existence—to make the Other exist—since it is the very existence of the Other that provides a space for transgression as a means of obtaining "obscene enjoyment," as Žižek calls it. This is the sense in which Žižek identifies the form of postmodern ideology as *cynical.* Drawing upon the Lacanian description of the perverse mechanism—of disavowal—and relying on the phrase used by Octave Mannoni, Žižek describes the cynical attitude as one of "*Je sais bien, mais quand même . . .*"—"I know very well, but nevertheless . . ."[92] It is even, in this way, that Žižek amends the Marxist logic of commodity fetishism with the Lacanian theory of the fetish.

The predominant Marxist approach to commodity fetishism is one in which the commodity masks or hides or conceals the positive—that is, existing—social relationship between people or, more specifically, the social relations of production and exploitation. But the psychoanalytic conception of the fetish, instead, refers to it as that which "conceals the lack ('castration') around which the symbolic network is articulated."[93]

Fetish, in other words, mirrors the operation of the signifier and the metaphor. It is that which allows the subject to disavow the lack or gap which it *is* within the Symbolic order; however, what fills the lack that *is* the subject in the field of the Symbolic is the fantasy structure that allows her to relate to her enjoyment. Fantasy, not as some dream of successfully obtaining the lost object of desire (the *object a*), but as that which regulates for the subject, teaches her about what she desires. Fantasy, in this way, becomes a support of ideology, especially when we appear to inhabit a post-ideological era. But that is not all.

As Lacan had claimed, desire is the desire of the big Other—of the Symbolic order. The Symbolic order, in other words, comes to figure for the subject her relationship to her desire and to her enjoyment. As the gap within the Symbolic order, fantasy supports the subject's approach to this position, filling in for her what is lacking; but she simultaneously attributes this position to the signifier that defines her. Žižek therefore describes how "a signifier (S_1) represents for another signifier (S_2) its absence, its lack $, which is the subject;" "the Master-Signifier, the One, is the signifier *for which* all the others represent the subject."[94] Simply marking the signifier as that which represents the subject would, however, also miss the relationship between the subject and the ideological implication of propping up a power that makes the subject ideological.

In contrast to the Althusserian claim that ideology interpellates individuals as subjects—which seems to imply that ideology is somehow *zapped* into the mind—Žižek adds that "ideology is the exact opposite of internalization of the external contingency: it resides in externalization of the result of an inner necessity, and the task of the critique of ideology here is precisely to discern the hidden necessity in what appears as a mere contingency."[95] This implies that, at the same time that the subject assumes a defining signifier that gives her substance within the spaces of the Symbolic, the task for the subject is to have recognized, by the authority of the big Other, the signifier that she confers upon herself, the signifier that has been conferred upon her by the big Other. Or, to be more precise, "it is never the individual which is interpellated as subject, *into* subject; it is on the contrary the subject itself who is interpellated as x (some specific subject-position, symbolic identity or mandate), thereby eluding the abyss of $."[96] The ambiguity as to the desire of the Other—*Che vuoi?*—"What do you want from me?" What am I to you?"—forces the subject into a precipitous identification, anticipating what the Other demands. But with the apparent loss of the Other in the postmodern, post-ideological condition of the *loss* of the signifier, it appears as though the Other is nowhere—nowhere, that is, *to confer* meaning. As I intend to argue, social media now figures for the form of the Symbolic big Other. It is the form of social media, both as a central metaphor and as the

character of the Other, that creates and establishes the lure of our desire
and positions us vis-à-vis our relationship to our enjoyment.

It appears in postmodern times that we enjoy so much freedom.
There is a loss of authority (in the form of the big Other, in the form of
political oppression, and so on). But what if what appears as a prohibition
of enjoyment is in fact its very condition of possibility? This is the trick of
the postmodern superego injunction: "Enjoy!" It becomes all the more
difficult to enjoy the more that we are increasingly and directly *enjoined*
to do so. There is, as Žižek describes, a transgressive dimension to enjoyment in which it is the transgression, itself—breaking the rules—that gar-
ners for us our enjoyment. This concerns the dialectical tension between
desire and drive. If I can be somewhat reductive for the sake of brevity,
we might see desire as "enjoying what we don't have" (to cite the title of a
book by Todd McGowan). We desire insofar as we are lacking. But if that's
the case, then drive has to do, in a way, with hating what we enjoy—that is,
the pain involved in *not* obtaining the apparent lost object of desire (that
only exists insofar as it remains lost), which actually procures enjoyment.
Jouissance, enjoyment, is thus caught up in an odd mixture of pleasure
and pain—we both enjoy what we don't have, but we still hate (insofar as
it is experienced as painful) what we enjoy. What separates the two, on
the one hand, is the fantasy that screens the experience of the drive—this
is why in working toward the analytical cure, the subject must "traverse"
the fantasy to arrive at the recognition that *jouissance* is firstly a treatment
of the relationship between desire and drive, and secondly that what we
desire is the obstacle.[97] The latter is the position arrived at, at the ends
of analysis. But in ideology, which also knows that the obstacle is a condition of enjoyment—the obstacle that we seek to transgress as the source
of our enjoyment—the subjective position becomes one of perversion.

In the conditions of postmodern culture, "perversion is not subversion."[98] This is Žižek's reproach to Judith Butler (and to Foucault), who
provides perhaps what is the most cogent explanation of this relationship
between ideology and enjoyment. Referring to what she calls "passionate attachment," Butler proposes (like Foucault) that power constitutes
the subject. Power, she says, "is not simply what we oppose but also, in a
strong sense, what we depend on for our existence and what we harbor
and preserve in the beings that we are."[99] How does it do so? Butler, on
the one hand, notes that this has to do with the discursive terms set out
by power and that we depend upon for our existence. But if we read
Foucault in *The History of Sexuality, Volume 1*, we also see that we come to
depend upon power for our existence because it is only by resisting power
that we become subjects. This is Foucault's critique of the "repressive hy-
pothesis," in which, among other things, he claims that desire is not something that is repressed—through a power that says "No!"—power, in fact,

becomes the very *raison d'être* of desire in the sense that "where there is power, there is resistance."[100] Where there is power, there is, in other (Žižek's) words, an inherent transgression. What the pervert knows, then, is that without the obstacle, without power, there is no transgression—there is no *jouissance*. It is the perverse subject, then, whose goal it is to prop up power, to impose an authority that says "No!" so as to be able to transgress. This is why, I claim, that the pervert, and not the schizo, is the typical subject of postmodern capitalism—the subject whose arrival is marked by the generalized acceptance of subversion, when subversion becomes the dominant ideology. This is how social media comes to figure as the dominant form of thought, understanding, and subjectivity today.

Cognitive Mapping with Social Media

The basic thesis of *Algorithmic Desire* is that social media is one of the central metaphors for coming to understand the totality of early twenty-first-century capitalism. However, my claim, too, is that social media has come to figure for us a central virtual agency against which we come to know the forms of the reigning contemporary consciousness, our subjectivity, and our relationship to enjoyment and our desire. Chun has argued that digital new media, or networks, end postmodernism or dissolve postmodern disorientation.[101] I am sympathetic to this argument, since the claim I defend in this book is that social media marks a new version of the agency of the Symbolic big Other. Social media resolves the kind of disorientation that Chun writes about. That is to say that social media provides ideological cognitive mapping for the postmodern subject incapable of locating or making sense of herself and her context. But it does so, as she points out, in spatial terms. The network, in other words, is a spatial metaphor. In this regard, like the typical postmodern aesthetic, the network continues to spatialize time. Although networks contain a temporal dimension, what they are missing is a historical one, by which I mean history in the Marxist sense. We might be able to say, then, that social media in some ways resolves some of the ontological problems of schizophrenic postmodernism; but we have not yet departed fully from the cultural logic of postmodern capitalism. Postmodern culture—and postmodern practices of subversion—still form the background against which we today try to find an adequate resistance to the historical form of the neoliberal and finance-dominated capitalist mode of production.[102] I take into account Chun and Jameson's objectives to map the current configuration through the dominant technological metaphor; therefore,

this book uses social media as a model for coming to terms with the totality of the present ideology. I am now in a position to map the trajectory
of what follows.

To start, the first chapter returns to the beginning of the second
decade of the twenty-first century. In *First as Tragedy, Then as Farce*, Žižek
notes that the first decade of this century was marked—bracketed—by
the two events: the terrorist attacks on the World Trade Center and the
Pentagon on September 11, 2001 and the financial crisis of 2008.[103] The
second decade, I claim, became fully pronounced with the so-called "year
of dreaming dangerously": the years 2010–2011 when we started to see
the first wave of protest movements, first with the Tunisian and Egyptian
uprisings dubbed the "Arab Spring," then with the rise of the Occupy
Wall Street Movement (#OWS), and other variations, such as the "Maple
Spring" and the #IdleNoMore movements in Canada. These social and
political movements, organized largely through social media, came to be
known as "social media revolutions." However, in recent years, we have
seen that, far from leading further toward utopian liberal democracy,
the rise of the Alt-Right and the election of Donald Trump as president
represents a force perhaps inherent to the form of social media and contemporary neoliberal capitalism. Chapter 1 begins by ascertaining the
rhetoric of the "social" in "social media" and "social media revolutions,"
by referring back to Laclau and Mouffe's thesis in *Hegemony and Socialist
Strategy*, that "society is not a valid object of discourse." Referring to this
thesis, I take the rhetoric of "social media revolutions" as an indication
of the rise of social media as a metaphor for the contemporary ideology,
signalling a kind of reconstitution of the ideological big Other. If the
Lacanian program is one of coming to terms with the nonexistence of
the big Other, then perhaps the correct response to the assertion of social
media as the new big Other, the new Symbolic order of our culture, is
that "*social* media does not exist." But if everyone already, in postmodern
culture, knows that the big Other does not exist, what then is the strategic
impact of this claim?

This question is taken up in chapter 2, where I engage with Jodi
Dean's conception of "communicative capitalism." Drawing on Lacan
and Žižek, Dean claims that in the context of a demise of symbolic
efficiency—of the postmodern "breakdown of the signifying chain"—
ideology is more a matter of drive than desire. In contrast, I argue that
with the reconstitution of the Symbolic through social media we must still
understand ideology through the logic of desire. I elaborate further on
this point in chapter 3 by discussing the role of social media algorithms
and automation in the constitution of subjectivity today. Here, though,
I engage with the distinction made by Maurizio Lazzarato—drawing on

Deleuze and Guattari—between social subjection and machinic enslavement. Lazzarato argues in a sense for the priority of machinic enslavement as the criterion for conceiving the relationship between subjects and machines, in which our subjectivity is more a matter of being interpellated away from our existence within the assemblage. I argue against this view and propose seeing subjectivity as prior, since it is through our formation as subjects that we come to desire, which is the basis for any and all integration into machinic processes.

In chapter 4, I move on to the concept of "curation." Returning to Stuart Hall's Encoding/Decoding model used for analyzing the relationship between content producers and consumers in the media, I show how social media programmers help to curate the big Other for each individual user. While my claim is that social media helps to reconstitute the Symbolic big Other, social media shows that the way to interpellate the user is by curating a particular image of the big Other, one that more forcefully and powerfully fuels our desire. Chapter 5, then, turns to the way that neoliberal subjects curate their own identities through the construction of the public profile. Here, neoliberal subjects are addressed as "entrepreneurs" or as "entrepreneurs of the Self," in which out of necessity, people are driven to curate their identities for the imagined big Other: the network of other uses who bear an influence upon our very social existence. Appearances, I claim, do matter, and it is by producing and reifying one's Self in the form of the signifier that we can understand the relationship, not only between the subject and her desire, but also in the form of the Self that she constructs for the other's gaze.

Chapter 6 turns to an interpretation of love and romance on social media dating apps. Considering the way that algorithms now model the instrumental rationality of the present, I take up the curation of love on social media as a manner of understanding the neoliberal entrepreneurial ethic as it applies to love and sex. The question I ask is whether or not this is enough to turn us on sexually, or does the rationalism of the algorithm deny sex to us.

In the final, concluding chapter, I return to some of the questions I have posed above about how New Materialism and Accelerationism envision a postcapitalist future. While many theorists of media and democracy posit the digital as a way forward toward emancipation and a postcapitalist future, I claim instead that the media offers us, analytically, a way to understand the contradictions and the gaps in the dominant consciousness. Rather than trying to build a postcapitalist emancipated future *through* the media or the technology, what we need instead is a movement to change and transform the institutional, legal, and political structures of society. This book concludes with an attempt to make the case for doing so.

1

Periodizing Social Media, or, "Social Media" Does Not Exist!

Žižek writes, in *First as Tragedy, Then as Farce*, that the first decade of the twenty-first century was bookended by two defining moments: first, the Al-Qaeda attacks on the World Trade Center in New York City and the Pentagon on September 11, 2001; and second, the global financial crisis that began with the crisis in the housing market that started in late 2007 and culminated in the credit crisis in the fall of 2008.[1] This latter event, of course, initiated in many ways the second decade of the twenty-first century, which arguably concluded with the election of Donald Trump as president in the fall of 2016. We are apparently talking about "decades" as eight-year periods, but the periodizing operation here is one that I use to identify points of historical consciousness in the moments being addressed. In the period between these last two events we have witnessed a much deeper integration of social media platforms into our everyday ways of living. We have seen, even, the concentration of power in the tech industry around only a handful of major players within this period: the so-called "FAANG" companies (Facebook, Amazon, Apple, Netflix, and Google). But the significance of social media has also played out to the degree that it has become not only a major source of information, but also a central site of communication and advocacy.

In the period between the financial crisis and the US 2016 election, we have also seen a proliferation of global social movements that have, in one way or another, organized around and through social media, including: the Arab Spring (in a number of sites, such as Iran, Tunisia, Egypt, and Turkey), Occupy Wall Street and the various other Occupy movements elsewhere in the United States, Canada, and Europe, #BlackLivesMatter (or #BLM), and #MeToo; in addition, there are the Maple Spring in Quebec (a student-led movement to fight increasing tuition costs caused by new regimes of austerity), the Indigenous-led #IdleNoMore, and the #MMIWG (the campaign for an inquiry into Murdered and Missing Indigenous Women and Girls) movements in Canada.[2] The proliferation of these movements has been signalled in the mainstream media as "social media revolutions," which have provided a lot of attention for social media, and less attention for the core demands of the movements themselves, and less attention to the forces that create limits for these movements in realizing their goals, namely the interests of capital, private property ownership, and a neoliberal regulatory regime more generally, to name but a few.[3] Despite the enthusiasm generated around these "social media revolutions," we have also seen how, beginning around 2013, a new force, self-dubbed the "Alt-Right," began to show up more often in the spaces of mainstream social media, including sites like Twitter and YouTube, advocating against social justice movements and using the derogatory term "SJW" (or, Social Justice Warriors), to attempt to discredit and challenge the forces of the Left, particularly Feminist, and Antiracist, Trans, and LGBTQ+ movements. The #GamerGate fiasco in 2013, led by figures such as Milo Yiannopoulos, formerly of Breitbart News, began to draw popular attention to these swarming forces, and have ultimately been represented as major sources of influence for the popularity of candidate Donald Trump in 2015 and 2016.[4]

Surprised, or blindsided, by Trump's electoral victory, attention began to turn toward the role of social media in generating misinformation, "fake news," and toxic communities in the construction of online group clusters where feedback enabled a kind of "bubble" think where echo chambers and informational silos created built-in limits to the dialogue promised to us by the advocates of the digital public sphere. Ever since, we have been hearing more and more about the fact that we now live in a post-Truth or post-fact society.

These most recent proclamations, I argue, have resulted from a now decades long transition whereby the very articulation of Truths or essences have been challenged by forces on both the Left and the Right, caught in a political conflict that has increasingly taken on a discursive form. All the while, although the surface level of debate may have shifted toward an apparent conflict of sliding signifiers, capital still remains the material basis underlying existing conflicts. The arrival, not only of social media as a platform communications technology, but also of the rhetoric of "social media," implies that the term itself seems now to occupy the space of a Master-Signifier, a referent against which we are able to somehow articulate the hegemony of the social order against the context of a "demise of symbolic efficiency," to employ a term used by Žižek and popularized by Jodi Dean as the "*decline* of symbolic efficiency."[5] As I will argue in the following chapter, social media appears to reconstitute the form of the Symbolic order at the moment when both the Left and the Right have made claims regarding the nonexistence of society.

Margaret Thatcher famously proclaimed in the early 1980s that there is no such thing as society, there are only individuals and families. Ernesto Laclau and Chantal Mouffe, on the Left, similarly also proclaimed that "society" is not a valid object of discourse, extending a logic that began with the structuralist rejection of humanism, and subsequently the poststructuralist reaction against structures themselves, which are held together by centers of power.[6] This, I will argue, may be true, but it is important to see and come to understand the historical trajectory of every new assertion of a norm, which arises out of its own reaction to the previous one. For me, the very term, "social media," represents the articulation of a new communicational norm that, even as deployed rhetorically, as a Master-Signifier, has become a referent against which all of the other signifiers determine the subject, as Lacan would have put it. "Social media," therefore, brings structure to the seemingly unstructured space of the internet, and in so doing helps us to identify precisely just how it represents a willing back into existence of the agency of the big Other (a topic that I will take up more directly in the next chapter). For now, let us develop a bit further this line of thinking about the relationship between social media and the internet architecture itself.

Contradictions of the Media Spectacle

The dilemma of the "fake news" or "post-Truth" society is not unrelated to the contradiction between the democratic and commercial logics of the media. One of the by-products of commodification has been a democratization of sorts. In art and culture this has meant widening access to those spaces previously open only to the elite—spaces of cultural consumption, like the art gallery. Oddly, though, commodification has the effect of veiling class antagonism when it now comes to accessing art, culture, and information. No one is barred from access, so long as one can pay the price of admission. For conservative cultural critics, like Matthew Arnold and F. R. Leavis, and especially for cultural critics of the Left, like Max Horkheimer and Theodor W. Adorno, the commodification of culture, however democratizing to a certain extent, still played a role in removing what was uniquely valuable about works of art—that is, their aura, or their uniqueness in time and space, and their ability to speak to the sublime essence of the human condition.[7] For Adorno, to a greater degree, modern art has the ability to truly challenge the reigning order, in contrast to the products of the culture industry, which simply help to reproduce capitalism.

The technological reproducibility of art, too, according to Walter Benjamin, is a factor in the democratization of art and culture.[8] Just as paying the price of admission grants access to the unique work, so too does new media make possible the widespread dissemination of the work so that it can be accessed far and wide, beyond the gallery's limited reach. In fact, this aspect of new media, its ability to share information widely, is part and parcel of democratization in a political sense. The term *media* has become synonymous with the practice of journalism. As journalism, the media serve an important function in democracy by providing the people with the information that they need to make critical rational decisions about how to participate democratically. However, this democratic (fourth estate) function of the media in the public sphere is contradicted by the commercial (that is, commodified) logic of the media.

As media scholars have long demonstrated, private media companies are principally driven, as businesses, by the profit motive. This includes contemporary new media and social media websites, such as Google, Facebook, and Twitter. As Edward Herman and Noam Chomsky demonstrated thirty years ago, the commercial logic of the media, particularly insofar as it is influenced by the role of owners and advertisers, works toward filtering out information that is either detrimental to the political status quo or at the very least to its bottom line.[9] This includes sifting out content that potentially offends advertisers or special interest groups. Nevertheless, the media interpellates viewers through the spectacularization and sensationalization of news and information. Since media revenues are still drawn by maximizing viewer attention, the "work" of which involves the so-called audience commodity, or online as the "prosumer commodity," building a sizable audience is still one of the primary motivating factors of media production.[10] In this regard, we can also see to some degree the "liberalization" of the media in the same sense, as has been already discussed in terms of the diffusion and branding of diversity. This gives some credence to criticisms of the mainstream mass media from both the Left and the Right.

On the Left, the political economic critique of the media demonstrates the existence of a right-wing, procapitalist bias. On the Right, however, the mainstream mass media is believed to contain an underlying liberal bias, which has become a favorite target for right-wing radio talk show hosts, like Rush Limbaugh, who see the push for political correctness and the positive representation of women and racialized minorities as a threat sparked by the "cultural Marxism" of the liberal university campuses of the 1960s and their culture wars. The rise of the right-wing website Breitbart News is also indicative of this trend, as the site was initially conceived as a locus for uncovering liberal falsehoods, cover-ups, and conspiracies. Regardless of which side is more correct—the critique of the Left is based more in terms of an organizational analysis, while the critique of the Right is based more on selective content analysis of the supposedly "liberal" media—both the Left and the Right apparently have cause for not trusting the mainstream media, which also makes pop protest songs, like Green Day's "American Idiot" (2004) and Katy Perry's "Chained to the Rhythm" (2017), both of which take media as their political targets, politically ambiguous. Evidently, everyone—whether on the Left or Right—is critical of the "fake news." This is one reason for understanding the techno-utopianism about the digital public sphere of the internet, first in the 1990s, with the development of the World Wide Web, and then again in recent times with the rise of the so-called social media revolutions, as a culture of not trusting the mainstream media. As Angela Nagle notes, "Just a few years ago the Left-cyberutopians claimed that 'the disgust had become a network' and that establishment old media no longer control politics, that the new public sphere was going to be based on leaderless, user-generated social media." This network, she says, "has indeed arrived, but it has helped to take the Right, not the Left, to power."[11]

If the protest movements that arose in the wake of the 2008 financial crisis, such as the Arab Spring and Occupy Wall Street, organized in part by using social media sites like Facebook and Twitter, energizing the techno-utopians on the liberal Left, this positive image of the new internet and social media culture was crushed by the election of Trump in November 2016. Not surprisingly, the enthusiasm for the social media revolutions that we saw in the mainstream media quickly dissipated in the election's aftermath. How could we have all been so blindsided? Social media became vilified with ensuing reports about online information "bubbles" or silos and the problem of "fake news."[12]

The "bubble" problem is exacerbated by for-profit social media websites, and if the prosumer commodity model is accurate—in which social media sites are capable of monetizing user-generated content and data—then there is an incentive to maximize user participation as much as possible. Instead of serving democratic interests, as profit-generating platforms, social media turns participation and communication into means of monetization and revenue building. Maximizing participation is key, and part of the algorithmic logic of sites like Facebook includes individuating user experience in the sense that the feedback loop becomes part of the normalized regimen of site activity.[13] Unlike an older conception of ideological passivity, social media use is paradoxical in that the more we participate, the more we are plugged into the feedback loop of the ideological choir club, so to speak, however lacking in any real encounter with the ideological other. In ideal terms, the liberal bourgeois conception of the democratic public sphere has meant more or less— and not without significant flaws—an encounter with the other.[14] The notion of critical rational public discourse is premised on the idea that people in civil society must come together to politely and openly debate opposing views. Not only do the feedback loops and information silos on social media prevent such an encounter; the new digital society of the spectacle is driven by maximizing the number of hits, clicks, likes, and shares that a post receives. The digital attention economy is very much an effect of the neoliberal entrepreneurial ethic of reputation management. In the cluttered spaces of the digital sea of abundance, attention is valuable currency, and getting noticed sometimes means being loud and obnoxious.

For the neoliberal ideology, it is primarily the entrepreneur as identity curator who is most publicly valorized by the reigning sensibility. However, it is the figure of the troll—an agent who builds a reputation by tarnishing the reputation of others—who has become one of the primary antagonists of the present, championed heroically by the racist and misogynistic meme culture of the Alt-Right. For a culture that privileges the troll as its antihero, Trump, then, appears as a godsend. Trolls, as Richard Seymour puts it, "are the self-styled pranksters of the internet. A subculture of wind-up merchants who will say anything they can to provoke unwary victims, then delight in the outrage that follows."[15] What drives the troll is the pursuit of "lulz"—a cynical form of enjoyment "that derives from someone else's anguish." And as an agent of the Alt-Right, the troll delights particularly in the harassment of feminists, cultural Marxists, PC liberals, and SJWs. In view of this use of the most advanced communications system and technology ever to exist, it is worth asking if the concerns of conservative elitist critics like Arnold and Leavis, or left-wing critics like Horkheimer and Adorno, were in fact correct about the commodification of culture, especially if digital democracy has been reduced to the anything goes, free speech fundamentalism of the masculinist Alt-Right troll. My own inclination is that social media can and does still fulfill a democratic function, but as with all forces of production, must be contextualized within the existing relations of production, exploitation, and the class struggle.

Finally, what makes the emergence of the Alt-Right troll—and Trump as a figurehead—so hard to bear for the traditional liberal Left is that the regular appeals to truth seem to have flown out the window entirely. Even the kind of political economic criticism of the mainstream media's propaganda model that is expounded by Herman and Chomsky still relies on an older notion of ideology as false consciousness. Part of the problem that they see with the mass media is that its system of filtration creates a barrier of access for people to the truth. They—and Chomsky in much of his political commentary in particular—seem to rely on the idea that "if only the people knew the truth," then they would revolt and demand back their democracy. The problem is that followers of the Alt-Right, and Trump in particular, already seem to know the truth, but continue to act as if this were not the case. In their cynical enjoyment of "lulz," truth simply does not factor in. As Seymour points out, "This is what the critique of 'post-truth politics' misses. Even when he lies egregiously, Trump's fans think he is demonstrating an important truth in exposing media fakery."[16]

Infoglut?

Let us be clear: today, we are, in a large sense, living in a "post-fact" society or era. We shouldn't misconstrue this problem. This situation has emerged, not merely because of a lack of facts, or due to a lack information, or simply because of misinformation. We are not, in other words, faced with a deficit of information. Quite the contrary. We are, in our current times, as a product of the "information age," plagued by the opposite problem of what the media theorist, Mark Andrejevic, refers to as an *infoglut*—we are now faced with the paradoxical problem of information overload.[17] How has it come to be that our problem is today one of *too much* information?

The problem, according to Andrejevic, has to do with the fact that our thinking about information and knowledge in democratic societies is based upon the media regimes of previous eras. Prior to our current times we relied upon and were dependent on newspapers and media companies, uncensored history books and encyclopaedias, as well as experts and opinion leaders, to help us to make sense of information and new knowledge. We had access to regimes of what Fredric Jameson refers to as "cognitive mapping"—that is, even if our access to information was limited, we still had maps of meaning that provided a narrative framework that allowed us to make sense of the world and our position within it.[18] We developed much closer and personal ties with media stations and personalities; and, in fact, in the past century, many of the struggles over information had to do with a problem of scarcity and restrictions on access to information. From this standpoint, it is easy to understand—in part, at least—why the arrival of the internet was greeted with so much democratic enthusiasm. More information, we believe, provides the building blocks to our liberation. From the perspective of a society initially founded in information scarcity, controlled access to information, and censorship, "technologies that make information more readily available and sharable carry with them a potential challenge to entrenched forms of power."[19] Knowledge, after all, is power, don't you know! Or, maybe we can amend this to claim to suggest that information leads to empowerment. Or does it?

A particular kind of informational utopianism certainly resonates in the discourses about the internet. In the early days of the World Wide Web, the internet came to be seen as a decentralized, horizontal, "rhizomatic," and nonhierarchical avenue of information production and exchange. The architecture of the internet was championed by critical theorists because it seemed to replicate the formulation of some theorists of ideology, railing against its top-down structure of authority and control.[20] For a utopianism of the Left, the internet came to be seen not merely as the actualization of the public sphere—the "digital public sphere"—it also came to represent the realization, or at the very least a representation of anarchy in practice; oddly—or maybe not so oddly— such an anarchistic utopianism would come to overlap with a variant of informational libertarianism championed by hackers of both the Left and the Right. The internet was decentralization, deconstruction, or de-structure ("destruction") realized. A flat, nonhierarchical space; a levelled playing field.

There is a kind of postmodern jubilation around the apparent decentralization of power on the internet. Thinking about its rhizomatic structure—the horizontality of the "network," or the "information superhighway"—we cannot but help to think it in terms set out by postmodern media theorists like Jean Baudrillard, Gilles Deleuze, or even Marshall McLuhan. The apparently deconstructed dimensions of the internet, its apparent decentering of some kind of "Master-Signifier" holding together the flow of meaning would seem to chide the role of any central point of reference (or "referent"): it appears to embody the society of simulation, or the hyperreality, theorized by Baudrillard. The form of the network seems to rail against the "tyranny of the signifier," in Deleuzian terms, and even reflects the sensorial "global village" described by McLuhan.[21] From these perspectives, the internet as an unstructured network seems to be the most appropriate forum for conceiving a radical democratic (should we even still talk about "democracy") politics. But what if, Andrejevic asks, models of power can incorporate the very horizontalism and decentering that radicals in previous eras saw as a complement to the liberation and deconstruction of knowledge? What if "that which was once challenged by the deconstructive arsenal now feeds upon it?"[22] Such a possibility, I claim, raises the potential for a post-fact or "post-Truth" politics, which of course makes sense in the context of a postmodern culture that challenges the very idea of a (capital "T") Truth. Allow me to explain.

The postmodern approach doesn't necessarily lead to the establishment of new norms or truths; but the attempt to "deconstruct certainty" itself—the deconstruction of all narratives, even counter-narratives that reposition our relationship to knowledge and truth—casts a complete doubt on any narrative's ability to even explain information and to put it into context. As Terry Eagleton puts it, postmodernism challenges universal Truths as a universal in its own right.[23] The postmodern "incredulity toward metanarratives," as Lyotard has it, puts into question some of the practices we might use—that might enable us—to place the newfound abundance of information into a particular (historical, geographical) rationale. No longer is there any single narrative, dominating over others—that would be too hierarchical; too tyrannical. Instead, various different (subjective, local, and particular) narratives are allowed to thrive in parallel with each other, each one given its legitimacy, in a new kind of networked relativity and democratic authenticity. Whereas in the past we contended with a dilemma of informational scarcity, in which the gatekeepers held onto so much power and control that we sometimes felt like we were sitting in the dark (lit only by the apocalyptic glow of the living room television set, positioned against the background of cultural paranoia of Cold War–era MAD—mutually assured destruction—fears; but "Make America Great Again," right?); now, in the information age, we are faced with the opposite problem: the problem of too much information, or "infoglut." The postmodern and poststructuralist delegitimization of authority and structure presents us with the problem of too much information that we are not even capable of ordering and organizing; that is, it is a problem of making sense. We are lacking a framework into which we can discern the meanings and ethical implications of what we know. We have become plagued by an overabundance of information. How do we process this?

Crisis of Hegemony?

The problem of the internet age is not (only) one of *mis*information. It is a problem of how do we decide? How do we choose or select the most suitable, or the most significant information? What is the most useful? What is the most necessary? What is the most important? We are, after all, caught in a "risk society," in which "safety nets" have been removed, and in which we are constantly forced toward a self-reflexivity that goes all the way down. Without any guarantees (of meaning, of answers), any choice we make is like a roll of the dice. Try as we might, to choose the right information, the correct options, we cannot be sure of anything until the proof (as they say) is in the pudding, and it is only retroactively that we can come to know the correctness of our decisions. Freedom is, in this way, quite radical! But it is also incredibly productive of anxiety. These types of questions add another dimension of infoglut that needs to be brought to the surface insofar as the latter contemplates the relationship between information, power, and ideology—that is: *Which* information gives us the most support for our position and place in the world? What information, in other words, helps us in our endeavor toward the "cognitive mapping" of our situation, our place in the world, and (more importantly) how to act in a way that supports our very being in the world. We are discovering more and more the contradiction between freedom and security, and we want both. As the singer Father John Misty puts it in his song, "Pure Comedy"—a perfect example of Hegelian lyricism— "Their idea of being free/Is a prison of beliefs/That they never ever have to leave . . . The only thing that makes them feel alive/Is the struggle to survive/But the only thing that they request/Is something to numb the pain with/Until there's nothing human left." We demand more freedom, but at the same time we search out forms of protection and forms of *the* guarantee. Is it only under the rubric of a guarantee that we can feel the most free? When we challenge power, what in fact do we want? Does power give us meaning? This is a problem that Nancy Fraser has recently described as one of hegemony.

According to Fraser our current moment of crisis—a crisis of meaning as well as economic and environmental crises, and of course political crises—can be viewed according to two overlapping levels: one of structure and one of hegemony. At a structural level, the crisis of capitalism (the credit crisis that began in 2007–2008) is due largely to capitalism's own inherent contradictions. Specifically, in our current moment we are dealing with a capitalism dominated by the financial sector; capitalism is dominated by the role of finance in organizing the circuits of production, distribution and exchange, consumption, and reproduction. But this crisis at the structural level has opened up another important structural fissure, which is that of hegemony. As Fraser puts it, hegemonic crisis is lived "as a restless search for answers to the following sorts of questions: who are my allies, and who are my enemies? What should I believe? What can I hope for? Who am I/ what is my community? Who are my fellows?"[24] This crisis of hegemony, in other words, is one in which the openness of the infoglut creates a dilemma whereby we are constantly in search of stabilization of some sort—of the kind that can answer what is perhaps the most difficult question: what is to be done? Or what should *I* do? Fraser concludes by asking whose narrative wins when the narratives of the Left are missing? We are here, in other words, caught, not between competing truths, but between competing narratives.

This, again, is the sense in which we might begin to think of our own period as one that is "post-Truth." I mean this, to repeat myself, not merely in the sense of misinformation or a lack of facts. No: "post-Truth" must be conceived as the disavowal of truth and fact; why? My claim here is that in a world so plagued by precarity and chaos, cognitive mapping provides for us the only means by which we can maintain our stability. If the material objective Truth is potentially damaging or harmful to that established sense of self and selfhood, then there is an incentive to disavow our knowledge. The problem for us, then, is not a scarcity of knowledge, but a return to the question of how do we give structure to our knowledge in a way that benefits us as subjects. Or, to be more precise, what structure, we might ask, is adequate to the task of Symbolically mediating the position of the subject who emerges at the limit points of the existing structure? This question forces us, I claim, to return to the abandoned nexus—abandoned, that is, in the movement from humanism, through structuralism, to poststructuralism and postmodernism—of the "structure-subject" paradigm in critical theory.

Structure and Subject

It is worth recalling that the passage from Marxism to structuralism, to poststructuralism, and even to postmodernism in theory and criticism, revolved around questions about the relationship between structure and subject in human history. The dilemma has partly to do with the oscillation in Marx's writings between the critique of political economy, the objective structural analysis of the contradictions in capitalism and all previous modes of production, and the subjective aspects of the class struggle. This is one reason why Fredric Jameson has claimed, "Marxism, owing to the peculiar reality of its object of study, has at its disposal two alternate languages (or codes, to use the structuralist term) in which any given phenomenon can be described. Thus history can be written either subjectively, as the history of class struggle, or objectively, as the development of the economic modes of production and their evolution from their own internal contradictions."[25] He goes on to say, "these two formulae are the same, and any statement in one can without loss of meaning be translated into the other."[26] Whereas the objective code concerns the structural dimensions of reality, society, history, and culture, the subjective code refers to the agency involved in registering and thus transforming or creating or constituting reality. Here, we are referring to the subject who either registers the structural contradictions of reality, society, and history or contributes to the evasion or disavowal of such contradictions, and contributes to the reproduction of the existing conditions and remakes things as they are. The goal, we might say, of historical materialism is thus to register the intersection of these two dynamics and to locate the points at which they overlap and make possible their mutual negation—a negation of the existing structural coordinates is at the same time the negation of the subject as constitutive of or constituted by these coordinates. Insofar as the subject negates the existing structure, it strikes at the heart of the hegemonic button tie keeping society intact. But history also shows us that every negation of a previously established hegemonic quilting point, or button tie, at the same time imposes a new one. Every negation of a norm imposes a new one. This is why, I claim, we cannot ever escape a governing structure, but we can still negate previous ones and create the new one: the negation of every Master-Signifier is at the same time the creation of a new one.

The movement away from Marxism, and eventually the movement toward poststructuralism and postmodernism in critical theory, began with a registering of this nexus between structure and subject in postwar French theory. The first advanced attempt to think this relationship between structure and subject in postwar France, according to Perry Anderson, came from the existential Marxism of figures like Jean-Paul Sartre and Simone de Beauvoir. In *Critique of Dialectical Reason*, for instance, Sartre set himself the project of uniting Marxist, psychoanalytic, and sociological concepts into a unitary method to account for the elementary formal structures of human history. The *Critique* was thus, according to Anderson, an attempt to understand the truth of humanity as a whole.[27] It was Claude Lévi-Strauss who, in *The Savage Mind*, responded to Sartre's humanism and historicism, now pitting humanism against an advancing Structuralism. According to Lévi-Strauss, the goal of the humanities is precisely not to constitute the human, but to dissolve it—that is, to de-substantialize the essence of the human subject—to prove that there is no essential core to human subjectivity. It was then Louis Althusser who, beginning with books like *For Marx* and *Reading Capital*, took up the mantle of a Structuralist Marxism, that later, with his essay on ideology and interpellation, addressed the very illusory question of the subject, claiming that subjectivity is merely a product of ideology. For Althusser, the subject is a construct produced by the bourgeois law, which makes possible in practice the ruling ideology.[28] By accepting Lévi-Strauss's claim, while incorporating an antihumanist dimension into Marxism, Althusser was also able to challenge a Marxist historicism, which comes across in his well-known statement that "history is a process without a subject or goal."[29]

As Anderson explains, "Lévi-Strauss had peremptorily sought to cut the Gordian knot of the relation between structure and subject, by suspending the latter from any field of scientific knowledge. Rather than resisting this move, Althusser radicalized it, with a version of Marxism in which subjects were abolished altogether, save as the illusory effects of ideological structures."[30] But in what way did the dissolution of the subject, beginning with Lévi-Strauss, and moving toward Althusser, pave the way for a more radical rejection of and turn away from structuralism? The arrival of poststructuralism, with figures like Foucault and Derrida, for instance, signals perhaps the effects that structuralism had, not in reviving Marxism, but in accelerating the theoretical critique of Marxism, which is itself a structuralism; in doing so, it came to develop an ethics of structure smashing. Along with declaring the death of man, Foucault was able to declare Marxism an outdated knowledge, and to demonstrate the limitations of a structuralism that ignored the historical dimensions of power. Derrida, likewise, was able to claim that the supposition of any stable structure is dependent upon the covert postulation of a center. The destabilization of the subject at the center of discursive structures of knowledge aided in the unhinging of the structures and interpretive frameworks. There is, after all, no metanarrative. This is how structuralism transforms into *post*structuralism. If structure and subject have always been interdependent—subjects, after all, are the product of structured discourse—then declaring the death of the subject eventually means overriding the structure. Death of the subject = death of the structure.

Taking a step back, now, we see that the problem that Fraser has identified as an overlapping crisis of structure and hegemony is therefore the present account of a project that has some roots (but of course, not all) in twentieth century critical theory. The crisis of hegemony, in other words, I claim, is not merely the result of a structural crisis in capitalism and neoliberalism—which of course it still is; it is also a crisis that is in part produced by the trajectory of radical and critical theory that has sought to dismantle, to tear down dominant structures and norms as such. For another view on the side of radical politics, it is also worth looking at the radical democratic politics of Ernesto Laclau and Chantal Mouffe, who have previously sought to develop a theory about the relationship between structure and hegemony—a poststructuralist or post-Marxist account of the role that hegemony plays, both in organizing the social structure as well as in articulating a democratic politics against the ruling order. Their concept of hegemony, in fact, is one that I find useful for thinking through the rhetorical implications of the term "social media."

"Society Does Not Exist"

Laclau and Mouffe's *Hegemony and Socialist Strategy* follows the trajectory of the structuralist reaction to a Marxist humanism, as well as a subsequent poststructuralist reaction to Structural Marxism. For me, one of the key claims of their book is the fact that society "is not a valid object of discourse."[31] In their assertion that society does not exist, they are more or less following in the footsteps of Foucault, who came to regard the Marxist conception of structured totality in terms of the topographical base-superstructure model. For them, the problem with the base-superstructure model, particularly as it was described by Althusser, is that it appears to represent the existence of a fully enclosed social totality. For Laclau and Mouffe, "totality" seems to imply a sort of closed loop: a pedestrian conception of the social whereby the base is said to determine the superstructure in a kind of unidirectional formation. Likewise, for them, as well as for Foucault whom they draw upon, the problem with the concept of ideology (especially in the Althusserian sense of the ideology interpellating individuals as subjects) is that it seems to be based too heavily on a notion of the false, of "false consciousness." As the Foucauldian conception would have it, the problem with ideology as "false consciousness" is that it always at the same time presumes an alternative position that is supposed to count as "truth." As Derrida, we have already noticed, has argued, the implications of this is that there always appears to be a central position of power-agency that would seem to order and arrange the structure. The assertion of a "false consciousness" is therefore itself fallacious insofar as it disavows its own relative position of power. For Laclau and Mouffe, then, as well as for Foucault, the category of discourse seems more appropriate for conceiving the way that power orders itself within the social. For Foucault, truth is an effect of discourse; but for Laclau and Mouffe, what remains central is the fact of antagonism between different discursive constructs.

Antagonism is for Laclau and Mouffe precisely where we come to locate the political at the heart of the social and is for them the very reason why society cannot be a valid object of discourse. "Society" assumes a position of totalization, of suturing or closing, creating the appearance of a fully defined totality. Society is never fixed completely; it is only partially and temporarily fixed through the operation of some hegemonic nodal

point, which they align with the Lacanian *point de capiton* (the "button
tie"). Laclau, in a piece that is closely related to the project of *HSS*, relies
upon the Lacanian discourse of the psychotic to assert that "meaning
cannot possibly be fixed," without the operation or mechanism of fixation, or without the operation of "domestication," which requires the
operation of a nodal point, or what Lacan referred to as the "Master-
Signifier."[32] In this way, he is not so dissimilar to the Derridean critique
of the transcendental signified, or to the Deleuzian-Guattarian railing
against the "tyranny of the signifier." In this sense, too, Laclau shares with
Fredric Jameson the idea that the historicizing operation occurs according to the logic of the signifier, and it is in this sense that Jameson claims
that postmodern culture identifies with the "breakdown of the signifying
chain." The loss of the signifier that is constitutive of the structures and
the subject of modernity, which, even here, Althusser credits Marx and
Freud for troubling—Marx with his conception of history as the history
of class struggle and Freud with his decentering of the liberal bourgeois
subject through the category of the unconscious, is one of the ways that
we might understand the arrival of the postmodern. But for Laclau and
Mouffe, it is the articulation of a nodal point, or of an empty Master-
Signifier that both creates a partial and temporary fixing and arresting
of the social, and at the same time articulates a particularly hegemonic
logic, a point Laclau articulates, too, in his essay, "Why do empty signifiers matter to politics?"[33] For Laclau and Mouffe, the radical democratic
project requires the articulation of a particular signifier that may bring
together the various relative discourses of the Left against some shared
enemy—a point articulated more precisely in Laclau and Mouffe's later
writings on the populism of the Left, in which they claim that a radical
politics assumes the character of a populism when it is formed according to an identifiable and articulable point of signification produced in
response to some enemy.[34]

Society, for Laclau and Mouffe, is impossible because it is always
fissured by irreconcilable antagonisms. However, society may be partially fixed through the articulation of a hegemonic signifier that links
together the political antagonism. What if the "social" itself is just such
a hegemonic signifier? What if the assertion, even, of a "social media"
is a hegemonic signifier holding together the field of the social that is
cleft by antagonisms? My claim, going forward, is that the rhetoric of the
"social" in "social media," and more precisely in the conception of "social
media revolutions," is a signifier meant to articulate the hegemonic ideology of post-crisis capitalism. It is the conception of "social media" that
creates the illusion of a totalized space linking together the apparent har-
mony of the neoliberal capitalist system. The assertion of the existence of

"social media revolutions" helps to create the image of a thriving digital and democratic public sphere, which lends legitimacy to this system. At the same time, it is worth pointing out in this way that the term "social media" serves rhetorically as a hegemonic signifier of twenty-first-century capitalism. The term helps to establish the very universalizing claim of a coherent social totality in post-crisis capitalism.

Social Media *as* Structured and Structuring Space

We have expected, since the dawning of the internet age, that the result of increased access to information in abundance would lend itself toward a new "Enlightenment" of sorts: a renewal of progress and democracy, perhaps, that "the truth shall set us free," so to speak. Or, perhaps, if not necessarily a new Enlightenment—the idea, seen from the perspective of the "dialectic of Enlightenment," being closer to the direction of tyranny—then maybe at least a greater and more horizontal freedom.[35] What we have here is, more or less, the libertarian, or maybe even a libertarian-anarchist fantasy of freedom: a kind of Chomskyan dream about the free flow of information leading toward greater freedom. What I'm calling the Chomskyan theory—mainly with reference to his collaborative work with Edward S. Herman on their "propaganda model" of communication—is the idea that barring any interference, barring any institutional censorship, a free media cannot but act in the collective interests of the society.[36] Chomsky's questioning of media institutions pertains less to their particular ideological predispositions (as is sometimes assumed) than to the question of whether or not the media are "free." Organized institutionally within the context of the capitalist system, the media according to Chomsky is absolutely not free; instead, the biased views of owners, shareholders, advertisers, and special interest groups prevail over those of the common people. The dream of the internet was that it would return to the people their open and free voice, uninhibited by the forces of domination. But what if the channels of information do become free only in the sense of a proliferation of competing (parallel) narratives, as we have seen?

We should be clear, though, that the internet is, of course, structured by the for-profit logics of the market, and therefore—and this is a point I still believe is missed by Laclau and Mouffe—the capitalist mode of production remains the underlying point of articulation of the overall field of antagonisms and the relative field of interaction of "floating signifiers." Nevertheless, it is worth questioning whether the proliferation of voices, rather than their restriction, is somehow conducive to the shaping and centralization of power. In some ways, perhaps it is the limitless freedom of articulation of competing narratives that now facilitates "communicative capitalism."

We could argue that in the internet age we are still seeing strong impulses that are not necessarily against fact, information, or truth; instead, we are witnessing a deeper relativization of truth, and we are witnessing a turn toward those facts that support our being and our identities. We are finding that, as Fraser puts it, the question of hegemony (or of ideology) is still central to a media system in which a proliferation (rather than a restriction) of voices prevails. The proliferation of voices helps the hegemonic goal of demonstrating that our society is still very much democratic in the sense that everyone is permitted one's own voice or opinion. But at the same time, where voice and opinion are privileged, we are witnessing increasing disdain for information, knowledge, and truth, which remains widely available and accessible, but which potentially threatens the subjective position of increasingly precarious subjects. One needs only consider the role of climate change deniers or antivaxxers to understand this point. Here, I would like to propose, we need to take into consideration two other elements leading to this situation: beyond the question of mere fact and truth, we should consider the role of rhetoric and the role of enjoyment. We should consider the way that ideology works both by way of rhetorical, discursive, and Symbolic dimensions, as well as the manner in which the latter is curbed by the logic of our desires.

Here we can see clearly the limitations of Chomsky's libertarian perspective, which still seems to cling to a more traditional conception of false consciousness, in the sense that "if only the people knew then they would revolt." Today, we seem to have access to the knowledge (it remains a liberal fantasy that only imposed ignorance is the cause of our dilemmas), but we continue to act as if this were not the case. In the precise psychoanalytic sense, the problem is more one of fetishistic disavowal than it is of ignorance; or, rather, we learn that where we are ignorant (where we disavow our knowledge) we are safe to enjoy. But this is one reason why rhetoric (along with interpretation and analysis) matters more, potentially, than all of the other fact-finding disciplines in the sciences (social or physical). Here, I do not mean to suggest that facts, science, and truth are no longer important. Of course they are! What matters, however, is how facts are deployed in a narrative context (as Fredric Jameson points out, the narrative context is socially symbolic). This last point reflects the ideological-discursive dimension. Our political future relies more on the combination of persuasion and enjoyment than it does upon fact and truth. Conflict, today, I claim, is related much more than in the past to the struggle over which narrative can best explain our circumstances and hegemonize the people to act toward a particular goal. The objective of analysis and interpretation is thus to identify the contradictions and fallacies in competing narratives. The implication is that we need to ask how best to think the actually existing structures that put information into context by giving order to truth, and how best to conceive a discursive and rhetorical response adequate enough to impact the material conditions of existence. In other words, it is necessary to think how best to deploy the Symbolic in order to have an effect in the Real.

Social media is distinguished from the internet by the fact that it gives structure to the latter, both through the platform interface and design and through the design of the algorithm. Tools, such as cookies and databases, also help to build and formalize the social media structure of the internet. As Claire Birchall notes, the basic architecture of the internet is one based simply upon sharing information. When we send information on the internet, we send all of the necessary coding commands and protocols needed for shipping, circulating, and receiving information, but the structure itself is not necessarily designed to store that shared information. It is only by adding a secondary layer of cookie codes, allowing platforms to track and store information and data about *what* is being shared, that social media builds more organized structure into the technology of the internet. This, of course—as it currently stands—is in the interests of capital, which is now the primary agent of power in this operation.[37] Although it is still correct to say that capitalist institutions and the political economy of capital (including state regulatory regimes that support the interests of capital) are central to the power dynamics of social media, it is difficult to say that censorship operates in quite the same way that it did pre-internet. Our dilemma is how to conceive the structures of power, given that people are increasingly encouraged and enjoined to participate, to contribute, to circulate, and to share information—in other words, to share information freely. Social media is very much a postmodern phenomenon in the sense described by Lacanian scholars, such as Slavoj Žižek and Todd McGowan, in which the problem is not the one of modern culture—a prohibition of enjoyment; in postmodern culture, we are less frequently prohibited from enjoying and more frequently enjoined to enjoy (and we are even made to feel guilty when we are not enjoying). But the point remains, however, that social media is, as such, at a formal level, a structuring mechanism of the internet, and we shouldn't dismiss the fact that as a communications and entertainment tool, a tool of representation and interpellation, it is very much involved in our daily (ideological) cognitive mapping. But does this mean that we need simply to deconstruct it? Should we merely attempt to return to the foundational architecture of sharing online and should we aim to eliminate the databases and archives of Big Data? In other words, is the problem here the structure that social media gives to the internet, or is it perhaps instead a question of who is in control?

At a formal level, social media remains ideological in the way that it structures, organizes, and formalizes—gives shape to—the information that we consume and distribute. It therefore embodies a digital rhetoric and aesthetic that interpellates users on an equal basis at the level of their desire. But the narrative of "social media"—that is, the way that it is itself represented as a technology, as a set of (corporate) platforms—is, at the same time, structured by other mainstream mass media that assign to it a particular meaning. This is worth noting, since the way that the latter builds a narrative around social media sets the agenda for how we are invited to think about it. Books such as *Why Social Media is Ruining Your Life* or *Anti-Social Media* certainly contribute to this narrative on the side of paranoia and negativity that is often present in the dawning days of every new medium, including cinema, radio, and television.[38] But on the positive side, the narrative around social media has also been shaped by the discourse of the so-called "social media revolutions" that took place, beginning in 2009 with the "Arab Spring" that struck first in Iran, and then in Tunisia, and then in Egypt, followed shortly afterward by the rise of the Occupy Wall Street movement in September 2011, and then the "Maple Spring" in Quebec, and then the #IdleNoMore movement, and then the #MMIWG movement (Murdered and Missing Indigenous Women and Girls) across Canada beginning in 2012, and later the rise of the #BLM or #BlackLivesMatter and #MeToo movements in the United States. These movements have all been evidence of the positive, democratic potential of social media as a tool for radical and progressive campaigns, helping to build worldwide solidarity, and helping to push issues of political and economic authoritarianism, corruption, contradiction, austerity, racism, colonialism, and sexism into the spotlight. Manuel Castells's book, *Networks of Outrage and Hope: Social Movements in the Internet Age*, is one example of the utopian sentiments about the radical possibilities of social media.[39] At the same time, though, these movements have lent themselves to the narrative and rhetoric of the "social" in "social media." That is, the narrative and rhetoric of the very discursive construction of "social media" as a hegemonic-discursive object. They lend credence, in other words, to the idea of the *social* in "social media" by helping to engage the utopian ideal of the digital public sphere, a corollary to the suggestion that the free flow of information will set us free.

What gets ignored here is the ideological-hegemonic dimension giving structure to the circulation of information. But also, when we ignore the ideological and rhetorical dimensions of the Symbolic, we are likely more easily blindsided by that other side of the internet—the one that also champions the free flow narrative, but not necessarily on the side of (what the mainstream refers to as) progressive politics. I am speaking, of course, of the new swarm mentality of the reactionary Right, or the "Alt-Right," themselves champions of a certain variety of internet "democracy," where anything goes. Trolling, in fact, has become one of the primary modes of interaction for the Alt-Right, which seeks to be as rude and crass as possible in order to prove the hypocrisy of liberal defenders of free speech and the free internet.[40] Oddly, in this formation, it is the reactionary Right that has, unlike the liberalism of the 1960s, become the primary champions of free speech and free expression. Oddly, as well, the Alt-Right and versions of a libertarian-anarchist Left share a common utopianism about the internet and social media, and (more importantly) what they both perceive as the structural-institutional limits to that vision.

Many have already highlighted the way that the media-capital nexus in social media has devolved into problems of surveillance and control.[41] Therefore, they pit against each other the democratic and social aspects of social media (that is, the digital public sphere) versus the antisocial and antidemocratic dimensions of surveillance and control. But what about the ideological element that cuts across these poles? On the one hand, there is certainly a rhetorical and discursive dimension to the ideology of the "social" in "social media"—who is the social? What does it mean to be "social"? What, after all, is so "social" about "social media"? Doesn't it in fact impede our actual ability to be social, plugged into our devices as we are? Social media, as the above reference suggests, is ruining our lives and is making us *anti*social. However, on the other hand, the problem with corporate social media is not merely surveillance and control as such. It has much more to do with the ties between surveillance and the mechanisms of information programming and curation—that is, with how platforms give structure to the information that interpellates users at the level of their desire, in what Deleuze refers to as the "control society." Furthermore, when we consider the political-economic dimensions of corporate platforms, we must think, not merely about how smashing the structures—the cookies, the databases—will liberate us from the tyranny of the corporation, in other words, how we might achieve the return to an unstructured internet. We should go further by asking how the tools for collecting big data might, under differently organized and more democratic legal and social structures, actually help to facilitate a more open society in a different way. What we should say, instead, is that *capitalism is ruining our lives, not social media; capitalism is making us* *antisocial.* The latter is a topic to which I will return in the final chapter. So the question I now turn to is how we might conceive the form and structure of social media, discursively and rhetorically, set against the background of structural crisis.

Mediating the Crisis

Our current moment is surely one of a structural crisis of capital, and a crisis of hegemony. I want to move on to explore the relationship between social media and the hegemonic crisis, but it is pertinent first to look at the background of the social media-hegemony dimension in the context of structural crisis of capital. In fact, to fully grasp the historical context that we are talking about here with respect to the rise of social media and the hegemonic crisis, it is necessary to place these factors in the light of the 2008 credit crisis that began in the US housing market in 2007. Social media, or Web 2.0, arose partly as a response to the previous crisis of the dot.com bust in the early twenty-first century. As Christian Fuchs explains, "In 2000, a crisis of the Internet economy emerged. The inflow of capital had driven up the market values of many Internet companies, but profits could not hold up with the promises of high market values. The result was a financial bubble (the so-called dot-com bubble) that burst in 2000, resulting in many start-up Internet companies going bankrupt. They were mainly based on venture capital financial investments and the hope of delivering profits in the future, and this resulted in a gap between share values and accumulated profits."[42] When investments in internet start-ups failed to yield realizable returns, a crisis broke out in the tech sector leading toward a new orientation of the internet around business and entrepreneurial incentives. The rhetoric and ideology of "Web 2.0"—the term was coined by media entrepreneur Tim O'Reilly—became more or less a marketing strategy to bring confidence back to investments in internet platforms.[43] As Alice Marwick notes, "Web 2.0" announced the coincidence between the new investment regime of platforms and an entrepreneurial ethic that inscribed social media fully into the neoliberal worldview.[44]

The story of Facebook, for instance, is usually told as the result of the creative genius of its founder Mark Zuckerberg. But as David Fincher's *The Social Network* (2010), for example, narrativizes, the foundation of Facebook was equally made possible by a series of social networking interactions (as the film's title suggests) between developers and investors seeking to find the next big venture in the tech world. The terms "social media" and "Web 2.0" were invented to give new life and new meaning to the emerging platforms giving structure to the internet, beginning with the new search engine platforms in the late 1990s like Google.[45]

Today, Google and Facebook are often the main points of entry for users surfing the internet. In fact, these days, in order to gain access to content from other platforms, users are often required to enter their Google or Facebook login information, which is a key indication of the way they both a) structure the entire medium of the internet and b) dominate at the level of concentration and centralization of the media market. On the one hand, the monopoly that these firms have over the entire terrain of the internet now demonstrates the way that they give very specific content and articulation to the space of the internet; on the other hand, this example also demonstrates the degree to which the recovery of the dot-com bubble has depended upon the excavation and expropriation of what is today probably one of the most profitable staple resources: user data. Data mining has become the primary resource extraction vehicle for profitability in the digital age.[46] But it is worth noting that data cannot be extracted without a prior legal arrangement between platforms and users. As we all know, signing (or agreeing) to the Terms and Conditions of Use and Service is the first step to gaining access to platforms.[47] However, even though many of us don't take the time to read through all of the documents contained in the Terms of Service, we should note that what they describe is the legal process by which platforms can appropriate, package, and sell user data as a source of revenue. None of this would be possible outside of the legal-discursive framework that transforms data into a commodity. My point is that the legal-discursive framework of data, more so than data mining itself, is the structural dimension that makes possible the formal framework of our control; this is more important than surveillance as such, I would say, since it is only the legal-discursive framework that transforms data into a commodity, alienated from those who produce it. The same discursive and Symbolic dimensions of the commodification of data share a formal dimension with financial commodities, like mortgage-backed securities and collateralized debt obligations (CDOs), or financial derivatives, like credit default swaps (CDSs). In fact, far from the open free market that neoliberal rhetoric promises, what we have seen in neoliberalism is actually a much stricter policy regime dependent upon the construction and creation of various forms of fictitious capital, like securities and data commodities.

The crash of 2008 is the result of a series of overlapping contradictions within neoliberal and finance dominated capitalism, itself the product of policy decisions inscribed into the space and governance of the market. The global crisis began in the housing market in the United

States due to an aggregate effect of defaults on subprime mortgages. Much of the push for lending at a subprime rate in the United States was due to a set of deregulations in the banking sector. "Deregulation" is, in fact, not the best term to use since what we are talking about is absolutely not the elimination of regulations. "Deregulation" is a term meant to conjure up the fantasy of the market operating outside of government control. It is the same kind of fantasy that creates the appearance of an open and free unregulated internet. This of course occurs nowhere since government and law are central to the very creation of the market as a space of exchange. The state backs the rules of exchange, even at the bare minimum of guaranteeing contractual ownership of property and the values of currencies. The state is the primary institution granting legitimacy to property contracts and currencies, which otherwise have no value. They are but mere representations of value ordained by the mechanisms of the state, which has its own implicit violent wing (the Repressive State Apparatus, or RSA) that, all things being equal, can enforce the rights of property and value when belief and trust in them fail—that is, when we cease to collectively believe in the value and rights that are secured by the paper on which they are written. A crisis, in other words, of ideological hegemony. Contracts therefore perform a fetishistic function. They embody the disavowed human social relationship (perhaps a relationship of inequality), for which they are a stand-in holding together the social bond.[48] What we are talking about, then, with "deregulation," is rather a change in the interests involved in the type of regulation: the state can either regulate primarily in the interests of the people or the public, or it can regulate in the interests of private wealthy individuals and corporations. In the neoliberal context, it is the latter interest that has dominated and has gained hegemonic control.

Neoliberal "deregulation" has therefore become a mechanism for changing regulations to favor capital unfairly. In the case of banking deregulation, this has meant, for instance, tearing down the barriers between savings and loans institutions and investment banks. Now, because of deregulation, savings and loans banks can lend out money for things like mortgages, and then package these loans together (loans that are essentially a bundle of IOUs) as new securities called collateralized debt obligations (CDOs), or "asset backed financial paper." They can then sell these new commodities to investment banks, getting the loans and debt off their ledgers, making a profit at the same time. Investment banks can then invest these commodities into the market, where the interest earned is much higher than in the mortgage sector because the risk is increased. Deregulation has permitted, in tandem, an easing on the prohibition of derivatives like credit default swaps, in which companies can buy insurance policies on investments not even owned, therefore standing to benefit when the price of the investment drops or crashes with a payoff in insurance monies. Because banks were making bigger profits by selling collateralized debt obligations to investment banks, they had an added incentive to give out more loans, hence the turn toward subprime mortgages.

At this point, it is very easy to understand what happened in the crash. Through an aggregate of defaults on loans, the CDOs lost their value, and at the same time, there was a drain on monies from insurance companies, like AIG, which were used to hedge the bet through credit default swaps. We see quite clearly how the crisis was a by-product of the structure imposed on the market by the neoliberal regime, rather than a result of "deregulation" or a deconstruction of the market.[49] Nevertheless, while the crisis was erupting, social media platforms like Facebook, Google, and YouTube seemed to be booming. The crisis in the financial sector was paralleled by the rising success of the tech sector.[50] How do we account for this? It is here that we can perhaps identify a co-incidence between the increasing pervasiveness of social media and the rhetoric of the "social media revolutions," which can be understood as a dimension of the crisis of hegemony; perhaps more appropriately, it is in the discourse regarding social media that we can locate the struggle for hegemony in our time.

With the rise of social media, we find, on the one hand, the prolif-eration of narratives about democratization in the wake of the crisis; on the other hand, we find a competing practice of increased surveillance and monetization of user data. This latter formation is best rendered by Jodi Dean's concept of "communicative capitalism," which will be the focus of the next chapter.[51] Before moving on, though, I want to briefly look at some of the political and radical formations that did emerge in the wake of the financial crisis, which have been dubbed "social media revolutions."

"Social Media Revolutions"

The apogee of the social media revolutions, I claim, came in the wake of the Occupy Wall Street movement.[52] This apogee is also shown in sub-sequent movements, such as the #BlackLivesMatter, #IdleNoMore, and #MeToo movements, and even in the rise of the online Alt-Right move-ment, arising in the aftermath of the failure of these movements to emerge as a leading contender in the struggle for hegemony. I see it this way in view of the fact that Occupy Wall Street, although inspired by the events of the Arab Spring, took as its target the financial sector itself, the main culprit of our current crisis. But history, certainly, never takes place in a vacuum, and it is important for a dialectical understanding of history to recognize each new formation as the product of the incorporation and sublation of prior instances. It is therefore significant not only that the Arab Spring arose in the years immediately following the financial crisis, but also that it made significant use of social media platforms like Facebook, Twitter, and YouTube as an organizational and informational tool for building global solidarity.[53]

The first rumblings of what has been called "social media revolutions," or "Facebook revolutions," or "Twitter revolutions," came out of protests in Iran during the 2009 election. Following the June election, mass street protests took place in Tehran claiming widespread irregularities and accusations of fraud in the reelection of Mahmoud Ahmadinejad. The international community, of course, took notice, because the West has largely been critical of the Iranian regime since the deposition of the Shah following the 1979 revolution. The protests found expression on Facebook and Twitter, where users wrote posts with the hashtag #IranElection or #1388, referring to the year in the Persian calendar. Around the world, Twitter users changed their location to Tehran to show solidarity and to confuse the Iranian police. One of the most significant blows, though, came from the video circulated on YouTube of the murder of Neda Agha-Soltan, a twenty-six-year-old protester who was killed by a sniper from a pro-government militia, Basij. The video circulated worldwide with its own hashtag, #Neda. Using Twitter and YouTube in support of worldwide solidarity for the election protests in Iran not only gave international recognition to the movement, it also helped to set a new standard of global online protest and solidarity.

What has subsequently come to be called the "Arab Spring" began on December 17, 2010, when a Tunisian street vendor, Mohamed Bouazizi, set himself on fire in protest of harassment by municipal officials, who had seized his merchandise. The following week, his relatives posted his picture and a video of a peaceful protest led by Bouazizi's mother outside a municipal building. The video was picked up by Al-Jazeera from Facebook. Following this event, protests began to erupt, with videos and messages increasing in number on Facebook and Twitter, using the hashtag #Bouazizi and then #Tunisia. This was the beginning of the Tunisian revolution and the Arab Spring, which continued into 2011, and moved into Egypt, perhaps the most pivotal moment in this sequence of events.

Although the Arab Spring, as it has come to be represented, really blossomed later in 2011, the catalyst for these events began on June 6, 2010, when two police officers dragged twenty-eight-year-old Khaled Saeed from an internet café in Alexandria, who was beaten to death for allegedly possessing a video showing police selling illegal drugs. After he was killed, a photo of Khaled's body from the morgue showing his beaten body was leaked on the internet, and the Facebook group "We Are All Khaled Said" was created by activists, including Wael Ghonim, the head of marketing for Google in the Middle East and North Africa. The Facebook group organized the now infamous demonstration in Cairo on January 25, 2011, which was titled "The Day of the Revolution against Torture, Poverty, Corruption, and Unemployment." The hashtags #Egypt and #jan25 became the highest trending topics on Twitter for two weeks following.

Inspired by the events in Egypt and Tunisia, the Occupy Wall Street movement began as a call from the Canadian culture jamming and anti-consumerist magazine, *Adbusters*, to occupy Zuccotti Park in Manhattan—redubbed "Liberty Park" by the movement—to protest the social and economic inequality in the United States and around the world, largely due to the influence of Wall Street and the financial sector. Christian Fuchs describes in *OccupyMedia!* the way that participants in the movement used social media as an activist tool, and he portrays their perceptions of social media in helping to build the movement. A theory of information, according to Fuchs, is necessary as a way to make sense of social movements' uses of social media, but this, he says, needs to be set against a political economic analysis of the media that takes corporate and anticorporate media usage into consideration. Political economy, he claims, is right at the heart of social movements' use of social media, because it expresses the political conflict at the center of the medium.

Fuchs's book is a report on a survey conducted of participants in the Occupy movement at Zuccotti Park. The aim of the project, he writes, was "to analyze Occupy activists' assessment of the role of social media in their movement, their actual usage of these and other media for obtaining and publishing news, protest communication and mobilization as well as their assessment of the relationship between commercial and non-commercial social media."[54] Based on the findings of the survey, the majority of respondents saw Occupy as a networked movement working toward the creation of a commons-based society. With respect to the role of social media in the movement, four groups of responses were ascribed: a dialectical one, according to which social media serves as a tool both of domination and of struggle; a techno-deterministic one, which argues that the media causes protests; a social constructivist one, which sees little import from social media; and a dualistic one, which sees contemporary

revolutions and protests as both social and technological. The most frequent assessment of the role of social media, according to Fuchs's study,
was that which he refers to as dialectical, seeing and emphasizing social
media as a terrain of antagonism. The respondents who opt for the dialectical assessment, he says, "point out social media's opportunities for
supporting protest movements' networking, mobilization and potential
to bypass the [traditional] mainstream media." However, these respondents also "stress that there are dangers such as surveillance, censorship,
separation from street protests, infiltration by the police and secret services, corporate and stratified visibility and attention economy."[55]

Fuchs's survey is useful for coming to understand the contradictory dimensions of social media set against the background of crisis
capitalism; however, although I agree with this assessment overall, it
strikes me as lacking attention to the ideological-hegemonic dimension
of social media; or, more specifically, it lacks attention to the formation
that social media takes both rhetorically and even aesthetically with its
degree of content curation, which serves as a lure for the interpellation
of the subject at the level of its desire. While Fuchs's dialectical category pays attention to the contradictions between the democratic and
participatory aspects and the surveillance and control society aspects of
social media, it still seems to miss an ideological component, not only
the hegemonic one, but also the elements of interpellation. As I have
argued in this chapter, the protest movements from the Arab Spring to
Occupy Wall Street somehow lend themselves, rhetorically, to the hegemonic framework of the "social" in "social media."

As Nick Dyer-Witheford points out, "No aspect of these revolts
attracted more attention than their use of digital networks."[56] Reports
about these movements focused more on their use of Facebook, Twitter,
and YouTube than they did about the movements themselves, what it was
that they were struggling against, what their demands were, and whether
or not they were justified in their struggles. "Facebook revolutions," as
Dean points out, became a reactionary trope used to diffuse the radical
politics of the movements, by shifting the attention to the media rather
than the message.[57] Overall, "social media" became the primary victor,
rhetorically speaking, in the struggles against tyrannical states, in the case
of the Arab Spring and in the case of Wall Street. It is for this reason,
I claim, that "social media," the term and the concept, has come to occupy something like an ideological and hegemonic Master-Signifier,
similar to the way the concept is deployed by Laclau and Mouffe, to help
to secure and suture the space of the social, which is cleavaged by antagonisms in the wake of the global credit and financial crisis and in the
wake of global protest movements against capitalism and tyranny. "Social

media," in other words, has come to congeal the space opened in the structure of neoliberalism and twenty-first-century capitalism.

"Social Media" Does Not Exist

In light of this, perhaps it is worth attaching Laclau and Mouffe's argument about the nonexistence of society—or the view that society is not a valid object of discourse—to the Lacanian claim that the big Other does not exist. In the course of the psychoanalytic treatment, the analysand is meant to come to the realization that, although her desire is positioned as the desire of the big Other, the big Other in fact does not exist, but is a mere virtual and reified formation of the social field. Žižek explains the category of the big Other in the following way: "If we are really concerned with language in a strict sense, with language as a social network in which meaning exists only in so far as it is intersubjectively recognized . . . then it must be part of the meaning of each name that it refers to a certain object *because this is its name*, because others use this name to designate the object in question . . . 'Others', of course, cannot be reduced to empirical others: they rather point to the Lacanian 'big Other', to the symbolic order itself."[58] What strikes me is the resonance between Žižek's description of the big Other and the kind of relationship instituted by social media as the *social network* that comes to (in)form the Symbolic order as such. But when we begin to assume the subjective position whereby we are capable of recognizing that we are the ones who presuppose the positing of the Other's existence—the Other exists only insofar as we are the ones who will it into existence as a condition of our enjoyment, a position that Lacan refers to as "subjective destitution"—then at that point we become capable of separating from the blind logic of our desire. We are capable of traversing the fantasy that positions our desire relative to the desire of the Other. If the constitution of "social media," rhetorically, makes possible the suturing of the social that is destroyed by structural crisis, can we assume, then, that the claim "social media does not exist" works in a way that is similar to the statement that the big Other does not exist? As I argue in the following chapter, this isn't necessarily the case.

2

Enjoying Social Media

In one of his most well-known essays, "Exiting the Vampire Castle," the late cultural theorist, Mark Fisher, warned about the dangers of social media for the Left. Fisher was concerned with a particular formation of online activism that he called "the vampire castle." The Vampire Castle represents a space of in-fighting on the Left, which began as a kind of "witch-hunting moralism" that, as Angela Nagle has argued, became a driving force for the establishment of the reactionary Alt-Right.[1] In the conclusion to his essay, Fisher writes prophetically, "we need to think strategically about how to use social media—always remembering that, despite the egalitarianism claimed for social media by capital's libidinal engineers, that this is currently an enemy territory, dedicated to the re-production of capital. But this doesn't mean that we can't occupy the terrain and start to use it for purposes of producing class consciousness. We must break out of the 'debate' set up by communicative capitalism in which capital is endlessly cajoling us to participate in, and remember that we are involved in a class struggle."[2] Fisher is inspired here by Jodi Dean's conception of communicative capitalism, which is referred to in several places in the previous chapter. Dean's concept draws out the idea that our period is one embossed by a "decline of symbolic efficiency," as she puts it, drawing on Žižek's Lacanian critique of ideology. Dean's concep-tion of communicative capitalism asserts that technoculture and social media facilitate the inscription of democracy into capitalist practices of exploitation, and in this way Fisher's claim about libidinal engineering rings true: online debates can sometimes serve as curated forums for the exploitation of our libidinal investments in the platform. This chapter examines in greater detail Dean's conception of communicative capi-talism, and more specifically it explores her claim regarding the decline of symbolic efficiency, in order to assess the assertion made at the end of the previous chapter about the possibilities for realizing the nonexistence of social media as akin to the nonexistence of the big Other.

My objective is to think critically about the ideological role of social media in Lacanian terms, and in the context of late capitalist consumer society—a society defined by what Žižek and Dean refer to as the "de-mise of symbolic efficiency," what Fredric Jameson has defined as "post-modern" (as the "breakdown of the signifying chain"), or what Fisher has called "capitalist realism."[3] With reference as well to Dean's pioneering work on "communicative capitalism," my aim is to argue that social media provides a good model for conceiving the connection between ideology and enjoyment at a point when digital media makes possible the conditions for the apparent erosion of the subject of desire. Like Dean, I draw on Žižek and Lacan to theorize social media. However, in contrast to her, my claim is that the ideological operation of social media is one that interpellates the subject in relation to its desire, rather than in relation to the drive as she has argued. It does this both through the form of social media, itself, as well as through the very rhetoric of "social media."

The promise of the internet, as we saw in chapter 1, is that it would give a voice back to the people, one that has been taken away by private media and entertainment. However, according to Dean, "the expansion and intensification of communication and entertainment networks yield not democracy but something else entirely: communicative capitalism."[4] Dean discusses the conditions of communicative capitalism by examining the world of technoculture, which functions by creating disconnection in the guise of community. Communicative capitalism makes this kind of disconnection operative by engaging users through the repetitive and reflexive circuits of drive, by imposing further gaps in older symbolic networks of community. In doing so, blogging and the use of social networks such as Facebook, YouTube, and Twitter facilitate the integration of users into the matrices of neoliberal capitalism.

Subverting Žižek, Dean argues that in the context of the demise of symbolic efficiency, drive is not an act[5]—suggesting instead that, in today's circumstances, drive makes ideology work. In contrast, my claim is not that drive is not an act, but that (to cite the title of one of the sections in Žižek's *The Ticklish Subject*) "perversion is not subversion." What we begin to realize in a period of the decline of apparent belief in the big Other is not that ideology is no longer a matter of desire, but that the "inherent transgression" that sustains the subject's attitude to her enjoyment works today, not by subverting power, but by "willing" it into existence. This is not unlike the masochist who takes a paradoxical pleasure from the violence of the sadist, because it allows the subject to return to a position of loss, from which all actual enjoyment takes place. The masochistic subject therefore enjoys turning herself into an object for the other's enjoyment.[6] In order to save her desire, the subject requires (at least the fantasy of) some figure of prohibiting agency whom she can transgress, whose gaze she wishes to impress. Today, we transpose this gaze onto the form of social media.

Dean, however, proposes that, given the demise of symbolic efficiency, since no prohibiting agency exists, desire gives way to drive, which according to her is the form taken by the subject's relation to enjoy-ment in the information age. She, therefore, argues against Žižek's claim that emancipatory politics follows an ethics of drive. As Dean explains, "conceived in terms of drive, networked communications circulate less as potentials for freedom than as affective intensities produced through and amplifying our capture."[7] Her argument is largely based on the idea that today, everyone knows that the big Other does not exist; therefore, no agency exists that can prevent the subject from realizing her desire. My point, though, is that, given these conditions, the subject of capitalist realism, rather than relating to the loss constitutive of subjectivity, pre-fers to disavow the fact of the Other's nonexistence in order to preserve the pleasure garnered in the pursuit of the lost object of desire. This is a subject that has yet to accomplish the traversal of the fantasy that sustains her relationship to the Other. The ideological function of social media is, then, one of "willing" the big Other into existence. Social media, in other words, is the answer to the question: "How will capitalism succeed in reintroducing lack and scarcity into a world of instant access and abun-dance?"[8] Social media has the function of reintroducing a limit into the social field that preserves the subject of desire—this is a limit constitutive of the Symbolic order as such.

While we know that the big Other does not exist, we act as if this were not the case. Why? The Lacanian joke about the man who thought he was a grain of seed—often recounted by Žižek—offers a possible ex-planation. After months of treatment, the man is convinced by his doc-tor that he is not a grain of seed, but a man. Weeks after he is cured, the man returns in a hysterical rage. "What is wrong?" asks his doctor. "You know you are not a grain of seed, but a man." "Yes," replies the man. "I know; but does the chicken know?" This is how the subject reacts to the nonexistence of the big Other. The problem is not the subject's own belief (in the big Other), it is rather the ambiguity of the Other's belief. Or, to take another of Žižek's examples, consider the operation of the stock market.[9] When we play the stock market, we are ultimately placing a bet on what public opinion believes public opinion to be. It is this be-lief in the Other's belief that accounts for our continued relation to the big Other, despite our own personal recognition of the nonexistence of the big Other. In the context of social media, we see how we perform, not necessarily for our own sense of self—we curate our identities, not to satisfy our own desire, but to satisfy the desire of the Other in the form of likes, shares, comments, follows, and so forth. It is this ambiguity that provides the pretense for our activity, and social media is the platform through which, today, in popular culture, the big Other continues to be operative. Nevertheless, the thesis that we are living in a post-ideological era—one based around the decline of symbolic efficiency—is an argument that needs to be explored. In what follows, I respond to this claim at multiple different levels as they relate to postmodern culture and to the impact of digital new media. The assessment that proceeds then wraps back around to my central claim, via a return to Dean's understanding of the demise of symbolic efficiency, that social media represents a return to—a new constitution of—the ideological big Other, constitutive of the ideology of twenty-first-century capitalism.

The End of Ideology

The problem of the decline of symbolic efficiency is very much a part of the postmodern thesis regarding the end of ideology. There is a problem, that is, with thinking about the critique of ideology, today, in what many view as a post-ideological era. Both the Right and the Left offer a position on the "end of ideology." On the Right, we have the Fukuyamist claim that Liberal Democracy and the market economy have triumphed, therefore ending the ideological disputes of twentieth-century politics. The world appears to have settled on one true answer. Meanwhile, on the Left, the conception of ideology as "false consciousness," on the one hand, has been thoroughly annihilated by poststructuralist thinkers, from Foucault to Derrida; while, on the other hand, the popular discrediting of every Master-Signifier, or point of ideological fixing, up to and including the Marxian conception of History (Lyotard's "incredulity toward Grand Narratives"), makes it difficult to claim that something like ideology still exists.

In the information age—a period that can be roughly associated with the consumer ethic of late capitalism—it is difficult for critical theorists to claim that ideology still exists, since new information technology has eased access to knowledge. Also, media sophistication is no longer something familiar only to scholars—who today does not know about media manipulation and the practices of photoshopping and airbrushing, editing, and CGI effects, in addition to the problems of media imperialism, concentration of ownership, and the role of advertising in commercial media? Who, in other words, is still "duped" by the media? Likewise, consumer society has provided everyone with access to the means that are necessary for realizing all of our pleasures. Consumer society, like the infoglut, creates the appearance of abundance and eliminates the notion that our society is one that is based on repression, prohibition, and scarcity. Given these circumstances, how can it be possible to claim that something like ideology (let alone "false consciousness") or Authority still exists? It is in this sense that we need to understand the contemporary critique of ideology in the context of the demise of symbolic efficiency, or the postmodern "breakdown of the signifying chain."[10]

The Demise of Symbolic Efficiency, or, the Big Other Does Not Exist

The problem for the critique of ideology is that today, with the "end of ideology," and the pleasure ethic of consumer society, no one seems to believe any longer in the existence of the big Other. The "demise of symbolic efficiency" and "the big Other does not exist" (similar to the claim that society does not exist) are two formulations for the same basic situation. The Symbolic order is no longer held together because every Master-Signifier articulated has been reduced to a mere effect of fixing or "suture." This is why Fredric Jameson is accurate in referring to the Lacanian formula for psychosis in his description of postmodernism as a "breakdown of the signifying chain." There is no totality that determines the flow of language; rather, what we have is a series of free-floating discourses and signifiers, local "language games," or mini narratives, unbound by a universal totality. Jameson's point about the postmodern breakdown of the signifying chain pertains to the specificity of the historical moment of the political mediations of postmodernism, particularly those of the postwar period, which saw the formation of new social movements (NSMs), including feminism, antiracism, and the gay rights and gay liberation movements, which took the place of the proletarian struggle against capital. The positive and progressive aspects of the NSMs destabilized (to some degree) the phallo(go)centrism, white supremacism, and heteronormativity of the reigning order—or, at least these movements have allowed the underlying elements of these aspects of power to be brought to the surface and to enter mainstream consciousness, if they were not necessarily able to eradicate these forms of power altogether.

It could, however, be argued that the end result of NSMs that are not based on class has been the triumph of consumer identity politics. The demands of NSMs are capable of being realized by consumer society. Identity politics and consumerism are natural allies. Consumer society asks of the individual not to repress who she is—consumer society does not prohibit. Its ethic is one of fully realizing the Self. "Be your true self!" The interpellative call of postmodern capitalism is, simply, "Enjoy!"

Because it appears as though there is no longer any agency of prohibition, it is possible to claim that the big Other no longer exists. But what the lack of prohibition presents is, however, a severe problem for the preservation of the desire of the subject. If enjoyment is procured through the transgression of the Other, how can the subject go on enjoying in the context of the disappearance of Authority?

Obligatory Enjoyment and the Logics of Transgression

Žižek argues that when ideology is no longer a matter of "false consciousness," then its mode of operation shifts away from the Symbolic and toward a "fantasmatic specter": an ideological fantasy that gives structure and support to our "reality." Reality, as such, is according to Žižek always already ideological, insofar as it is structured by some underlying fantasy formation that puts us in relation to our desire. The Symbolic surface level of every ideology is supported by a "sublime object" of ideology that subjectivizes us in relation to our enjoyment. The problem of ideology is not that people are not aware of their actions and how they contribute to the reigning order. The problem is that people are fully aware, but they continue to act as if this were not the case. Further, it is our very resistance to ideology—our attempts to transgress (what we perceive to be) the reigning order—that traps us even further within its grasp. Subversion and transgression are the very conditions for our capture by ideology precisely because this kind of action procures a perverse pleasure. From this perspective, too, it is not difficult to understand the specific historical conditions giving rise to the transgressions of the Alt-Right.

As Angela Nagle puts it, "The rise of Milo [Yiannopoulos], Trump and the alt-right are not evidence of the return of conservatism, but instead of the absolute hegemony of the culture of non-conformism, self-expression, transgression and irreverence for its own sake—an aesthetic that suits those who believe in nothing but the liberation of the individual and the id, whether they're on the left or the right. The principle-free idea of counterculture did not go away; it just became the style of the new right."[11] The Alt-Right is, on the one hand, a by-product of ideological postmodernism and, on the other, the result of the contradictions of subversion and transgression within postmodern culture. To understand this, it is necessary first to recall in what sense subversion itself became part of the dominant ideology of postmodern capitalism. In this regard, Jameson's cogent application of the Lacanian logic of the psychotic's discourse still provides an illuminating aesthetic description of the historical, political, cultural, and ideological dynamics of contemporary postmodern society. What he describes, borrowing equally from Gilles Deleuze and Félix Guattari, as the "breakdown of the signifying chain" not unlike the demise of symbolic efficiency operates as a kind of shorthand to describe some of the various tenets of postmodernity and postmodern culture, including, on both the Left and the Right, an incredulity of sorts toward metanarratives, otherwise encapsulated by the "end of history" thesis or by Daniel Bell's notion of the "end of ideology." The "breakdown" metaphor highlights what Perry Anderson means when he says, "Modernism, from its earliest in Baudelaire or Flaubert onward, virtually defined itself as 'anti-bourgeois.' Postmodernism is what occurs when, without any victory, that adversary is gone."[12] Postmodernism is equally, according to Terry Eagleton, defined not by a victory on the part of the antibourgeois but by an imagined defeat—that is, by a cynical resignation that, in Thatcher's words, "there is no alternative," a feature that Fisher aligns with "capitalist realism."[13]

This sentiment of the loss of the adversarial relationship between the bourgeoisie and the proletariat—whether in the form of the perceived triumph of either side—is not at all disconnected from the logic of capital. It is tied to the very persistence of capital to break down all barriers to accumulation. This includes, in some cases, the breaking down of political and cultural barriers, which is partly what the "breakdown" metaphor describes; or in Deleuze and Guattari's terms, this includes the constant pursuit of accumulation and the breaking down of barriers to force a deterritorialization of capital, unleashing it in different modalities or "lines of flight."[14] Politically, this has resulted in the sublation of existing antagonisms into the very logic of capital, save (of course) for that antagonism that is its absolute point of negation: the class struggle, which instead of being eliminated is simply displaced onto other, cultural antagonisms—that is, class war turns into "culture war." This last point helps, in part, to explain the rising influence of the Moral Majority and neoconservatism among the working classes in the United States from the late 1970s up to and including George W. Bush's two terms as president. With the sublation of class war into culture war, it often appeared as though the Right more than the (liberal) Left spoke the language of the working class.[15] It is also in this sense that, as Anderson puts it, modernity "comes to an end . . . when it loses any antonym," that is, when the terms of antagonism get so confused that the image of the actual enemy gets blurred.[16] The driving force of the existing postmodern culture, therefore, differs from the propulsion of the modern culture, insofar as postmodern culture is fueled by antagonism and contradiction.

As a logic of production, capital is driven by its dialectic of development, constantly in need of destroying the old to produce the new. As such, it consistently requires breaking down those older ideological—as well as material—barriers that prevent exponential expansion. Modernity was therefore culturally contradictory in the sense that, for instance, it relied on traditional culture—say, the culture of the conjugal, patriarchal family—as part of its own processes of social reproduction while it worked to break down the structures of traditional culture to produce new subjectivities that could act as agents of consumption, the latter of which is required to ensure that a crisis of effective demand in the market does not ensue. This logic of antagonism and contradiction operated similarly in art and in culture.

The significance of the political formation of the bourgeoisie as a class is matched by the emergence of the market as the material and ideological space of shared individual equivalence. Regardless of one's identity outside the market, inside it we are all supposedly free and equal individuals engaged in acts of (fair and equitable) exchange. The market logic applied as well to art and culture, as the rise of capitalism broke down the older relationships between the artist and his patron. The commodification of art and culture is a contributing factor for the emergence of modernism. No longer producing for the patron, the artist—now, too, "liberated" as "entrepreneurial" labor—produced art for the market. But modern art was able to carve out for itself its own separate sphere, a field of cultural production, the latter defined by two points of negation, first, by its vocation not to become mere commodity. In this sense, modern art sought to distance itself from what was later termed mass or popular culture—or the "culture industry." The second point is the negating influence of new media, beginning with the daguerreotype. What the technological reproducibility of the image instituted in modernism was a formal criterion to "make it new!" From impressionism onward, through cubism, surrealism, and abstract expressionism, visual art sought to distance itself formally from the production of verisimilitude found in popular culture.

On the other hand, the modern avant-garde found definition by distancing itself, again, from the culture of the bourgeoisie. Culturally, modern artists carved out a space for themselves by setting up a concept of the bourgeoisie to demonstrate precisely what they were not. At the same time, modern artists sought to distance their work from the political sphere, completely—hence the tautology "art for art's sake." So, it is in these two ways that modernism found definition: by railing against what it was not—a process of negation—both in terms of its object (the work of art itself as noncommodity) and in the identity of the artists (antibourgeois).

However, capital, being what it is, did not take very long to saturate this antagonism. While modernism may be understood by its vocation not to become commodity, postmodernism, we could say, is what emerges at the point of total commodification in postwar consumer society, in which art and commodity begin to fold into each other, as in the case of pop art, like Andy Warhol's *Campbell's Soup Cans*, and later with works of pastiche, like Cindy Sherman's *Untitled Film Stills*. But postmodernism is also what emerges when the rebellious art of modernism, which constantly sought to negate the existing world, becomes the official art of the canon, the gallery, and the university. Put differently—and this is one of my central claims—if modernism defined itself as a process of subversion and negation, postmodernism, culturally, is what emerges when subversion itself becomes the dominant ideology. If subversion is now part of the ruling ideology, how might we imagine the subversion of subversion?

Alongside these developments in the cultural sphere, a parallel conundrum emerged in the political spheres of Western Europe and North America in the 1960s, in the moment of the postwar welfare state and Cold War-era class compromise between capital and labor, which saw the emergence of new subjects of history, in place of the apparently nonexistent proletariat. NSMs appeared to replace the class struggle between capital and labor. But just as modern art and culture were absorbed into the mainstream, first by the logic of commodification and then by way of institutionalization, so too were the NSMs similarly diffused.

A positive feature of the NSMs was the kind of criticism that they launched against the phallocentrism, heterosexism, and Eurocentrism of both the dominant culture and the labor movement. However, in the campus protest culture of the 1960s and 1970s, there was a concerted effort to ensure that fights against sexism, racism, and homophobia were still conducted in the context of a class awareness: hence the cultural studies mantra, "race-class-gender." With their increasing political influence, NSMs had a profound impact on the curriculum of humanities departments in the 1960s, 1970s, and 1980s, with more attention being paid to nonwhite and female scholars, writers, and artists, launching a kind of academic "culture war." Again, positively, the culture war in the universities drew attention to issues of cultural representation in the media and to the stereotypical representation of racialized and gendered minorities, which by the 1990s came to include the representation of gays and lesbians, with the addition of queer theory to the literature.

Not surprisingly, and not unproblematically, the rising attention to cultural representation and to questions of diversity in the media was picked up by the consumer culture. Just as the threat of subculture is diffused by and incorporated through commodification, so have the identity politics of the NSMs and the institutionalization of the culture wars been incorporated into the branding logic of the consumer society, which is interested less in multiculturalism and diversity, or in intersectionality, than with maintaining a steady base of diverse consumers—the interpellation of new subjectivities— in order to avoid crises of market demand. Unlike the mass audience culture of the early entertainment industries, the contemporary consumer culture is "demassified" in the sense that it makes diversity a marketing tactic to broaden its reach. But what this context also reveals is that here too, rebelliousness, difference, and subversion have become part of the reigning ideology when it comes to questions of identity. Demassification and branding are both tied to the commercial diffusion of subversion. Rather than ideology interpellating individuals as compliant subjects, the ruling ideology today is grounded on the inherent transgression of the ideology that seems to rule. Here we face one of the central cultural and political contradictions of our time. If, as I have shown, in both art and culture, and in the identity politics of the NSMs, subversion, far from being antagonistic to the existing system, has actually become part of its interpellative call or hail—that is, if subversion has itself become the dominant ideology (in the case of art and culture, the ethic of innovation reigns over tradition; in the case of identity politics, diversity subverts conformity)—if all of this is the case, what does the subversion of subversion look like?

This is how the situation must be approached from the perspective of the new Alt-Right. What the Left sees as the subversion of bourgeois, elitist, phallocentric, and Eurocentric ideology, the Alt-Right sees as the formation of a new culturally dominant ideology, best encapsulated in the much-disdained call for political correctness. The Alt-Right, too, is antibourgeois, but it perceives and constructs the Left as just such a bourgeoisie, trapped in its own libertine elitist bubble. What the Alt-Right, particularly in its white nationalist and masculinist bent, finds most objectionable in the politically correct postmodern identity politics is what its members perceive as a double standard on questions of diversity and identity. From their perspective, all identities are permissible, save for white and conservative identities, or even "normative" identities. In this scenario, when political correctness and postmodern identity politics are posited as the ideology that seems to rule, for the Alt-Right, its conservative politics cannot but appear subversive. The Alt-Right, in fact, is caught up in the postmodern interpellative call to subversion. What makes this formation additionally troubling is that it also, at times, seems to rail against the consumer culture of postmodern capitalism, making it both ironically populist and at times seemingly anticapitalist, not unlike the depiction of Project Mayhem in David Fincher's *Fight Club* (1999), an iconic film for members of the Alt-Right.[17] Although the film appears radical in its anticonsumerist posturing, the film is outrageously misogynistic in its equating of consumerism with femininity. In the fight club, a prototypical men's rights association (MRA) if ever there was one, the men literally beat each other up, metaphorically beating the consumerism and femininity out of themselves. The paradox, however, is that in order to enjoy transgression, the subject requires a force to transgress. The call to enjoy is therefore difficult to bear, since enjoyment is procured only when it has an Other to transgress.

There is, thus, a perverse core (in the strictest Lacanian sense) to the form of ideology: specifically, ideology, in the context of postmodern capitalism, takes the form of fetishism.[18] In part, this has to do with the interpellative call of consumer society, the call to 'Enjoy!' The prohibition to enjoy has been replaced by an *obligation* to enjoy. However, this also has to do with the mode of ideology today, which according to Žižek is premised on cynicism, and the psychoanalytic category of disavowal, best encapsulated by Octave Manoni's phrase, "*Je sais bien, mais quand même . . .*"[19]—I know very well, but nevertheless. . . .

From a Lacanian perspective, the price of entry into the Symbolic order is a constitutive loss. As McGowan puts it, "no subjectivity exists prior to this structuring loss."[20] But the subject has two possible modes of relating to this constitutive loss—desire and drive:

> Desire is predicated on the belief that it is possible to regain the lost object and thereby discover the ultimate enjoyment. Desire represents a belief that a satisfying object exists and can be obtained. In contrast, the drive locates enjoyment in the movement of return itself—the repetition of loss, rather than in what might be recovered.[21]

These two modes—desire and drive—are, however, tied to each other: the "continuing frustration of desire—this failure to obtain the truly satisfying object—is the precise way that the drive satisfies itself. Through the drive, the subject finds satisfaction in the repetition of failure and loss that initially constitute it."[22] Desire, in other words, serves the drive as a mechanism for facilitating the repetition of the loss, "which is where enjoyment actually lies."[23] There is a problem, though, for the subject of desire in the context of postmodern, post-ideological, consumer capitalism: without a prohibiting agency; with the demise of symbolic efficiency; when no one believes any longer in the existence of the big

Other—what is to prevent the saturation of desire? The constant injunction to 'Enjoy!' presents a dilemma: we can only enjoy insofar as we are prohibited from enjoying.

For Žižek, fetishism disavowal expresses the contemporary reigning cynical approach to ideology. Cynicism, as McGowan puts it, "is a mode of keeping alive the dream of successfully attaining the lost object while fetishistically denying one's investment in this idea."[24] The post-ideological subject can fully recognize the fact that investment in the object of desire is doomed to failure, but she continues to invest herself in the search for this object. True satisfaction is achieved, not by the successful attainment of the object, but by the enjoyment of returning to the position of loss through failure. Drive is definitely a central aspect of contemporary communicative capitalism; however, we should be hesitant about claiming that the subject of communicative capitalism is one of drive.

The (Digital) Delay of Desire

"Communicative capitalism" is an attractive way to theorize the current configurations of networked media, and it is difficult to disagree with Dean's characterization of the ideological operations of information technology and social media.[25] Her theory allows media scholars to grapple with the conditions of space-based media, where the limits of time are increasingly eroding. Noting the similarities between early blogs and search engines, Dean points out that both originate in the problem of organizing information online. Filled by "the fantasy of abundance,"[26] online users had previously been plagued by the problem of locating the desired information. Like the Lacanian theory of the unconscious, Dean points out that in cyberspace, "the truth is out there," but is difficult to find within the sea of abundance. Dean notes that the first blogs were lists of websites, links, and articles that were noteworthy to the "blogger." Bloggers also added comments about the links that they posted. Like search engines, blogs emerged in place of the "subject supposed to know" (the Lacanian analyst). The search engine and the online database also work in combination to avoid the time lag, or the delay, the result of which is the "spatialization" of time. This adds to the difficulty in grasping a conception of prohibition in postmodernity. Everything is available; there are no limits to access. Desire is no longer prohibited by time—the time necessary to locate and achieve satisfaction; everything is present, located in the database. The result is a crisis for the subject of desire—how to prevent the saturation of desire. This is how we might concede Dean's claim that drive makes communicative capitalism operative, and therefore drive is unlikely to work for a political act of resistance and transformation. The disappearance of the delay, which made satisfaction of desire appear possible, leaves only the drive on the other side of fantasy.

New media, information technology, and social media add to this mix. There is no longer any denial of access (that is if we ignore the global "digital divide"). Everything is open and available online. But does instant access suffocate desire? There is an important temporal dimension to desire, which is that of the delay. Desire exists only insofar as the object remains lost. Increasingly, as the delay is reduced closer to zero, it can become apparent to the subject that there is a limit point to desire. The temporal limit is spatialized—delay is no longer the primary factor in distancing oneself from desire. It is now a matter of space—the space of the database. The object is there; it is no longer lost. The suffocation of desire—the reduction of the delay to zero—appears to leave only the drive that circles around the void of the loss. From Žižek's perspective, this is what can potentially lead the subject toward some kind of break from ideology.

Desire involves the endless search for an (impossible) object that will bring satisfaction. But desire is, by definition, insatiable. It continues to follow along a cycle in which the object attained is never *it*, the thing that is desired. This constant search for the object produces an unconscious satisfaction in being able to reset the coordinates of desire, thereby continuing the search. Drive speaks to this other side of insatiable desire. It achieves enjoyment for the subject by failing to get the object. With desire, one can never achieve full enjoyment; however, with drive, one is condemned to an unbearable enjoyment. According to Žižek, "desire and drive are two ways of avoiding the deadlock of negativity that *is* the subject. . . . The two ways . . . involve two thoroughly different notions of subjectivity."[27] The subject of desire chooses, whereas for the subject of drive, choice is inverted into making-oneself-chosen. The only freedom I am granted in drive "is the freedom to choose the inevitable, freely to embrace my destiny, what will happen to me in any case."[28] That is, the subject of drive recognizes the constitutive aspect of loss, which the subject of desire disavows. The reversal of desire into drive, therefore, involves the subjectivization of that which is beyond representation. That is, we subjectivize the traumatic kernel—the negative limit—of the Self. Žižek argues, therefore, that an ethical act is in line with an ethics of the drive.[29] If desire is that which attaches the subject to ideology, the drive moves the subject in the direction of emancipation. In the psychoanalytic sense, the drive is all that remains once the subject has "traversed the fantasy." That is, "if no object can satisfy desire, desire must proceed for its own sake, which means that it must become drive. The drive is what remains of desire after the image of realization has been stripped away. It is desire without the hope of obtaining the object, desire that has become indifferent to its object."[30] The instant access of technoculture leads, potentially, to this stripping away of the subject of desire. As McGowan notes, "the immediacy created by digital technology plants the seeds for the recognition of the subject of drive."[31] But it is here that we see how ideology is still structured and supported by fantasy:

> There is, of course, nothing necessary about the emergence of the subject of drive. The contemporary spatialization of time may simply continue to produce dissatisfied subjects of desire who continue to increase their investment in the illusory promise embodied by the commodity. As long as we experience the object's failure as contingent rather than necessary, we will remain subjects of desire devoted to the capitalist mode of production.[32]

Flatline Constructs

Mark Fisher's writing on "capitalist realism," particularly with respect to his writing on media, adds another layer to our conception of communicative capitalism: what happens when technoculture tethers us to its matrices below the surface level of Symbolic mediations? Through Fisher, we may come to understand the technological component of the decline of symbolic efficiency via the cyberculture itself. In his blog, *K-Punk*, Fisher's short reflections addressed themes ranging from popular film and television, pop music, electronica, rave culture, Jungle music, and alt-rock, to some of the denser aspects of contemporary postmodern theory, ideology, and cyberculture. In *Capitalist Realism*, his most famous book, Fisher develops a critique of the reigning ideology, which he describes as a form of cynicism, drawing on the claim, often attributed to Žižek and Jameson, that it is easier to imagine the end of the world than the end of capitalism. This small but effective point, according to Fisher, signals the manner of disavowal fetishism specific to late postmodern capitalism, and it especially applies to the view on both the post-Marxist Left and the Right about the nonexistence of society, or the Thatcherite thesis that there is no alternative to capitalism.

Fisher's writing in *Capitalist Realism* oscillates between two lines of interrelated critique, similar to Noys's view about accelerationism: there is, on the one hand, a transcendental and dialectical materialist line of inquiry that questions the possibilities for radical change, and there is the subjective agency that can bring about such change; but there is also, on the other hand, an immanentist line, concerned with the material forms of social control, the desacrilization of meaning, and the stripping away of the subjective. It is this latter line that reflects and coincides with Fisher's earlier affiliations with the Cybernetic Culture Research Unit (CCRU) in the 1990s—an unofficial research collective at the University of Warwick—and his mentorship by the group's directors, Sadie Plant and Nick Land, the latter now famous for his association with Right Accelerationism, the Neo-reactionary, and the Dark Enlightenment movements that some tie to the emergence of the online Alt-Right. While the influence of CCRU scholarship and Land in particular is still felt in *Capitalist Realism*, it is clear that Fisher's allegiances had by the time of writing this book shifted closer to the transcendentalist and dialectical materialist line of inquiry in what the cultural studies scholar, Jeremy Gilbert, has referred to as Fisher's "Lacanian period," influenced largely by Žižek and by his friendship with Dean, in addition to his break from Land's influence.[33] Still, the book reflects back to Fisher's earlier affiliations at the CCRU, particularly with respect to some of his reflections on media in his doctoral thesis, *Flatline Constructs* (1999).[34]

Flatline Constructs is Fisher's attempt to define what he calls "gothic materialism." The term itself is more or less a rendering of Deleuzian transcendental empiricism articulated through the lens of cybercultural theory and cyberpunk fiction.[35] A theory of media influenced by McLuhan is also apparent in Fisher's writing. Fisher states that McLuhan did the most to advance a nonrepresentationalist theory of the media, developing instead a concern with the relationship between bodies and the media environment. By taking account of Fisher's writings on McLuhan, we see how media theory plays a role in his theoretical project overall and in his more influential conception of capitalist realism. There is a certain cynicism present in Fisher's writing on media that establishes the parameters of our control dilemma today.

Fisher's interest in media environments is still very much present in *Capitalist Realism*, for instance, as he writes about the postdisciplinary media environment of spaces like the university. The dissolution of modern disciplinary systems in the Foucauldian sense has not, he says, resulted in the increased use of newfound freedoms, but has instead conditioned people into "hedonic lassitude," in which, as he puts it, "the soft narcosis, the comfort food oblivion of PlayStation, all-night TV and marijuana" now dominate as flows of control. "Ask students to read more than a couple of sentences and many . . . will protest that they *can't do it*. The most frequent complaint teachers hear," he says, "is that *it's boring*." Not the content, but the act of reading itself is considered boring. What we are facing, according to Fisher, is the contradiction between the postliterate "New Flesh" that is "too wired to concentrate" and the "concentrational logics of decaying disciplinary systems." "To be bored," he writes, "means to be removed from the communicative sensation-stimulus matrix of texting, YouTube and fast food; to be denied, for a moment, the constant flow of sugary gratification on demand."[36] As a consequence of "being hooked into the entertainment matrix," people become twitchy, agitated, and interpassive, with an inability to concentrate or to focus. Such a plugged-in culture, according to Fisher, numbs us to the future—the "incapacity to connect current lack of focus with future failure," the "inability to synthesize time into any coherent narrative, is symptomatic of more than mere demotivation." This condition, he writes, is similar to Jameson's breakdown metaphor—as a series of pure and unrelated presents in time—whereby we come to experience the technological exhaustion of the pursuit of desire in communicative capitalism. It is this interpretation of the present media environment, one that appears eerily familiar from cyberpunk dystopia, that relies very much on Fisher's earlier reading of McLuhan.

If there is a sense in which Fisher's McLuhan appears close to the Lacanian-influenced schizoanalytic writing of Deleuze and Guattari, it is perhaps the sense that McLuhan's theories that are most in the mode of science fiction can be read as an inheritance from Freud. He writes that "in a direct anticipation of McLuhan, Freud describes technical machines as extensions of the organs," proposing that McLuhan's "extensions of man" thesis goes back to Freud in *Civilization and its Discontents* and *Beyond the Pleasure Principle*.[37] Freud in fact states in *Civilization and its Discontents* that "as a member of the human community and with help of technology guided by science, one can go over on the attack on nature and subject it to the human will."[38] For Fisher, following Freud, "McLuhan conceives of the organism as an homeostatic system whose aim is to neutralize, or *disintensify, stimuli.*"[39] But if technology is a human creation to save us from the shock and overstimulating threats of nature, what is there to protect us from the shocks unleashed by the technological sublime?

The media, according to Fisher, functions ambiguously. What McLuhan misleadingly describes as "extensions of man" forms an artificial system of perception, connecting the external environment to the perceptual apparatus of the body. What McLuhan then designates as "auto-amputation" arises as a mechanism to protect the body from the potentially threatening shocks of stimuli from the external media environment.

This point is not so dissimilar from the way that early- to mid-twentieth century theorists, such as George Simmel or Walter Benjamin, describe the effects of anomie or the "blasé" attitude; they describe the self-imposed isolationism of individuals, resulting from the overwhelming shock experience of the new urban environments of one hundred years ago. The same can be said about the kind of "whatever-being," as Dean calls it, of the response to the overstimulation of contemporary new media; alternatively, the same can be said of what Susan Buck-Morss describes as the "anaesthetics" of media developed to absorb the overwhelming dimensions of the new aesthetic.[40] Auto-amputation is thus the product of the subject trying to regain a sense of equilibrium—it is a kind of numbness or blocking of perception enacted to protect the organism or the body from overwhelming sensory stimulation. On this point, can we not also claim that such a sensation creates the need to escape into the protective field of the big Other? I will return to this below.

It must be noted, as Fisher does, that the technological acceleration that he is talking about is also, as we have seen above, a feature of capitalist development. It is, in other words, a product of capitalism's incessant need to revolutionize the means of production that, in another register—and from perspectives as oppositional as Freud and Deleuze—points to the emergence of ever newer devices to ground the exhausted energy and affects that are (potentially) lost as a result of the disequilibrium unleashed by the new.

This is one reason why, drawing on Deleuze and Guattari, contemporary Accelerationists on the both the Left and the Right see the only way past capitalism as going through capitalism—to accelerate the process to the point of its limits. For Freud, however, the unleashing of libidinal energy is reprocessed through transforming mechanisms of repression, from religion to modern civilized discourse; for Deleuze, it involves newer processes of territorialization or processes of fixing in ever new cultural constructions. But as Fisher writes, for McLuhan, "the attempt to become a closed system results in a *freezing out* of stimuli, resulting in a kind of auto-amputation of the body induced by the transition into fully mediated environments."[41]

Fisher writes, "for McLuhan, the modern technical environment . . . is continuous with the human nervous system, misrecognized as something separate because the sheer amount of stimuli cannot be dealt with except by an enormous numbing, or 'auto-amputation' of the electronic sense organ transmitting stimuli."[42] McLuhan is therefore distinguished, according to Fisher, from later postmodern theorists such as Jean Baudrillard and Jameson, because of his sense of the failures of screens adequately to protect the subject. For Baudrillard, the hyperreality of new media more deeply *integrates* the subject into the space of the screen;

for Jameson, it results in a fragmenting of the subject, uncoupling the modern mechanisms of repression, depth, and essence.

McLuhan's notion of Narcissus as Narcosis helps us to see another possibility: for him, the problem of Narcissus is not one of self-love, but of the difficulties of separating self from other, such that there is a dissolution of the divide, for instance, between private and public.[43] Baudrillard (similar to Deleuze and Guattari) associates this dilemma with the emergence of cybernetic networks. In another cultural register, we could (as Jameson does) identify this transformation with the decline of the paternal metaphor. For McLuhan, television—we could extrapolate further to include contemporary new media—cyberneticizes the environment. For him, the forms of media are not tools, but environments. Likewise, Deleuze and Guattari describe TV as the technical apparatus of enslavement—"one is enslaved by TV as a human machine," they write, "insofar as the television viewers are no longer consumers or users, nor even subjects who supposedly 'make' it, but intrinsic component pieces, 'input' and 'output', feedback or recurrences that are no longer connected to the machine in such a way as to produce or use it."[44] Through the repetition of images, media play a crucial role in anaestheticizing the subject from overwhelming stimuli.

If we are to turn back then to a political register, which is much more evident in Fisher's post-Lacanian phase of writing, then we can consider the potential direction that McLuhan's writing on auto-amputated cybernetic environments can lead us. Writing after the publication of *Capitalist Realism*, Fisher returns to McLuhan to think through these conditions. From the way that McLuhan has written about media environments, we get the sense that "new media-logics stealthily impose themselves while we look in the rearview mirror [of past media development], importing concepts from the past to explain what is actually in front of us."[45]

For McLuhan, the forms of media are not neutral—"any medium has the power of imposing its own assumptions on the unwary."[46] The point of the Narcissus myth is that people become fascinated by any extension of themselves, but "the more cyber-blitzed we are by media, the more numbed we become" to its implications.[47] Self-understanding lags behind what we actually do.

Only artists and designers, then, according to McLuhan, are capable of bringing an environment into view, because of their ability to construct counter-environments. "Artists, being experts in sensory awareness tend to concentrate on the environmental as the challenging and dangerous situation."[48] But, as Fisher concludes, "artists are by no means the only agents capable of snapping us out of a narcissus trance. In the era of Web 2.0 . . . there are all manner of consultant-manipulators and hyper-engineers who can also control 'the future' because they see the present. They deliberately build rearview mirrors into all the new architecture of Web 2.0, making users feel that they are empowered, participating, involved—convincing all the digital narcissuses that there is after all, a substance to their subjectivity."[49]

Citing Dean's conception of "communicative capitalism," Fisher addresses the lack of equitable distribution of wealth in new media environments, saying that "the deluge of screens and spectacles coincides with the extreme corporatization, financialization, and privatization across the globe."[50] Rather than rendering it as a space of potentially radical transformation, the new media environment tends to *accelerate* the present conditions of control, with the rearview mirror creating only the appearance of satisfactory change. For Fisher, then, "there's no way back through the (rearview) mirror. The possibilities for a different politics depend upon waking from a Narcissus trance and seeing the new potential in what is in front of us. But McLuhan's most important lesson," he writes, returning to the cynical register of capitalist realism, "is that what is in front of us is the hardest of all to recognize."[51] It is from this perspective that we can return to the question of desire and the Symbolic in communicative capitalism; or, more precisely, we can return to the question: How do we save desire from its suffocation in an age of instant access and abundance?

Symbolic Identities

Social media, I claim, is the manner in which capitalism has succeeded in reintroducing lack and scarcity into a world of instant access and abundance. In social media, the subject, who no longer believes in the existence of the big Other, works toward a willing of the big Other back into existence. The subject caught in social media is not duped by ideology, but seeks it out, unconsciously, in order to save herself from the saturation of her desire; to save herself from the anxiety of living under the conditions of the demise of symbolic efficiency; and to save herself from the traumatic encounter with the impossible-Real that has been opened up by the limit points of the Symbolic. Social media is (one example of) the secular solution to the lack of a big Other, which is paralleled by a fundamentalist turn to conservatism and tradition. People, in other words, engage with social media, "not to *escape from*, but rather in order *to escape to* a social reality that protects (mediates) us more effectively from the truly traumatic issues and concerns that belie our 'normal' lives."[52] Social media is a new frontier for desire. This can be seen in three operations of social network sites defined by boyd and Ellison: the public profile; the connecting to a network; and the operation of "sharing."[53] For the sake of brevity, I will rely on examples from Facebook in the analysis that follows.

One of the central questions we need to pose about the profile page is whether it is a representation of the subject's Imaginary or Symbolic sense of Self. According to Dean, the "society of control" and "communicative capitalism" make possible the conditions for replacing Symbolic identities with Imaginary ones. The latter is one aspect of the dominance of neoliberalism and its emphasis on the cult of the individual, away from the welfare state's emphasis on community. Communicative capitalism, then, "does not provide symbolic identities, sites from which we can see ourselves. Rather, it offers in their place new ways for me to imagine myself, an immense variety of lifestyles with which I can experiment."[54] In communicative capitalism, we are not interpellated into "symbolically anchored identities;" instead, we are enjoined "to develop our creative potential and cultivate our individuality."[55] This characterization, however, is perhaps more appropriate to the brief decade-long period between the popular arrival of the internet and the arrival of social media. In the 1990s, the attitude was that nobody on the internet knows who you really are (best encapsulated by the parody cartoon, "on the internet, nobody knows you're a dog")[56]—online, we can perform a different persona and no one will know, which is perhaps the ultimate victory for identity politics. Today, though, the mechanisms of control and big data are so precise that it is possible to determine one's offline identity by way of one's online activity. The profile page provides some indication of how this works.

On Facebook, details about one's city of residence, contact information, marital/relationship status, date of birth, employment history, and education are all provided in the public profile. What is even more important is that this information is provided freely and willingly by the user herself. Of course, providing a minimum of this information is required in order to join the site; however, the necessity of joining is another significant aspect of social media. The price of inclusion is the willful submission to the mechanisms of surveillance. Additional information is also provided on the profile page: photographs in which one is "tagged"—thus providing a true life image of the subject on the site, as opposed to the "avatar"; places that one has visited; and interests, such as music, film, television, books, etc., with specific titles and names of artists and authors—the latter are provided by the operation of "liking." The profile page also lists the names of Facebook "groups" in which the user is a member. To whom is all of this data presented? The answer, of course, is another piece of data that makes up the profile page: the "friends" list—that is, the user's online social network.

The network is a list of people with whom the user maintains contact online. These may or may not be those with whom the user is actively engaged in offline life. This, though, is the list of others to whom the user is presenting herself as an objectified entity: a combination of the commodification of the Self and the entrepreneurial ethic of neoliberalism. In fact, in some cases, it is the user's friends list, or network, that makes her desirable to others, a demonstration of her "symbolic capital"—this is even more pronounced on the professional social media site, LinkedIn, where it really is "who you know" that counts. What is important, though, is that it is the "friends" in social media that are the target of one's activity, whether it is the operation of "liking," sharing, commenting, or updating one's "status."

"Liking" is the operation of demonstrating—through the simple click of the mouse—something about one's taste. "'Sharing" similarly presents something about one's taste, but can also add detail about an opinion on anything from humor to politics—it is a demonstration of one's "cultural capital." One may share articles and images that are of interest to oneself, and potentially to one's "friends." Sharing, though, is also an operation of showing to others something about one's own sense of humor, political sensibility, etc. Images, as well, can be shared—most popular in recent years is the "meme": an image or video that is passed electronically online. Recent memes often take the form of images with short and quick, catchy captions, often expressing either some cynical or ironic observation about contemporary life and politics. Liking and sharing act symbolically. They are articulations of one's subject position within the field of the Symbolic. Likes and shares are enunciated contents. It is the operation of articulating signifiers which "represent a subject for another signifier."[57] Similarly, comments and status updates articulate in language the subject's Self-representation for the benefit of others. Comments and status updates take the form of the blog and reduce it to short, simple statements. The furthest extreme of this, so far, is Twitter, in which users are able to express themselves in 280 characters or less. Beyond the word, though, Instagram has reduced this function to the mere image. With Instagram, users can upload images taken with their mobile phones, without the labor required for articulating their images in words.[58]

Mobile media, such as smart phones, simplify these operations. Not only can we participate in social media wherever we roam—without the use of a personal computer—but also, it is possible easily to share images and videos captured on one's phone, thereby easing the signifying aspect of Self-representation in social media. This is of course the operation of the control society moving beyond the disciplinary mechanisms of surveillance. But the degree to which we are integrated into these mechanisms, despite the fact that we are aware of how they work, demonstrates the way in which social media acts as the willing into existence of the big Other. Not because we are monitored, but because it is the agency of the Other for whom we perform our Symbolic identities in social media, which is increasingly connected to the world offline. I tweet, therefore I exist; and the compulsion to (re)tweet is the symptom of our need to feel affective recognition from the Other.

Analyst or Pervert?

Since the subjects of communicative capitalism are, according to Dean, already subjects of drive, it certainly appears as though an ethics of drive is off the table for a revolutionary politics—or does it? Perhaps what the demise of symbolic efficiency demonstrates is that the line between ideology and emancipation is disappearing. A political ethics of drive depends largely upon the way in which the demise of symbolic efficiency is interpreted and approached. If it is read, in Lacanian terms, as the nonexistence of the big Other, pure and simple—the Other of the Symbolic order, regulating and organizing symbolic reality—then surely it is necessary to concede Dean's main argument, that a politics of drive is not possible today, or the "drive is not an act." But what if the postmodern subject's recognition of the nonexistence of the big Other is *only* apparent?

Dean further argues, contra Žižek, that in the context of the demise of symbolic efficiency, the position of the analyst, as defined by the Lacanian discourse of the analyst, loses its radical subjective positioning. The analyst's position of subjective destitution is one of drive. But, according to Dean, if we think of the social link of the discourse of the analyst within the context of the demise of symbolic efficiency, the position of the analyst as one of pure drive is no longer radical.[59] This, however, makes sense if we conceive the position of the agent in the analyst's discourse, not as that of the analyst, but as that of the pervert, which carries the same form as that of the analyst (a–$\$$, in Lacanese).[60] The pervert and the analyst are separated by a thin line, which we can attribute to fantasy. That is, they share the same basic structure, and are grounded in a certain kind of knowledge; however, the analyst has successfully traversed the fantasy—she acknowledges loss as constitutive—while the pervert has not—he wishes, still, to be the object for the Other's *jouissance*, since it preserves his own enjoyment. The analyst accepts the position of subjective destitution, while the pervert wills the Other back into existence in order to preserve his perverse pleasure.

It is worth conceiving the demise of symbolic efficiency, then, not necessarily as the loss of the Symbolic order as such (the nonexistence of the big Other), but rather as the loss of the symbolic efficiency of the analyst's interpretation. According to Žižek, postmodernity is marked by a crisis in interpretation, leaving the symptoms intact.[61] The problem, then, is how to bring about a rupture in the subject's symptomatic chain, when she herself already recognizes the interpretive procedure of locating its cause. According to Žižek, the loss of the efficiency of symbolic interpretation is one way to diagnose the postmodern condition of the demise of symbolic efficiency. This, too, is how one should read Fredric Jameson's notion of "cognitive mapping"–lacking the symbolic weight of interpreting her position in the world, the subject remains lost, trapped in a situation, without any means of making sense of herself and her position in the world. This means that—while agreeing with Dean's characterization of communicative capitalism—the conditions of emancipation involve, not redirecting the loop of drive, but sticking to the "cognitive mapping" of the analytical discourse: the analytical position is one of willing to sacrifice desire, or of acknowledging that the limit to desire is where we enjoy; while the position of the pervert recognizes the failure of the object, but nevertheless enjoys her symptom. The latter is the type of subject position interpellated for our enjoyment of social media. While enjoying social media we are still subjects of desire.

3

Subjection before Enslavement

Social media is, as I claim, a desire machine. It is a metaphor, as I have suggested, for the algorithm of our desire. I want to explore this logic of the algorithm further by drawing on Lacan. In fact, there is an endnote to Lacan's paper, "The Subversion of the Subject and the Dialectic of Desire," which indicates something particular about this problematic. There, Lacan explains that the printed version of the text differs from the original presented at the colloquium on "La Dialectique" in 1960.[1] Lacan notes that the published version of the paper includes a final section on "castration," about which he lacked the necessary time to address in his presentation. In his presentation, the concluding section about castration was replaced with a few short and quick remarks regarding "the machine," by which, he says, "the subject's relation to the signifier can be materialized."[2] This substitution of castration with the machine, and vice versa, seems to presage the distinction made by Deleuze and Guattari, more recently elaborated by Maurizio Lazzarato, between what they call "social subjection" and "machinic enslavement."[3] On the one hand, "castration" implies the priority of subjection, precisely in the sense that it is this very cut that produces the desiring subject within the register of the Symbolic order; on the other hand, placing an emphasis on the machine seems to displace the centrality of castration in the desiring-*machine*, as it is dubbed by Deleuze and Guattari. The Lacanian parallax between castration and the machine conveniently introduces the topic that I address in this chapter.

Continuing from my assessment of communicative capitalism in the previous chapter, I now intend to argue against Lazzarato for the *priority* of "social subjection"—or simply subjectivization (and hence, castration in the logic of producing a desiring subject)—over "machinic enslavement." Social media provides a tactical model for making this argument, because of the kinds of activities that it now encompasses. Social media overlaps the functions that are tied to the political divides of democracy and surveillance, but it also overlaps the functions of (exploited) labor and enjoyment, a point expressed by the term "communicative capitalism." Social media is a communications medium, and therefore plays a role in the production and circulation of information and meaning. However, my claim is that ideologically, the production of meaning in social media is tied principally to processes of social subjection, which then (secondarily) help to incorporate subjects into the matrices of machinic enslavement. My own reference to subjection is located at the intersection of "castration" in the Lacanian-psychoanalytic sense and the class struggle in the Marxist sense. The overlapping contexts of the subject's entry into the Symbolic order, and her positioning relative to the class struggle, as I see it, logically precede her enslavement in the machine, regardless of the fact that the machine is definitively and retroactively a force of subjection both in terms of exploitation and in terms of the circulation of desire. The forms of social media, as "meaning machines," to use Langlois's term,[4] in this respect are not unlike the ideological apparatuses theorized by Althusser,[5] but they are distinguished by the way that they also overlap processes of exploitation and interpellation directly.

Just as Althusser's interest was in coming to understand the way that capitalist relations of production are *reproduced,* so too do my interests lie with the way in which the forms of algorithmic media facilitate not only the formal matrix of exploitation, but also the modes of interpellation that tether people to these matrices. Expropriation is still made possible in (neo)liberal capitalism because of the wage relation and commodity fetishism, which veil the social relation of exploitation by giving the worker *something* back; however, the value of this *something* remains far below the value of the expropriated surplus value inscribed into the commodity.[6] Although recent literature proposes viewing capitalist relations of production in terms of the real subsumption of labor, and in terms of social production rather than simple commodity production,[7] my claim is that the commodity form (and hence fetishism) still factors heavily in the precipitous subjection relative to the class struggle that facilitates the subject's enslavement to the machine. The logic of fetishism is key and works at a formal level, in the exploitation of the prosumer commodity, but it also works in the exchange of data for meaning, meaningfulness, and enjoyment. How then can we conceive these overlapping and converging apparatuses of exploitation and enjoyment?

When we look at the forms of algorithmic media, we find that these interrelationships are compressed into a single form. When using a popular social media site, like Facebook, for instance, we find that it is at once a source of exploitation, expropriation, and interpellation. But Lazzarato's view, which prioritizes enslavement, or the intersection of enslavement-subjection, *misses* the priority of exploitation, and therefore the role of the class struggle at the heart of the mode of production. I argue instead that the forms of algorithmic and social media make possible a deeper identification between the production of surplus value through exploitation and the lure of desire in what Lacan referred to as surplus-enjoyment. Although I believe that Lazzarato goes too far in reifying the subject in the assemblage of the machine, my claim is that the machine still occupies a component part in reproducing both the capitalist processes of exploitation and interpellation, particularly in the new age of algorithmic media, like social media and digital automation. Nevertheless, it is the context of the class struggle (socially and politically) and "castration" (subjectively), I claim, that positions our understanding of the role played by the machine in reproducing capitalist class interests and power.

(Re)Inventing *The Matrix*

When discussing the convergence of labor and enjoyment in algorithmic media, it is difficult not to draw an analogy with the Wachowski siblings' *The Matrix* (1999), in which humans are exploited by the machines as sustenance, in such a way that their pleasure and enjoyment provide the main source of energy fueling the machines. Yet it is this imagery that frames the contentions I have with the kind of perspective held by Lazzarato, in which the subject-object dualism is dispelled with the effect of displacing the centrality of the subject-subject *antagonism* of the class struggle, which is an objective antagonism insofar as it expresses the material contradictions of capitalism.

    The historical materialist analysis of capital demonstrates the contradictory logics of capital and labor, in which capital, in order to secure its own interests, is logically and rationally required to pursue profit by whatever means necessary. This includes the contradictory requirement to displace human waged labor-power, which is also the source of value production in commodities. Likewise, to best secure its own survival, labor must continuously challenge the interests of capital. It must act according to its own rational and logical imperatives for survival, which is ultimately antagonistic and contradictory to the interests of capital, since it can create a barrier to the further appropriation and accumulation of capitalist wealth. It is in this sense that I refer to the subject-subject antagonism as "class struggle," since capitalism is incapable of negating its logical and collective requirement for exploiting labor and remaining intact (whether consciously or not—although capital tends to have a higher degree of class consciousness than labor), just as much as it is impossible for labor not to fight for its own survival needs collectively (again, mostly an unconscious collectivity, making it easily cooptable by other dominant-hegemonic forces), which are oppositional to the interests of capital.

Class struggle is, in this way, an objective and material antagonism. It is also for this reason that I reject non-dialectical or non-materialist approaches to the political and the contradictions of the social, such as the radical democracy or the populist rationality of Laclau and Mouffe.[8]

The difference between the views of Laclau and Mouffe and my own view is that for me, the subjective agency of radical politics (which is nevertheless still quite diverse with regard to race and gender, for instance) has its origin in the material and objective contradictions of capital rather than in merely discursive formations, organized around shared demands toward a common enemy. Laclau and Mouffe defend the latter position. The difficulty with their view of populism is that it bears a resemblance that is too close to the discursive formations of proto-fascisms, which lack an objective or material basis for demands regarding the ideal form of the social.[9] It is also in this sense that I place emphasis on subjection over enslavement, in contrast to Lazzarato, while still attempting to maintain the significance of machinic enslavement in the apparatus theory of ideology and subjectivity, again because of the material role of technology set within the class struggle.

Social subjection and machinic enslavement encompass the intersection of politics and technology. In the history of capital, machinery developed as part of the class struggle in order to reduce the amount of necessary labor time, to make processes of production more efficient, and to discipline the labor force through automation, the threat of unemployment, and deskilling. Machinery also proved critical in what Marx refers to as "relative surplus value," when the length of the working day was shortened, and capitalists needed to find mechanisms for producing the same amount (or more) of surplus value in a shorter period of time in the working day than what was produced in longer periods of the working day (what Marx refers to as "absolute surplus value"). Machinery therefore made possible the production of relative surplus value within the limits of shorter working days, in which labor-power could only be put to work for a fixed and given amount of time. Automation in machinery thus helps to reduce the amount of necessary labor time within the context of the capitalist mode of production, increasing the amount of surplus labor as the source of surplus value and profit.

It's important to point out, too, that revolutions in productive technology (from the early-nineteenth to the mid-nineteenth century onward) also emerged in parallel with the rise of new (analogue) entertainment technology and media, from the daguerreotype and film to radio and television.[10] However, the machinery that changed everything was the development of digital automation and information technology, from the desktop computer to the laptop, the internet, the smartphone and the tablet, software, algorithmic new media, and social media.[11] The latter have converged in ways that now make possible the overlapping functions required to discipline populations and to enforce contemporary mechanisms of control, so that we have, in a single device, machinations of enjoyment *and* labor, but also of democracy, surveillance, and control.[12] We can see why, for this reason, social media operates as a useful metaphor for the current stage of capital.

When we consider the productive and the consumptive aspects of algorithmic new media—labor and entertainment—we start to see in what sense the logics of surplus value and surplus enjoyment overlap. Surplus value and surplus enjoyment have a parallax relationship in the same way that exploitation and ideology, historical and dialectical materialism, and the subject and object share parallax relationships.[13] We cannot necessarily comprehend the matter at hand unless it is viewed through an identifying gaze that approaches the object from the inverse sides of the same problem. To better explain this overlap, let us take the example of the episode, "Fifteen Million Merits," from the Charlie Brooker series, *Black Mirror* (2011–).

In this episode, which takes place (like all episodes of the series) in the not-too-distant future, people "work" in "factories" that combine physical labor with entertainment. Workers perform labor by riding stationary exercise bicycles. While doing so, they watch television on a large LCD display screen positioned directly in front of them. Work stations are lined up in rows, with each worker cycling side by side. Each has his or her own television monitor, which they use to select and watch a program of their choice, or to play an interactive videogame. The purpose of this labor remains unclear (conceivably it is to generate energy to power this dystopian society). There is no mention of what kind of value is being produced and for whom. However, the more each worker cycles—the longer he or she spends performing his or her work—the more each worker accrues in wages that are measured in "merits." A worker's wealth in merits is displayed whenever he or she plugs into an interactive display, which is located at various locations on every wall in this claustrophobic world that only seems to support indoor living.

The episode follows the life of Bing (Daniel Kaluuya), a quiet loner who goes back and forth, every day, from his small wall-to-wall display screen bedroom to the cycling center where he works. In his bedroom, just like at work, he watches TV and plays videogames. From time to time, banner ads for pornography websites pop up in the middle of his viewing. He is able to ignore the ads, but is forced to pay a fee from his merits. If he chooses to close his eyes during the ad, an alarm bell sounds and red lights flash until he once again continues to consume.

This is truly a society of the spectacle, in which people are continuously enjoined to "amuse themselves to death," in which entertainment and labor converge in ways that demonstrate the homology between surplus value and surplus enjoyment. Ideologically, people are driven by the superego injunction to "Enjoy!,"[14] and even when they attempt to evade this injunction, it is reinforced through threats of indirect (punitive) violence (a reference to contemporary postmodern culture in which the prohibition to enjoy has been transformed into the obligation to enjoy). In this world, media is hyper-personalized—it is "mass" media, in the sense that the masses consume simultaneously, but personalized because of the direct individualized engagement with the sites of consumption. Materially, then, this engagement fuels the drive to produce—or, at the very least, it provides distraction and amusement at the same time that workers are driven toward laboring activities, not unlike the dangling of the carrot in front of the horse. This model best explains the overlap in algorithmic and social media between labor and enjoyment, between the production of surplus value and surplus *jouissance*. It demonstrates precisely the way in which I here conceive the role of algorithmic media in interpellating subjects through the lure of desire, while they at the same time participate in the production of surplus value. But it also encapsulates the intersection of what Lazzarato refers to as social subjection and machinic enslavement. Therefore, in the following section I outline the distinction between these terms. I do so, however, in order to lay claim to the fact that social subjection takes precedence over machinic enslavement.

Subjection and Enslavement

Drawing on Deleuze and Guattari,[15] Lazzarato contends that subjectivity is produced by and within capitalism in two ways, or through two apparatuses: that of social subjection, and that of machinic enslavement. According to Lazzarato, subjection "equips us with a subjectivity, assigning us an identity, a sex, a body, a profession, a nationality, and so on" (Lazzarato, 12; see note 3). Machinic enslavement, conversely, "occurs via desubjectivization by mobilizing functional and operational, non-representational and asignifying, rather than linguistic and representational semiotics" (Lazzarato, 25). With machinic enslavement, the subject loses her individuality and becomes a mere cog in the machine, or "a component part of an assemblage," which includes structures not normally conceived as "machinery," such as businesses, the financial system, the media, welfare state institutions like schools, hospitals, museums, theatres, and (of

94

course) the internet (Lazzarato, 25). Subjection, in other words, deals in the construction of *individuals*—it is interpellation in the sense attributed to Althusser; enslavement, however, incorporates people as "dividuals"—that is, to paraphrase Deleuze,[16] as samples of data and data sets (Lazzarato, 25). Machinic enslavement, therefore, refers to the way that people are incorporated into a human-machine assemblage.

Lazzarato is keen to emphasize the role that machinic enslavement plays in producing capitalist subjectivity, particularly since, according to him, several contemporary social theorists, such as Alain Badiou, Jacques Rancière, Judith Butler, and Žižek,[17] ignore this aspect, preferring to focus on questions relating to social subjection (Lazzarato, 13). Against these thinkers, Lazzarato claims that unlike feudal society, power relations in capitalism are impersonal and emerge out of the organization of machines (Lazzarato, 29). As he puts it, "capital is not a mere relationship among 'people', nor is it reducible to an intersubjective relationship." Power relationships do exist, but according to Lazzarato they are constituted by "social machines"—by which he refers to corporations, collective infrastructures of the welfare state, and communications systems—and are "assisted" by technical machines, such as the algorithmic media (Lazzarato, 28). Unlike subjection (this seems to be one of his central claims), enslavement dissolves the subject-object dualism, replacing it with "ontologically ambiguous" entities, hybrids, or what he refers to as "subject-object bi-face entities" (Lazzarato, 30).

Theorists that place their focus on subjection, according to Lazzarato, would seem to draw out too rigidly the subject-object dualism. Lazzarato remains somewhat critical of this stance, particularly since, for him, this would also seem to be the same process as drawn out by capital: "by dividing the assemblage into subjects and objects, [property rights, for instance] empty the latter (nature, animals, machines, objects, signs, etc.) of all creativity, of the capacity to act and produce, which they assign only to individual subjects whose principle characteristic is being an 'owner' (an owner or non-owner)" (Lazzarato, 35). By prioritizing the assemblage of machinic enslavement in this way, Lazzarato, it would appear, seems to place class antagonism in a secondary position, relative to the machine.[18] That is to say, by viewing the production of capitalist subjectivity primarily as a product of "dividuals," who are only then interpellated as individuals, Lazzarato seems to want to do away with the subject-object dualism, which he regards as central to the interpellation of the subject. This formulation, in some ways, is not too dissimilar from the Althusserian one, in which individuals are interpellated as subjects. By comparison, Lazzarato sees the interpellation of the subject as something that withdraws her from the assemblage, forcing her into a subject position that only then, secondarily, divides us between subject and object. However, while working to disparage the subject-object dualism, Lazzarato misses, not the dualism, but the *antagonism* between *subjects*. Not an "intersubjective" relationship, but a subject-subject *antagonism*; in other words, the class struggle. In pointing to the subject-subject antagonism of the class struggle, my point is not to ignore the side of enslavement, but to draw out the fact that the technical object, regardless of the fact of enslavement, is that which is caught at the intersection of the tension of class power.

If I can put it somewhat differently, I claim that machinic enslavement is in a secondary position relative to the class struggle, which does in fact prioritize what Lazzarato refers to as social subjection. The machine is that object which is caught in the tension produced by the class antagonism. Therefore, while I agree with Lazzarato that attention to machinic enslavement is pivotal to any theory of exploitation and emancipation, it must still be understood in the context of the class struggle. It is within the class struggle that the kinds of subjectivization required for machinic enslavement are produced, first in the sense of reproducing the kinds of inequality (including the kinds of inequality that are tied to our embodiment, such as race and sex) that are necessary for the continued (re)production of surplus value, second in the sense of interpellating subjects by way of enjoyment. Lazzarato is quite clear on this point when he explains, "enslavement does not operate through repression or ideology . . . [Rather] it takes over human beings 'from the inside', on the *pre-personal* (pre-cognitive and preverbal) level, as well as 'from the outside', on the *supra-personal* level, by assigning them certain modes of perception and sensibility and *manufacturing an unconscious*. Machinic enslavement formats the basic functions of perceptive, sensory, affective, cognitive, and linguistic behaviour" (Lazzarato, 38, emphasis added).[19] In this sense, Lazzarato's lineage is fixed precisely on Deleuze and Guattari's productive model of desire in their schizoanalytic methodology, which sees the signifier as a tyrannical territorializing mechanism similar to the way that, as they see it, social subjection, secondarily, interpellates the subject out of the assemblage.[20] My claim, however, is that machinic enslavement is only productive as a critical category if it assumes a prior desiring subject, or if it assumes a desiring subject that precedes its interpellation by the machines of enslavement.

However, one of the benefits of using machinic enslavement as a valence of comprehension is that it helps to renew contemporary questions about the relationship between smart technologies, such as algorithmic media, capitalist exploitation, and interpellation. In this way, the logic of enslavement is useful for rethinking the modes of ideology critique.

Rather than conceiving enslavement in the manner described by Lazzarato, it is worth conceiving it in terms of the subject-ideology logic introduced by Althusser in his theory of the state ideological apparatuses, including the relationship between exploited labor and ideological interpellation. The two converge in algorithmic media and in social media, in which users are exploited as prosumer commodities, but are also inscribed into the productive assemblage through their own participation in the production of surplus enjoyment.

Inside the Meaning Machine

Just as Lazzarato seems to prioritize machinic enslavement in capitalist subjectivity, recent approaches in critical social media studies afford the same priorities to algorithmic media. Ganaele Langlois, for instance, claims that in the age of social media, meaning is no longer simply a human process—it has become tied to technological and commercial processes (Langlois, 24; see note 4). What she refers to as "meaning" is not so much the content of a medium as it is the way in which algorithmic media and technology assign "meaningfulness" to pieces of content. With participatory media, governance processes are geared toward "enabling and assigning levels of meaningfulness" (Langlois, 44). Meaningfulness involves both processes of "assigning cultural value to information" and "strategies to foster a specific cultural perception of the platform" (Langlois, 44). Assigning meaningfulness becomes important when one considers the fact that platforms are geared toward fostering as much participation as possible (Langlois, 44).

Langlois's central argument is that software itself is a cultural actor (Langlois, 46). To make this case, she draws on a range of theoretical perspectives, most notably Actor Network Theory (ANT) and autonomist Marxism. As she describes it, ANT "defines nonhumans such as technical objects as possessing agency, as being able to influence, reshape, and bend to their will other nonhuman and human actors" (Langlois, 52). As an actor, software is not just "a neutral conduit, or a mirror of our desires: it can impose a specific will, it can transform us, it promises to reveal new meaningful horizons, yet at the same time, it is not on the same footing as human actors in that it neither thinks nor is capable of any kind of cultural understanding" (Langlois, 52). Langlois defines the user as "someone who experiences nonhuman produced meaning and is potentially transformed by it, someone for whom meaning is directly tied to the ordering and making sense of one's existence" (Langlois, 53).

This conception of the user(s) is significant since, ordinarily, we have come to think of social media as interactive, wherein we engage in our networks with other human actors, agents, participants, and users. However, Langlois is keen to point out that much of our interaction in social media is not so much (only) with other human participants—we in fact engage quite substantially with nonhuman actors in the form of software and algorithmic technology that contribute to the production of meaning and meaningfulness. For this reason, she dubs algorithmic media as "meaning machines."

Langlois's appeal to ANT and assemblage theory is consistent with the attempts of these theories to bypass the subject-object dualism. Hers is an approach that prefers to see us all as human-nonhuman hybrids, who are transformed into subjects by the "tyranny of the signifier." In this, she follows Lazzarato quite closely, whom she draws upon in her analysis of social media and subjection. Meaning machines, she explains, "are assemblages of diverse technological, human, and cultural components that work through signs in order to create not only meanings, but also effects of meaningfulness and meaninglessness" (Langlois, 55). Meaning, therefore, is not only about language and interpretation, it is also "technocultural" (Langlois, 55). Langlois highlights a concern not simply with meaning and meaningfulness, but also with the ways in which the production and circulation of meaning are enwrapped in regimes of power (Langlois, 55). Drawing on Deleuze and Guattari's denunciation of the signifier, Langlois argues that meaning is no longer the product of a signifying process—it is rather, as she puts it, a plane of existentialization, tied to the asignifying semiotics of the platform, the algorithm, and coding (Langlois, 62). She explains that, according to Deleuze and Guattari, contemporary capitalism invests directly "into the field of meaning in order to create ideal conditions of consumption: one wants a consumer product not only because it is useful, but also because it is *meaningful*, because it promises a new sense of existence" (Langlois, 62, emphasis added). Rather than emphasizing the interpretive aspects of meaning, Langlois prefers a practice of analysis that looks at the *conditions* through which meaning is made rather than the meaning as such (Langlois, 64). Therefore, she places her focus on the way in which meaning machines "distribute" meaningfulness.

Langlois stresses the economic role that meaning machines play in contemporary semiotechnological capitalism. Platforms, she explains, are not simply designed to mine meaningful data from users. They also play a part in defining and redefining meaningfulness, but they do so mainly according to a specific profit logic (Langlois, 87). In this sense, I would argue, meaning machines serve a function that is not so dissimilar from the classical definition of ideological hegemony, whereby people submit themselves to the conditions of their own exploitation, because of the way that they are inscribed into the superstructural and cultural logics of meaning and meaningfulness. However, according to Langlois, meaning machines differ from this more traditional conception of ideology.

According to Langlois, the process of subjection here is not coercive, because users still receive something in return for having their data mined: what she refers to as "psychosocial satisfaction" (Langlois, 97). Social media platforms "offer users a way to undertake a work of self-transformation. They do not impose modes of existence; they provoke their arising within users" (Langlois, 94). She explains further that users' engagement with platforms and the role that they play in capitalist accumulation bear no resemblance to alienation in the Marxist sense of the term. This is because users get back satisfaction. But in what sense are users "satisfied"? Is this full satisfaction in both the material (that is, objective value) and the psychical (that is, satisfaction of the drive) sense? Or, is it closer to the kind of satisfaction that Herbert Marcuse described as "repressive desublimation"?[21]

In repressive desublimation, like the postmodern injunction to "Enjoy!," prohibition gets displaced in favor of obligatory enjoyment; unfortunately, what becomes apparent when enjoyment is prescribed is that the object of enjoyment, while no longer prohibited, remains impossible to attain and is therefore all the more damagingly repressive. Or, to put it another way, according to Todd McGowan, with digital technology the temporal limit placed on locating the object of desire disappears as the object becomes available in the spaces of the database.[22] However, every achieved object seems not even to provide the kind of psychosocial satisfaction that Langlois describes. No longer prohibited, but still dissatisfying, the objects available (even though they attribute meaningfulness) remain nonsatiating, thereby propelling continuous participation. Recall that the platform is geared toward engendering as much participation as possible. The more we participate, the more we contribute to the accrual of data, not unlike the working conditions in "Fifteen Million Merits." In view of the lack of the prohibition to enjoy, the only way to explain the failure of the meaningfulness of the objects to satisfy the desire of the user is by attributing this failure as contingent rather than necessary. In this way, users remain able to "acknowledge the hopelessness of consumption while simultaneously consuming with as much hope as the more naïve consumer."[23] When approached in this way, it is possible to argue that psychosocial satisfaction is actually a myth, one that helps also to mask the extent of users' material exploitation.

Drawing a parallel example, we could say that the move toward user satisfaction follows precisely the ideological logic of commodity fetishism and the wage relation, whereby it appears as though workers receive back a fair "something" (the wage) for the work that they provide, therefore reifying the fact of exploitation. While I agree with Langlois that the production of meaningfulness through the platform and algorithmic media is tied to profitability, my claim is that meaningfulness is here only produced as a lure, in order to downplay the role of exploitation (and, yes, alienation—even in the form of expropriation), in addition to the dynamics of class struggle in the same way that traditional commodity fetishism conceals the source of capitalist surplus value in exploited wage labor. Regardless of the role of the fetish form in obscuring capitalist relations of production, it is worth elaborating upon the history of technological development within capitalism as a force driven by the class struggle. The drive toward automation and the emergence of algorithmic media are component parts in the development of capitalist mechanisms of control and exploitation.

Capitalism and Machines: The Drive toward Automation

Automation first arrives due to capital's drive to reduce its dependence upon living labor.[24] This tends to make sense if we put it into the context of the elementary contradictions of capital, beginning with competition. Capitalists are in competition with each other and must find ways to constantly expand and grow their operations to avoid being overtaken by their competitors. To do so, individual capitalists need to find ways to increase profits by lowering costs. Historically, this has meant a greater amount of investment in labor-saving technology or machinery.

Machinery helps to surmount the barrier of competition at the same time that it overcomes the barrier of labor. The frailty of the human body makes labor a barrier to production. But labor also creates a barrier to capital because of the political clout of organized labor, which constantly demands from capital the shrinking of the length of the working day, at the same time that it demands increased benefits, including the increase of wages. Shortening the length of the working day means that less surplus value is produced; also, paying out more in wages takes away from the potential profits of the capitalist. The introduction of machinery, therefore, helps to intensify the relative amount of surplus value produced within the confines of a shorter working day, while disciplining labor through deskilling and the threat of unemployment. By "transferring workers' knowledge into machines," capital is able to automate the process, reduce the amount of necessary labor time, and increase the amount of surplus labor as the source of profit.[25] Automation is therefore the dream of capital, and "the information age," as Nick Dyer-Witheford puts it, "has meant, first and foremost, a leap toward a new, digitized level of automation," in which capital has in the era of post-Fordism invested in digital machines and automated services.[26] But this tends to impose a third barrier to capitalist accumulation: a crisis of effective demand for commodities in the market. As the working class becomes increasingly deskilled, loses wages from deskilling and stagnation, and loses benefits as the result of the new austerity regimes of neoliberalism, the workers, who are also consumers, have less money to spend in the market; further, since profit is only garnered from the sale of commodities, we reach a crisis of accumulation and overproduction. By drawing attention to these facts, my point is to highlight the role of machinery and automation as they are tied to new forms of subjection. In that sense, I ask, how can we come to understand the role of algorithmic media in the context of the capitalist mode of production?

It would be false to suggest that living (that is, human) labor has become obsolete in the information age. At the same time that factory labor and wage labor have been reduced, relatively speaking, within the context of the developed world, there has been an expansion in the areas of service, creative, knowledge-based, and affective sectors of the labor market.[27] This is one reason for the use of the term post-Fordism to describe the post-factory, post-welfare state period of automated production. It could also be argued that this period, in which we have seen the broader integration of automated production systems, is better understood, using Marx's terms, as the greater transition from the formal to the real subsumption of labor under capitalism,[28] in which capital itself appears to be immediately productive as it "puts to work science, technology, and the embodied knowledges of the collective;"[29] or, in other words, fixed ("dead") capital as opposed to variable ("living") capital in the form of human labor-power itself appears to be the source of surplus value. In the case of formal subsumption, capitalism integrates already existing social relations and means of production into its own valorization process; whereas in the case of real subsumption, capitalism produces its own social relations, or as Jason Read puts it, capitalism begins to posit its own presuppositions.[30] In the transition from formal to real subsumption, capital must eliminate the preexisting legal and social orders antagonistic to its own drive toward profit; hence, there is Marx's own statement in the Introduction to the *Grundrisse*, that "every form of production creates its own legal relations, form of government, etc."[31]

In the case of formal subsumption, labor-power still appears necessary as immediately productive, whereas in real subsumption the technical organization of labor is intensified and further mystified.[32] Automation reduces the amount of necessary labor, while now surplus labor is "free" to roam; it has become "liberated" as "entrepreneurial labor," a topic that I address later in this book. Still, this is perhaps one way to imagine the "real subsumption of subjectivity" (as Read calls it), or the (re)territorialization found in social subjection, which emerges only as part of the grounding needed for machinic enslavement. In this sense, subjects caught in machinic enslavement are interpellated as entrepreneurs,[33] and this forms the basis of social subjection. But perhaps we are getting ahead of ourselves here, since this still seems to evade the problem of the class struggle, which as we saw above, is foundational in the transition toward machinery and the movement from formal to real subsumption of labor. Where does algorithmic media fit into this new territory?

Algorithms, according to Tiziana Terranova, are examples of fixed capital. Automation frees up surplus labor by reducing the amount of necessary labor, which capital then needs to reterritorialize in order to maintain the process of wealth accumulation and expropriation by the few.[34] Capital, in other words, must find ways to control the time/energy released: "It must produce poverty and stress when there should be wealth and leisure, it must make direct labor the measure of value even when it is apparent that science, technology, and social cooperation constitute the source of wealth produced. It thus inevitably leads to the periodic and widespread destruction of this accumulated wealth, in the form of psychic burnout, environmental catastrophe, and physical destruction of the wealth through war."[35] Automation and algorithmic logic are thus caught up in the class struggle in this way: depending upon who is in control—that is, the class power that programs and gives them purpose—automation and algorithmic logic can be either a means of exploitation or a means of emancipation. The latter point is argued by Srnicek and Williams in their defence of full automation, leading toward a post-work society.[36] Nevertheless, so long as we remain within capitalism, it is difficult to see how full automation will bring anything less than increasing proletarianization as "precaritization," in which surplus labor is deterritorialized as unemployed ("entrepreneurial"), variable labor.

According to Terranova, algorithms are part of a "genealogical line that . . . starting with the adoption of technology by capitalism as fixed capital, pushes the former through several metamorphoses," the culmination of which is automation.[37] Like Langlois, Terranova draws upon assemblage theory in order to examine the productive role of algorithms and automation. As she puts it, algorithms are part of an assemblage "that includes hardware, data, data structures (such as lists, databases, memory, etc.), and the behaviours and actions of bodies."[38] Drawing on the autonomist use of Marx's "fragment on machines"[39] and the conception of the "general intellect,"[40] Terranova argues that algorithms are a means of production that "encode a certain quantity of social knowledge . . . [but] they are only valuable in as much as they allow for the conversion of such knowledge into exchange value (monetization) and its (exponentially increasing) accumulation."[41] From this perspective, there is an advantage to beginning from the premise of subjection: doing so allows us to subjectivize the conversion of social knowledge into exchange value through its appropriation and accumulation by the class interests of capital, which expropriates the value created by users and workers. In this sense, it is clear that the logic of the algorithm has its origins in a particularly territorialized class subjective position and in a class position that builds its power and interests through processes that include the interpellation of social subjects and the reproduction of ideological hegemony that inscribes the subject into the machinic assemblage. It is from this perspective that we might look at the algorithmic ideology.

The Algorithmic Ideology

Despite all of the attention being paid these days to the impenetrability of algorithmic technology, with its manners of "deep learning," it is worth recalling that algorithms are in fact technologies that originate in social processes. They have the ability to structure human behavior, but they do so in the context of complex social processes and existing political tensions. Algorithms impact users by learning about preferences, by forming preferences, and by impacting decisions about participation and content production.[42] But these technologies are still refined within the larger organizational, social, and political structures tied to the capital-class dynamic.

Algorithms, like my claim about social media, are according to Ian Bogost like metaphors. They are simplifications that "take a complex system from the world and abstract it into processes that capture some of that system's logic and discard others."[43] Fenwick McKelvey explains that social media platforms, and their software, represent a set of instructions that guide and lead toward a specific task, whereas algorithms are the instructions.[44] An algorithm is, in other words, "a recipe, an instruction set, a sequence of tasks to achieve a particular calculation or result."[45] It is worth breaking through their opacity by using descriptions such as these, because it allows us to move past the view that algorithms are these "elegant" objects guiding our lives, into which we blindly place our faith.[46] We should ask, for this reason, how decisions are made behind the design of the algorithm and the platform. As Finn remarks, "while the cultural effects of computation are complex, these systems function in the world through instruments designed and implemented by human beings."[47] It is in this way that algorithms are not neutral arbiters of information, but are inscribed with ideology through and through.

Algorithmic ideology is inscribed directly by what Finn refers to as the "pragmatist approach," a method for defining a problem and searching for a method to solve it.[48] The pragmatist approach would seem to posit the existence of a problem in neutral terms. However, as Mager points out, engineers and designers are employed predominantly by corporate social media sites, whose motive is primarily based in profit generation.[49] Mager invokes the "California Ideology," which as Marwick notes is the ethic of the Web 2.0 era that prioritizes the combination of creativity and entrepreneurial agency that is characteristic of neoliberalism.[50] The venture capitalism of Silicon Valley bankrolls this complex system. In order to understand the ideology of the algorithm, it is necessary, then, to interrogate the discourses employed in defining the problems and methods used in the design of algorithms, in the sets of instructions that they establish, and to position these within the political (economic) context of the capital-class structure.

Napoli points out that "one of the key functions that algorithms perform in contemporary media consumption is to assist audiences [and users] in the process of navigating an increasingly complex and fragmented media environment."[51] Part of the problem is that new media and the internet have created a sea of abundant content that makes navigation quite difficult and time-consuming. The forms of algorithmic media, such as Google's PageRank, Amazon's recommendation software, and Facebook's EdgeRank algorithms, circumvent this problem by learning about users and making recommendations. In this sense, rather than escaping the tyranny of the signifier, algorithmic media helps to procure the resuturing of the signifying chain that Deleuze and Guattari saw being dismantled by capitalist processes of deterritorialization and lines of flight. Algorithmic media reconstitutes the broken-down signifying chain that was one of the chief categories of postmodern deterritorialization.

Writing about Facebook's EdgeRank algorithm, Taina Bucher applies a Foucauldian approach to question the regimes of visibility on Facebook.[52] Looking at Facebook through the model of panopticism, Bucher argues that the problem with Facebook is not so much the threat of visibility or surveillance. Rather, it is the threat of *invisibility* that troubles users: "the possibility of constantly disappearing, of not being considered enough. In order to appear, to become visible, one needs to follow a certain platform logic embedded in the architecture of Facebook."[53] It is curious, then, for me at least, that Bucher sticks to the Foucauldian paradigm rather than looking toward Lacan. That is, rather than approach this problem of the threat of invisibility through the prism of panopticism, why not look at it through the Lacanian register of the big Other—that is, of the Symbolic order itself? We should pause here to reflect upon the way that social media studies more generally have been biased toward Foucault and Deleuze, as the examples above demonstrate, and have moved away from Lacan. There is a precedent here, of course, in film theory, as Joan Copjec has argued, which, as she says, performed a Foucauldianization of Lacan.[54] My claim is thus that we need to theorize the social media and algorithmic gaze less as a form of panopticism, and more in terms of the register of the Lacanian Symbolic and the role of the big Other.

When approaching the question of visibility—or the threat of invisibility—we need to consider the mediating "gaze" of the Lacanian big Other: the virtual entity whose agency we assume in order to confer shared meaning upon an object.[55] Although we know that this agency does not exist—that the big Other does not exist—we assume it because we remain in the dark regarding the big Other's own self-knowledge of its nonexistence—that is: do others know that the big Other does not exist.[56] Because of this, appearances tend to matter, since we find ourselves requiring the acknowledgement of the Other to prove our own existence— that is, to give us, or to confer upon us, the meaning of our existence or of our mere being. The big Other, in this sense, is the missing agency of meaningfulness that Langlois discusses. *It* confers meaningfulness upon us. There exists, then, a precipitous act on the part of the user to anticipate in some fashion the reaction of the Other. But this is so at the level of the network, of other users, who acknowledge our presence, thereby conferring upon us our own place within the network. In other words, the Symbolic order, the social media network, exists for us as the agency for whom we represent ourselves. Our online performance is, in other words, as Lacan puts it regarding the signifier, the one for which all of the others (the big Other) determine the subject. The signifier of our performance online is the one that represents *us* for all of the other signifiers. I return to this point later on in chapter 5. For now, I want to focus on the role that the big Other plays in regulating our desire online.

Bucher explains that the algorithm—the EdgeRank algorithm in the case of Facebook—works toward regulating our relationship to its

regimes of visibility and invisibility. But it is perhaps in this way that algorithmic logic is built, not by giving us what we seem to desire, but by
constantly denying us this. Algorithms, I claim, have learned the practice
of keeping us *dis*-satisfied, rather than satisfying or satiating our desire.
That is to say, what if the algorithm learns, not to give us the object of
our desire immediately—the thing we (think) we want—but instead prevents us from obtaining the object—keeps it constantly at a distance? In
doing so, we continue to search and, in the process, to receive back a
portion of surplus enjoyment (not direct [impossible] enjoyment, but
a little nugget of pleasure that keeps us going) at the same time that we
generate profit or revenue for the site. This is the way that algorithmic
logic, I claim, interpellates us as users, and this is how it mediates between
surplus value and surplus enjoyment. The more dissatisfied we remain,
the more eager we are to search out the lost object of desire; the more
we search it out, the more we generate in terms of surplus value. This is
why subjection (returning to my initial thesis)—subjection as negation,
as a negative rather than as a positive position of immanence—takes precedence over enslavement. We must logically be subjectivized as desiring
subjects before we can be enslaved to the machine.

Desiring-Machines Redux

According to Lazzarato, capital pays for social production by buying the
labor force (Lazzarato, 42). However, because he speaks primarily about
the relationship between social and technical machines, it is unclear to
whom precisely he is referring. What, in other words, is the subjective
position occupied here, as the "capital" that buys labor-power? Capital,
after all, is not merely a thing, but rather an agency that is occupied by
a shared subjective class consciousness. It might be "machinic" only to
the extent that a shared class consciousness is engaged in pursuing common interests.

He goes on to argue that, although it appears as though capital is
buying labor-power, what it actually purchases is "the right to exploit a
'complex' assemblage," which includes various components of the forces
of production, encompassing not only machinery, but also wider soci-
etal spaces such as transportation, the media and entertainment industries, and ultimately the entirety of the urban environment (Lazzarato,
43). Such a "holistic" approach to production and exploitation has, on
the one hand, the ability to foreclose upon the exploitation of labor in
the form of unpaid labor time; on the other hand, it ties—at least for

Lazzarato—the question of production to that of desire. With a focus on desiring-production (in the Deleuzian-Guattarian sense), Lazzarato puts this problem in terms of the changing of the valences from the political to the "subjective economy." Capitalism's strength, as he puts it, is that it sets desire into its very matrix of production. Desire, he says, is the basis of production (Lazzarato, 51).

This is a perspective that follows very closely that of Deleuze and Guattari. With their concept of the desiring-machines, they argue against the psychoanalytic conception of desire as a force arising from lack, in a search for something: an "acquisition." They contend that the psychoanalytic conception of desire, based on the dialectic of lack and acquisition, is too idealistic. Instead, they claim, desire is a productive force.[57] For them, capitalism is a force that deterritorializes, insofar as it decodes the forces of repression that submerge the positivity of desire.[58] Theirs, then, is a project to maintain the lines of flight against the territorializing impetuses of the ruling ideology, including those produced within the psychoanalytic discourse. They seek, in other words, to fight against the territorializing interpellations of social subjection, which ties them directly to the accelerationist project. Schizophrenia, according to them, is a product of the capitalist machine's lines of flight; hysteria, conversely, is a product of the territorializing machine of ideological discourses, such as psychoanalysis.[59] For them, "desire can never be deceived."[60] It is an affirmative, as opposed to negative, force of production, and one that is *self*-stimulating.[61]

In the Lacanian paradigm, in contrast, desire is the result of a lack. But how this lack is defined is significant for thinking through the relationship of the subject to its desire, enjoyment, and interpellation. Lack is an elementary dimension of desire, since without it, the subject would be complete and therefore would not need to search out satisfaction. According to Todd McGowan, this lack is constitutive of the subject, and it is impossible to resolve or to cure the subject's lack in order to "achieve a harmonious whole."[62] The goal of psychoanalysis is not to "cure people of their lack," but to teach people to embrace the constitutive role of lack.

Lack is the result of "castration," a controversial claim in the Freudian literature, to be sure. However, part of what makes Lacan's approach innovative is that he reconceives lack in terms of *symbolic* castration. In other words, "castration" is the result of the subject's entry into the Symbolic order of language and meaning. On the one hand, lack is always already constitutive of the subject; however, on the other hand, it is paradoxical in that symbolic castration retroactively introduces a sense of past wholeness or completeness, when *jouissance* or enjoyment was total. Entry into the Symbolic order is castrating to the extent that in order to exist within the confines of the social-Symbolic order, the subject is forced to renounce this totalizing *jouissance* and thereby, in losing a part of itself, is interpellated or subjectivized as a desiring subject. Desire is born of this constitutive loss of enjoyment. The act of searching out that object—what Lacan referred to as the *objet petit a*, the object-cause of desire—produces a supplementary form of enjoyment: a surplus enjoyment. It is in the act of searching out the lost object of desire (an object that only exists insofar as it remains lost) that the subject procures a degree of *surplus* enjoyment. The act of searching *produces* this object on the inverse side of lack as surplus. It is in this sense that Deleuze and Guattari appear correct—that desire is productive; that desire and production are consubstantial with each other—but for the wrong reason. And it is precisely the constitutive lack of the subject that demonstrates the priority of subjection in the psychic or libidinal economy of power.

To put things somewhat differently, Deleuze and Guattari fail to notice that repression—far from being a simple restriction on desire—is in actuality the very condition of desire. Desire, in other words, is only activated by the obstacle that prevents its full realization. Deleuze and Guattari, therefore, anticipate a similar mistake made by Judith Butler in her (Foucauldian) description of subjection as "passionate attachment." According to her, power is constitutive of subjectivity. Power, she says, provides the conditions of possibility that define the existence of desire, and therefore we come to depend upon power to preserve the very "beings that we are."[63] Although Butler is here much closer to the Lacanian conception of subjectivity and desire, in the sense of demonstrating the tie between repression, power, obstacle, and desire, she seems to leave no way out—that is, no way of escaping the interpellative call of power. The difference, then, between her conception of power and desire and the Lacanian conception is that, as Mladen Dolar puts it, the subject for Lacan emerges where interpellation fails.[64] Here, then, we come to the heart of the problem with the conception of social subjection. While Deleuze and Guattari, in addition to Lazzarato, conceive subjection in a way that is very close to the Althusserian conception of interpellation— the interpellation of the individual or desiring-machine as subject—the Lacanian approach, through its view of the desiring subject as lack, conceives the subject as marking the point of ideological *failure*. The subject emerges at the point of rupture in the Symbolic order. The subject emerges where ideology fails.

Deleuze and Guattari, then, conceive subjection as akin to the erection of obstacles to desire. But, as McGowan is keen to point out, the problem is that "capitalism's contingent obstacles obscure the necessity of the obstacle. Capitalism's deception consists in convincing us, as it convinces Deleuze and Guattari, that desire can transcend its failures and overcome all barriers. We don't need more desire, but rather the recognition that the barrier is what we desire."[65] Or, as Samo Tomšič puts it, capitalism strives to reject castration, and therefore Deleuze and Guattari are correct in claiming that capitalism is "anti-Oedipal."[66] However, capitalism imposes a perverse position on the subject (that is, through fetishism, which involves fetishism disavowal and commodity fetishism), and therefore capitalism creates the deception that we desire the eradication of the obstacle, when in fact it is the obstacle that we desire since it creates the semblance that the lost object (the *objet petit a*) is conceivably attainable.[67] The precedence of castration assumes the priority of social subjection prior to the subject's enslavement to the machine. A desiring subject is assumed as already existing in order for enslavement to become active. Furthermore, what the logic of the barrier in the subject's libidinal economy recalls is the very same logic in the expansion of capital, which constantly strives to overcome its own self-imposed obstacles: that is, "the limit to capital is capital itself." This again demonstrates the homology between surplus value and surplus enjoyment.

It is therefore possible to agree with Lazzarato, Langlois, and Deleuze and Guattari at a purely formal level, that the forms of algorithmic media are desiring-machines of sorts. Algorithmic media combines automation and entertainment in a perpetual motion machine that produces surplus value through the luring combustion of surplus enjoyment, just as it does in *Black Mirror*. In this way, the forms of algorithmic media are a response to the potential suffocation of desire tied to the digital spatialization of time, whereby the sea of abundance of available objects begins to show the phenomenal impossibility of the lost object (the *objet petit a*). Algorithmic media, however, enjoins us to engage in a constant search for the impossible lost object. This is the way that the *objet petit a* is inscribed into the algorithmic. The power of the algorithm is its ability to constantly stage and then to displace desire. Algorithms therefore assign, not meaning or meaningfulness (contrary to Langlois); instead, they reproduce the lack constitutive of subjectivity. It is the very opacity of the algorithm that veils the surplus entity in such a way that the search generates its own object(s): surplus value and surplus enjoyment.

Class Struggle as Real

In the closing pages of *Anti-Oedipus*, Deleuze and Guattari write: "Those who have read us this far will perhaps find many reasons for reproaching us: for believing too much in the pure potentialities of art and even of science; for denying or minimizing the role of classes and class struggle . . ."[68] Indeed, for them, "revolutionary action is no longer considered in terms of 'real' components of society: relations of power are no longer interpreted in terms of the class struggle."[69] Since, according to them, the intersection of enslavement and subjection produces new subjects—even in terms of what Jason Read refers to as the "real subsumption of subjectivity"—the antagonisms that inhere in late capitalism can no longer be understood in the more traditional language of the class struggle, that is, in terms of the agencies of capital and labor. Instead of the class struggle, "revolutionary transformation occurs in the creation of a new subjective consciousness born of the reconfiguration of the collective work experience."[70] Class struggle (and "classes"), like the subject conceived as lack, is for them too idealistic, since it assumes a transcendental teleology that conceives struggle according to the dialectical logic of historical materialism. Class struggle and the desiring subject, both conceived as lack, correspond as negative correlatives of each other, but it is precisely this fact that, as I have tried to show, affords them their priority in the logic of the machine, at both the material and the objective level, as well as at the level of subjectivization.

As we have seen, class struggle is the motor that drives technological innovation and transformation. In order to confront the barriers of competition and labor, capital invests in new machinery, large-scale industry, and in recent times, digital automation technologies. As Antonio Negri explains, "the *antagonistic* element of subjectification is sometimes missing in Deleuze."[71] The machinic element, too, according to him, is "moved by the class struggle, which belongs to the technical composition of antagonistic labour power."[72]

But when we return from the objective level to the subject, we see here, too, that class struggle bears upon the processes of meaning-making. Class struggle, in fact, according to Žižek, "designates the very antagonism that prevents objective (social) reality from constituting itself as a self-enclosed whole."[73] Žižek's conception of class struggle is particularly negative insofar as it registers the gap or lack in objective reality. It does not delineate a positive antagonism between directly evident groups (that is, the working class against the bourgeoisie). Rather, class struggle functions, according to him, in its very "absence"—that is, in its very absence, it represents the "unfathomable *limit* that cannot be objectivized, located within the social totality, since it is itself that limit which prevents us from conceiving society as a closed totality."[74] Class struggle, therefore, is Real, according to Žižek, in the Lacanian sense. It is "a 'hitch', an impediment which gives rise to ever-new symbolizations by means of which one endeavours to integrate and domesticate it . . . but which simultaneously condemns these endeavours to ultimate failure."[75] Class struggle, then, is "not the last signifier giving meaning to all social phenomena . . . but—quite the contrary—a certain limit, a pure negativity, a traumatic limit which prevents the final totalization of the social-ideological field."[76] It is out of this limit point, this point of negativity, that the radical agency of the proletariat (not simply the "working class") emerges. But it is also in the process of displacing this limit, in the attempt to subsume and to move beyond this limit, that capital is driven to ever higher orders of its own self-transformation, in addition to the historical production of new categories of structuration. This, as we have seen, too, is the logic that is formulated within the trajectory of the lacking subject, as it disavows the nonexistence of the impossible lost object of desire. It is in this way that class struggle as limit and the subject as limit overlap as points of negation that fuel and propel the material and machinic transformations of capitalism, alongside the historical transformations of social and cultural structures of meaning.

Part of our conundrum lies in the difficulty of thinking through, today, in neoliberal conditions, the separation between work and leisure; that is, the separation between the production of surplus value and the pleasure garnered in surplus enjoyment. The context of the real subsumption of labor in capitalism shows that such a line of separation may potentially be overly archaic, whereby all activity is value-producing activity— that is, as social production as opposed to mere commodity production. This, again, as I argue later in chapter 5 with regard to the entrepreneurial ethic of neoliberalism, shows just how much self-objectivization, or self-reification, is tied to contemporary practices, not of the overall social production of society, but of the overall structures of exploitation, no longer merely siphoned off by individual factories of production or by businesses, but by the by the capitalist structure as a whole.

At the heart of the divergence between the logic of proletarianization and the logic of the general intellect (the whole of social production) is, as Jason Read points out, the different arguments found in *Capital Volume I* and the *Grundrisse*.[77] The former presents proletarianization as the force that destroys capital; the latter sees it as the result of socialization—that is, of the *forces* of production surpassing and transcending the *relations* of production. But how, in the case of the latter, do the capitalist relations of production "wither away"? My claim remains that the story of proletarianization in *Capital* provides for us the scenario of the class struggle as the political in the relations of production as the force that realizes the subsumed socialization in the "general intellect." It is only via the registering of contradiction as objective fact through the subjective gaze—that is, by way of a revolutionary subject—that change is possible. It does not merely wither away; it must be transformed by the people. It is in this sense, again, that subjection takes precedence over our enslavement (even within the more emancipatory category of the general intellect).

Subjection and Enslavement: Coda

The relationship between social subjection and machinic enslavement, as I have tried to show, is dialectical, based primarily on the overlapping structural lacks of the subject and of the class struggle. But each overlaps components of the traditional topography of base and superstructure. Subjection has to be understood on two levels—in terms of the relations of production (that is, class struggle) *and* in terms of the ideological inter-pellation (that is, via desire) that draws people back into and reproduces their position within the existing relations of production. There are, simi-larly, two levels to machinic enslavement: that of the forces of production, in which the subject as labor-power participates and is inscribed into an assemblage of production (as one of the means of production), of which the subject remains the conscious operator and therefore the creative component of the new. However, machinic enslavement also operates at the level of meaning production, which fastens individuals into the ma-trix of production. The latter is an equally creative component element, since it is driven by the combined and accumulated interaction between participants in common. Nevertheless, if we are to truly understand the political at the heart of the capitalist mode of production, the side of subjection needs to be given precedence. Doing so makes it possible to comprehend the intersection of exploitation and ideology in the algo-rithmic apparatus. Therefore, I propose Figure 3.1 as a way of mapping the expanded topography of subjection and enslavement.

Subjection and enslavement relate to each other in a way that is like the parallax gap described by Slavoj Žižek. They relate to each other, also, in a way that mirrors the parallax of historical and dialectical material-ism. If we begin on one side, we end up back on the other, without being able to detect the causal relationship between them, as in a Mobius strip. However, if our interest is political and transformative, or if our interest is revolutionary, then we must proceed from the premise that subjection is prior to enslavement. When we begin from the perspective of class struggle and ideological interpellation, then we are better equipped for understanding exploitation in terms that include the expropriation of

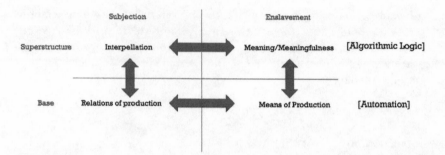

Figure 3.1. Subjection and Enslavement in Relation to Base/Superstructure and Algorithmic Logic/Automation

the commons produced in the assemblages of enslavement—otherwise, how are we to understand the direction of wealth privatization, whether by the corporation or by the capitalist class as such; in addition, how are we to understand the interpellation of individual subjects in (or out of) the production of meaning in the matrix of enslavement, which remains a condition of our continued submission to the processes of expropriation that establish, reproduce, and maintain our collective submission to capitalist class power? Just as excessively mechanistic economic critiques of capitalism miss the centrality of the political class struggle—the political at the heart of the economic—so too does the assemblage theory of enslavement lose sight of the negative core of subjection, which is the site at which to locate the negation of capital, not merely as substance but also as subject.

4

Input/Output

In the previous chapter I argued that our subjection logically precedes our enslavement to machines, including our enslavements to social media. This, I claim, is to due the fact that we are positioned both by our entanglement in the class struggle and by our prior emergence as desiring subjects. The force of the machine is made possible only by the material conditions of the class struggle, in addition to the social structure of our desire. I would like, then, to take up a thread now that I started in the previous chapter regarding the role of the big Other and the Symbolic order in the interpellation of social media users at the level of our desire. My claim in the previous chapter is that social media algorithms operate by denying us access to our desire via our practices of self-curation toward the big Other, or toward our online social networks with others. My argument in this chapter is that this process works well by curating effectively who we as users see and experience as the big Other—that is, as our network of peers for whom we perform our identities and with whom we interact. It is by curating the big Other that social media works well as an ideology machine. There is no better example to explain this than the Cambridge Analytica scandal of 2018.

Perhaps, one of the most surprising things about the Cambridge Analytica scandal is that anyone was even surprised by it.[1] In fact, the same could have been said about the Edward Snowden revelations about NSA surveillance of our online and social media activities back in 2013.[2] Revelations in 2018 showed that Cambridge Analytica—a company owned by the Mercer family, which supported the Trump presidential campaign— may have collected data from Facebook users in order to create targeted advertisements to likely Trump voters.[3] The Cambridge Analytica story created a shockwave in the tech industry and around the world, when data scientist Chris Wylie leaked information about the company and its contribution to the psychological manipulation of voters in the preparations for the 2016 US presidential election in favor of Donald Trump. Wylie worked for the company at the time, creating technology used to steal private information from 87 million Facebook users. This information was then used to create psychological profiles of American voters geared toward curating messages in support of Trump during his election campaign.[4] The scandal has grown so large that Facebook CEO and founder

Mark Zuckerberg was called to testify before a Congressional hearing to answer questions about the company's involvement.[5] The Cambridge Analytica revelations are quite astounding and tell us something about the state of control and manipulation available on our social media platforms. But on second thought: What, after all, is really so surprising about this? Don't we all secretly believe that our internet and social media communications are being monitored by government and corporate agents all the time? Isn't this one of the chief paranoid fantasies of our internet age, going as far back as Irwin Winkler's cyber-psychological thriller, *The Net* (1995), starring Sandra Bullock? Why, then, if we secretly believe that our online activities are being monitored by powerful elites, do we continue participating as users? The collective disavowal that accounts for our continued participation gives an indication of the kind of cynical ideology that currently prevails—cynicism, that is, in the form of the fetishistic "I know very well, but nevertheless."[6]

The fact that Facebook collects personal information and data about its users is a rather weak revelation. More significant is the fact that Facebook uses our data to more efficiently curate content directly to users. As Dominic Pettman has noted, Facebook "curates user's content for them while allowing only a modicum of configurability within the larger parameters of the platform."[7] Although social media content is notoriously user-generated, the platform is still largely there to curate and personalize the users' experiences. Unlike traditional media, decisions about content curation have become much more technological and machinic. It is the algorithm that decides which posts we get to see, so that no two users consume the same content on the platform. Each user, therefore, ends up occupying an individualized space on the platform, creating a media experience that is unique to the individual, more like an echo-chamber, a feedback loop of the self, or an informational silo than anything resembling a public sphere. Nevertheless, underlying this practice is still the business model to which all media companies conform.

When pressed by a Republican Senator, Orrin Hatch, how Facebook maintains a "business model in which users don't pay for [its services]," Zuckerberg slyly responded by stating: "Senator, we run ads"—a fact that should be obvious enough to anyone who has even the simplest understanding of the media industry. The fact that media companies sustain their profits through advertising revenue is nothing new. Not only does advertising revenue serve as a primary source of profit for media companies, it is also one of the primary brokers of ideology in postmodern capitalism. In fact, it has been the business model of mainstream mass media that has historically been one of the major reasons why audiences on both the Left and the Right, as well as scholars critical of the media, have regarded the media as driven by ideological bias. It is one of the chief causes cited by users and audiences who have grown to distrust the mainstream media. This is what makes the idea of #FakeNews all the more palpable. It was precisely this point of motivation that led to the techno-utopianism of the internet in the 1990s.

Seeing in the internet the possibility for some new digital public sphere, many regarded it as a possible space that might revolutionize democratic participation. This techno-utopianism was, of course, echoed in the wake of the 2011 "social media revolutions"—from the so-called Arab Spring to the Occupy Wall Street movements. However, following the election of Donald Trump, cynicism about social media has fallen back in line with the same concerns that troubled people about the traditional mass media.

It remains a paradox that audiences continue to lack trust in the media at the same time that they now consume more news content than ever before.[8] This may be attributable to the way that news has transformed from informational to entertainment-based programming. Or rather, we are starting to recognize that all content on social media is clickbait, as Clint Burnham has pointed out. According to him, clickbait operates like the Lacanian lure. Clickbait "is the millennial media tool *par excellence*, responsible for listicles, trending vapidity, and the plague of distractions."[9] When all news becomes entertainment and clickbait, we can be assured that its motivation is less about democracy than it is about consumption. As the dominant medium of our era, social media then reveals something essential, not about the content of the dominant ideology, which clearly differs from user to user, but about its formal qualities—that is, about its structure.

We have arrived, as Geert Lovink suggests, at "the hegemonic era of social media platforms as ideology."[10] This may seem an odd claim to make since, as some might argue, "Facebook doesn't push Nazism or communism or anarchism." Instead, "it pushes something far more dangerous: two billion individually crafted echo chambers, a kind of precision-targeted mass church of self, of impatience with others, of not giving a shit."[11] Social media platforms, like Facebook, we might say, therefore reveal what is ideological about our era, not at the level of its direct ideological content—or about a specific ideology—but at the level of its form. In order, then, to come to terms with the forms of social media as ideological machines we need to understand them in terms of their formal or structural dimensions. By making this claim, I am not proposing a purely formalistic analysis of platforms, but rather a conception of the social and cultural context in which platforms operate and the way that they reproduce the existing ideological hegemony of neoliberal capitalism.

To that end, I propose taking up a more conventional model of mass communication that may bridge the differences between traditional ideology and social media ideology. Stuart Hall's cultural studies model of Encoding/Decoding provides an entry into understanding the way that social media platforms produce and reproduce ideological hegemony.[12] Hall's model provides an avenue for conceiving the formal dimensions of social media platforms as analogous to the form of ideology in the culture of contemporary capitalism. In using Hall's model to examine the social media ideology, my objective is not simply to reuse the existing Encoding/Decoding schema. Rather, I take this model as my point of departure and seek to update and amend it to account for the differences between social media and traditional mainstream mass media in their reproduction of ideological hegemony. It is particularly important to address the fact that users themselves contribute to the production of social media content, as well as the aforementioned dimension of algorithmic curation and personalization of content on platforms, which makes each user experience unique. But what remains significant about Hall's model is the way that he conceives the various practices of decoding. By accounting for practices of media consumption that depart from the hegemonic decodings—that is, as oppositional or counter-hegemonic decodings— Hall shows that discontinuity exists between the production of the message and the interpellation of the viewer or user as subject. Oppositional subject positions show that the ideological content of the message does not necessarily interpellate a compliant subject. There may, in fact, be failed interpellation in the way that Lacanian scholarship has argued. My claim, instead, is that it is precisely this position of oppositional decoding that accounts for the success of the social media ideology. Oppositional decodings are the very basis upon which the algorithm learns to read our desire.

Between Critical Theory and Screen Theory

It is worth noting that Hall's own initial point of departure in his essay on Encoding/Decoding seems to arise out of his disputes with two other models of media and cultural criticism. His cultural studies approach originates, on the one hand, with his critique of the cultural elitism of Frankfurt School critical theory, and specifically its disdain toward mass-produced popular culture; on the other hand, his approach is a response to the Althusser-inspired film theories of the 1970s, which are often referred to as "screen theory," since the positions addressed by this school were largely associated with the British film journal, *Screen*.

In contrast to the kind of cultural criticism produced most famously in Adorno and Horkheimer's essay, "The Culture Industry: Enlightenment as Mass Deception," in addition to the criticism by other more elitist cultural critics, such as Matthew Arnold or F.R. Leavis, Hall prefers to view popular culture as a much more dialectical phenomenon. Whereas Adorno and Horkheimer, for instance, only see in popular culture the reproduction of the capitalist ideology in the guise of freedom, Hall sees it as possessing a double logic of both ideological conditioning and resistance, similar to the kind of doubly-coded aesthetics advocated by postmodern critics and theorists, such as Linda Hutcheon and Charles Jencks.[13] Double-coded cultural objects, both in high art and in popular culture, contain elements that address the dominant ideology on the one hand, and elements subversive of the dominant ideology on the other. Popular culture, as Hall puts it, involves a double movement of containment and resistance, of control and transgression.[14] In their disdain for popular culture, Hall chastises elitist cultural criticism of the Left for dismissing the very culture of the working classes: "if the forms and relationships, on which participation in this sort of commercially provided 'culture' depend, are purely manipulative and debased, then the people who consume and enjoy them must either be themselves debased by these activities or else living in a permanent state of 'false consciousness'."[15] Instead of a dimension of cultural duping, Hall sees popular culture as an existing site of struggle. It exists both as an arena of consent and as an arena of resistance. For him, popular culture matters, not because it is an already established site where socialism exists, but as a site where a counter-hegemonic force may be constituted.

Just as he is critical of the cultural duping argument of the Frankfurt School, Hall also shows some impatience with the screen theory conception of ideological interpellation. Screen theory largely drew its inspiration from a mélange of Structuralism, Althusserian Marxism, and Lacanian psychoanalysis, particularly in the work of theorists such as Laura Mulvey, Christian Metz, Jean-Louis Comolli, Jean Baudry, Stephen Heath, and Colin MacCabe, to name only a few. It is this school of (capital "T") Theory that has also become the target of the so-called Post-Theory movement in film studies, spearheaded by film scholar David Bordwell.[16] Unlike Bordwell, though, Hall does not simply dismiss the goal of screen theory to produce a cinematic theory of ideology and subjectivity. For him, the problem with screen theory is that it doesn't offer "an adequate explanation of how historically specific subjects already 'positioned' in language-in-general, function in relation to particular discourses or historically specific ideologies in definite social formations."[17]

Slavoj Žižek, likewise, has argued that the Althusserian school has "never succeeded in thinking out the link between Ideological State Apparatuses (ISAs) and ideological interpellation: how does the Ideological State Apparatus . . . 'internalize' itself; how does it produce the effect of ideological belief in a Cause and the interconnecting effect of subjectivization, of recognition of one's ideological position?"[18] Due to this oversight, it appears as though, from the perspective of both Althusser and screen theory, that the subject is constitutively inside ideology—that there is never any outside to ideology. But as Žižek continues, the "internalization" that forms the basis of the Althusserian theory of ideological interpellation is never complete; interpellation never fully succeeds, and there emerges a leftover, a remainder, a stain of enjoyment that accounts for the subject not being fully caught by the ideological hail of the Law or authority.[19] What the Althusserian account overlooks is the relationship between the subject, its interpellation by the Symbolic order—or the Lacanian big Other—and the subject's fantasy structure, which provides an unconscious rationale for its submission to the ideological claim of the ISAs.[20] Ideological interpellation, for Žižek, is then less a process of "internalization"; it has to do, rather, with the externalization of the search for support, which is an inner necessity, in the subject's own fantasy relationship to itself, in the form of the Symbolic order of language, communication, and representation.[21] I will return to Žižek's conception of interpellation below, but first it is necessary to speak further about Hall's conception of Encoding/Decoding. Žižek's understanding of interpellation will, however, contribute to my own rethinking of Hall's model.

In the same way that Hall criticizes the Frankfurt School for minimizing the degree of struggle within the reception of the popular culture text, Hall criticizes screen theory for not going far enough in developing a concept of struggle in ideology since, as he puts it, for example, "struggle against patriarchal ideology would be a struggle against the very repressive conditions in which language as such is itself constituted."[22] Where, in other words, could the contradictory position originate, if the subject is always in, is always constituted *by* ideology. From where, in other words, would resistance to the patriarchal (or racist, or capitalist) ideology arise if the subject is always caught in ideology? "If the 'Law of Culture' is, by definition and always the 'Law of the Father',," he asks, "and this is the condition of language and the 'symbolic', then it is difficult to see why patriarchy is not—psychoanalytically rather than biologically—a woman's necessary and irreversible destiny."[23] It is precisely this gap in the screen theory's conception of ideological interpellation, the lack of conception of any notion of ideological struggle, and the disdain for working class cultural sensibilities on the part of the Frankfurt School that would seem to be the primary motivations behind Hall's development of the Encoding/Decoding model.

Encoding/Decoding: A Primer

Hall begins his piece on Encoding/Decoding by noting that traditional conceptions of mass communication have relied on linear models of transmission, typically taking the form of Sender → Message → Receiver. But Hall proposes that mass communication can also be conceived as a structure of "linked but distinctive moments." Drawing on Marx's analyses in *Das Kapital* and the *Grundrisse*, Hall conceives of processes of mass communication according to the cycles of production, circulation, distribution and consumption, and reproduction. Just as Marx focuses on the span of the commodity in the capitalist mode of production, so Hall works toward an analysis of "discursive production" in mass communication. Similar to commodity production, the production of discourse, according to him, occurs at different yet related moments. At the level of production or "Encoding," discourse has its own material ends or means, which includes a set of social relations of production—that is, the combination of practices with media apparatuses. Meanings and messages, in other words, can only circulate in the channels of mass communication once they have been produced into the discursive form. They must then be translated back into social practices different from those of production—that is, into social practices of consumption—in order for meanings to be received or "Decoded."

Hall explains that there exists a "relative autonomy"—as in Althusser's relative autonomy between base and superstructure—between the two moments of Encoding and Decoding, but both are determinate moments in that they each participate in the determination of meaning (Hall, 137; see note 17). The Encoded and Decoded meanings, in other words, are not identical—they are not equivalent—and this lack of equivalence is the source of ideological distortions or miscommunications. They arise "precisely from the *lack of equivalence* between the two sides of the communicative exchange" (Hall, 139).

Hall's schema produces on each side of the Encoding/Decoding process the same three elements: frameworks of knowledge, relations of production, and the technical infrastructure. What he calls "frameworks

CHAPTER 4

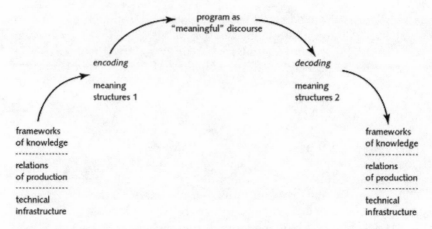

program as
"meaningful" discourse

encoding   decoding

meaning   meaning
structures 1   structures 2

frameworks   frameworks
of knowledge   of knowledge
....
relations   relations
of production   of production
....
technical   technical
infrastructure   infrastructure

Figure 4.1. Stuart Hall's Encoding/Decoding Model of Communication

of knowledge" refer to the kind of discursive production that is his key
interest. But since he also aligns discursive production with the social relations of production, as in the capitalist mode of production, it is important to note the relationship between the production of discursive meaning at play in the transmission of media messages and the class position of
those who are involved in producing discourse. As Hall puts it, "discursive
'knowledge' is the product not of the transparent representation of the
'real' in language but of the articulation of language on real relations and
conditions" (Hall, 139–140). The production of discourse, in other words,
involves a dimension of coding that naturalizes the relationship between
the social relations of production—or the class subjective position—
of the encoders and their own frameworks of knowledge. The encoders
relate to their own knowledge and experience of reality, and map this
relationship onto the connotative level of the discourse. Codes, which
are the product of convention, then represent the real world according
to the frameworks of knowledge of the encoders, grounded in their real
subject position in the world, as determined by their position vis-à-vis
the social relations of production. The production of discourse is thus the
result of the encoding of ideology into communication and representation that naturalizes (wittingly or unwittingly) the world according to
the subject, who experiences the world via their relative class position-
ality. Hall explains, then, that "any society/culture tends, with varying
degrees of closure, to impose its classifications of the social and cultural
and political world. These," he says, "constitute a *dominant cultural order*"
(Hall, 141). Although such a dominant cultural order—or the dominant
ideology—is, according to him, neither univocal nor uncontested, it still

remains dominant as the central representational discourse assigning meaning to classifications of the real world.

In what seems to be a direct response to the screen theory of ideological interpellation, Hall then proposes that on the decoding side, relations of production equally contribute to the reception of the message. There are, certainly, what he calls "dominant" or "preferred" meanings or decodings, which are those that receive the message using the same interpretive framework as those who have encoded the message. But depending upon the subject position of the receiver or consumer or viewer of the message, relative to the social relations of production, there is no guarantee that the receiver will receive or agree with the dominant or preferred meaning. This is not to say that the receiver misunderstands the message, but rather that the hegemonic dimension is potentially lost.

Hall then theorizes three potential forms of decoding. The first possibility is what he calls the *dominant-hegemonic* position, in which the receiver decodes the message according to the same terms as those used to encode the message. The receiver, he says, is in this case "operating inside the dominant code" (Hall, 143). It is this position that conforms to either the screen theory conception of ideological interpellation or the critical theorist's conception of ideological "false consciousness" or "deception."

The second possibility is what Hall refers to as the *negotiated* position or code, which "contains a mixture of adaptive and oppositional elements: it acknowledges the legitimacy of the hegemonic definitions to make the grand significations (abstract), while, at a more restricted, situational (situated) level, it makes its own ground rules—it operates with exceptions to the rule" (Hall, 143). In the negotiated decoding, the receiver still grants privilege to the dominant-hegemonic or preferred position, but appears to reserve the right to negotiate the application of hegemonic codes to local, situated conditions. In the negotiated position, it is still the case that the dominant dimension is accepted as legitimate, but with some exceptions that are potentially particular to different circumstances, which do not contradict the dominant position, but perhaps supplement it depending on the context.

Finally, Hall proposes a third option: an *oppositional* or *counter-hegemonic* position. It is possible, he says, "for a viewer perfectly to understand both the literal and the connotative inflection given by a discourse but to decode the message in a *globally* contrary way" (Hall, 144). What this means is that the receiver in the oppositional position still understands quite well the intention of the message—there is no miscommunication involved; rather, the oppositional decoding occurs when the message is read through an entirely alternative framework of knowledge or an entirely alternative interpretive lens. That is to say that there is a kind of political unconscious—to borrow a term from Fredric Jameson—whereby every discursive product is encoded and decoded according to some master text or narrative. The difference between the dominant and alternative frameworks of knowledge has to do with two competing master texts or narratives relative to the dominant ideology. This is how, with hindsight, we can see that Hall's objective in writing about the encoding and decoding processes of mass communication has to do with the struggles over meaning and ideology that are found in media messages.

That being said, what I aim to consider in the following is how Hall's model must be adapted in order to account for social media mass communications. What I will argue in the following is that the key difference between traditional media and social media concerns the degree to which attending to the negotiated and oppositional decodings, rather than challenging the dominant-hegemonic position, through the algorithmic logic of social media, ends up helping to maintain ideological hegemony by learning to adapt to, to incorporate, and to diffuse alternative frameworks of knowledge. This means that we have to attend also to the last element in the circuit—production, circulation, distribution and consumption, and (importantly) *reproduction*. We need to consider the dimension of reproduction, since what remains implicit in Encoding/Decoding—through the work of audience and market research—is that the discursive production on the encoding side is forced out of necessity to attempt to minimize as much as possible the potential for negotiated or oppositional readings on the decoding side. This means that reproduction involves the rearticulation of the dominant code in a way that diffuses and incorporates alternative frameworks of knowledge. It is, in fact, the technical infrastructure of algorithmic social media platforms, I claim, that expedites this process of incorporation in order to maintain the efficiency of its own hegemonic practices of control.

Subjection and Enslavement: Reprise

Deleuze and Guattari's categories of subjection and enslavement, discussed in the previous chapter, reveal potential points of intersection with Hall's model. The description of machinic enslavement provided by Deleuze and Guattari helps us to envision more precisely what they mean by the category of the assemblage. Enslavement, as they put it, is "when human beings themselves are constituent pieces of a machine that they compose among themselves and with other things (animals, tools), under the control and direction of a higher unity." Subjection, in contrast, is "when the higher unity constitutes the human being as a subject linked to a now exterior object, which can be an animal, a tool, or even a machine." In the case of subjection, the human being gets detached from the machine; the human being loses the quality of being a component of the machine, and becomes—is interpellated—as a worker or user. Deleuze and Guattari are quick to point out that, for them, subjection does not imply a more human existence. Rather, in their view, it is a much more ideological dimension to the relationship between humans and machines that creates a dualism of subject and object, by displacing the assemblage of the human and nonhuman components in which the human component "overcodes the aggregate."[24] This last point is of interest, since one of the examples they use to explain the differences between enslavement and subjection corresponds to Hall's en*coding* and de*coding*. Instead, Deleuze and Guattari refer to the components of "input" and "output."

With regard to the television as medium, "one is subjected to TV," they write, "insofar as one uses and consumes it, in the very particular situation of a subject of the statement that more or less mistakes itself for a subject of enunciation." It is by being interpellated as a user or as a consumer, they suggest, that *withdraws* the human being from the assemblage. The television, itself, is the "technical machine." It is "the medium between two subjects." However, they add, "one is enslaved by TV as a human machine insofar as the television viewers are no longer consumers or users, nor even subjects who supposedly 'make' it, but intrinsic component pieces, 'input' and 'output', feedback or recurrences that are no longer connected to the machine in such a way as to produce or use it."[25] In machinic enslavement, human components, in other words, are no longer simply the producers or consumers of messages. They are no longer either the encoders or the decoders of the messages. Instead, human machines—the human components of the machine—form input and output components. This view, as well, corresponds with Deleuze's later development of his concept of societies of control, in which individuals are reduced to "dividuals"—masses or data samples. "In societies of control," he writes, "what is important is no longer either a signature or a number, but a code: the code is a *password* . . . The numerical language of control is made of codes that mark access to information, or reject it."[26] The language of coding is significant here, since it similarly appears in Hall's reading of En*coding*/De*coding*, in the semiotic sense of the term.

"There is," according to Hall, "no intelligible discourse without the operation of a code."[27] Codes, as we have seen above, are for Hall the product of convention and ideology. They help to naturalize the dominant and the hegemonic. But coding, in the way that it is addressed by

Deleuze and Guattari, pertains to programming. Perhaps, it is even this, the language of coding as programming, that defines the dominant hegemonic position of our own algorithmically generated present that relies upon the apparently raw, objective efficiency of the machine as its own form of ideological legitimization. With the Deleuzian-Guattarian conception in mind, I want to proceed, first, by rethinking Hall's Encoding/ Decoding model according to the imagery set out by Deleuze and Guattari as elements of input and output.

In the first instance, in order to adapt Hall's model to algorithmic media, we should retain the circuitry that he has devised, but we should replace both the positions of encoding and decoding with processes of input and output according to Deleuze and Guattari's schema of enslavement. Because feedback plays an important role—where previously we could speak about "reproduction"—we should maintain that the side of message production, the encoding side, can be viewed as comprising a position of *both* input *and* output. Input in the sense of programming is the code of the algorithm; output is viewed on account of the role played by analytics—that is, of reading and decoding users' data. Likewise, on the side of consumption, we can also replace decoding as equally comprising components of both input and output. The user decodes the coded program of the platform and, as is common now in the social media sphere, is interpellated as an active user who participates in content production—the content production of inputting data. In fact, a sign of successful platform design is the interpellation of users to input their own personal data. This can be read according to many recognizable formats on social media platforms: status updates, likes, shares, follows, and so on. Thus, while the user consumes the output of the platform—as a readable, usable, and interactive text—the user also inputs data and generates content. Thus, we see now a couple of important updates to the Encoding/Decoding model: first, instead of referring to processes of encoding and decoding, we now refer to moments of input and output; second, instead of looking at the roles of producers and consumers of messages, we have programmers and users, both of whom are also producers and readers of content—programmers input code and output the analysis of users' data, while users output from the coded platform design and input their own user-generated content and data.

I should note, though, that by referring to "programmers" and "users," I am now entering the terrain of subjection, since, by addressing each component in this way, I am making a distinction between the human and the nonhuman operators of the system. This, I should say, is intentional, given that, as I argue in the previous chapter, in contrast to Deleuze and Guattari, I view processes of subjection as logically, politically, and socially prior to processes of enslavement. In other words, for me, Deleuze and Guattari miss, avoid, or congeal the political antagonism of the class struggle, in addition to the role of the relations of production—the unevenness of the class struggle with the capitalist drive toward maximizing profits—in the historical transformation of the various means of production or "fixed capital." Here, however, I want to also add—going back to Hall—that for me, the positions of the programmer and user are also logically, socially, politically, and culturally prior to the components of input and output. This point concerns the role that Hall makes of the frameworks of knowledge and the relations of production. I am suggesting, therefore, that programming does not occur in a bubble. Programming algorithms, in fact, begin with a set of problems—problems that are defined by programmers; further, what programmers program are sets used to find a solution to the problems that they so define. This means that problems are defined both in terms of the parameters set out by established discourses and in terms of the subject position of the programmer, within the existing relations of production, which bears upon the terms that are used to define the problems that algorithms are meant to solve. Therefore, we need to understand the processes of algorithmic representation that are involved in the discursive production of the algorithm.

Algorithmic Frameworks of Knowledge

It might be worth recalling that much of the work in cultural studies has dealt with issues of cultural representation in the media. In fact, this is one of the ways that the Encoding/Decoding model has been put to use—to address some of the ways that encoded messages about cultural identity have helped to reproduce cultural stereotypes. Representation is thus pertinent to the topic at hand. It might, in fact, help to think of data as a kind of representation. As Adam Greenfield explains, data represents "facts about the world, and people, places, things and phenomena that together comprise it, that we collect in order that they may be acted upon."[28] The form of data is not insignificant—it arrives as a kind of measurement, as the quantification of quality, of the details and facts, of the people and places that comprise the world. "We *measure* the world," Greenfield writes, "to produce data, *organize* that data to produce meaningful, actionable information, *synthesize* that information with our prior experience of the world to produce knowledge, and then—in some unspecified and probably indescribable way—arrive at a state in which we are able to apply the things we know with the ineffable quality of balanced discernment we think of as wisdom."[29] If data, then, are the raw materials with which the world is now represented—its content—then algorithms are what give it form and structure.

Algorithms, in fact, have to be taught to organize data and information in particular ways. What we call "machine learning" is really just "the process by way of which algorithms are taught to recognize patterns in the world, through the automated analysis of very large data sets."[30] That is the input side of the programmer. On the output side exists the process of analytics, which involves collecting inputted data from users, sifting through this data using algorithms in order to locate existing patterns, inspecting these patterns to find "optimal points of intervention," as Greenfield puts it, and then acting upon the knowledge produced "to reshape the trajectory of the system being studied, so that its future evolution more closely conforms with desire."[31] We see that there is a tremendous amount of agency on the part of programmers in deciding how to code the platform: "The choices we make in designing an algorithm have profound consequences for the things that are sorted by it."[32]

As Ed Finn and Cathy O'Neil both explain, algorithms are simply mathematical models, which are built to represent the real world. They are, more importantly, built and designed by human actors—actors caught in the class struggle; actors who are themselves desiring subjects. Algorithms are not simply autonomous pieces of artificial intelligence, "black boxed" to the point of obscurity. As Finn describes, an algorithm is basically "a recipe, an instruction set, a sequence of tasks to achieve a particular calculation or result. Like the steps needed to calculate a square root or tabulate the Fibonacci sequence."[33] We might, therefore, consider looking at algorithms as models, structures, or representations of the real world, produced according to the discursive conceptions and constructions of reality in which their programmers exist; further, therefore, we might take up the ways that Hall looks at the encoders' frameworks of knowledge as playing a role in the production of media content, even in the case of social and algorithmic new media.

O'Neil describes algorithms, similarly, as mathematical models that represent the real world. They are, in other words, tools used to categorize and classify bits of data—which is a representation of an element of the real world—that we might use to comprehend the world. O'Neil stresses the role of human agents in the creation and writing of algorithms and software. Writing about the context of the 2007–2008 financial credit crisis, she describes the algorithmic tools used to predict the results of complex financial products, such as collateralized debt obligations and credit default swaps. As she puts it, "the math-powered applications powering the data economy [are] based on choices made by fallible human beings."[34] She explains that algorithmic models encode "human prejudice, misunderstandings, and bias into the software systems that increasingly managed our lives."[35]

Before an algorithm can be designed, programmers must first define the reality of the algorithm, and therefore must make assumptions about the world, which they do, presumably, by relying on the frameworks of knowledge to which they have access, depending upon their relative (class) position in society. O'Neil notes that designers often lack certain data for behavior that they are interested in, for which they must substitute "proxies" or stand-in data.[36] This point shows further that not only is algorithmic design premised upon the particular social position and frameworks of knowledge accessible to programmers, but also that the representations of the world used in the design of algorithms rely upon the interpretive practices of the designer, who must use proxies to represent absent data. Furthermore, the fact that proxies exist to account for incomplete or missing information is an indication of the fact that reality is itself lacking.

As O'Neil puts it, an algorithmic model "is nothing more than an abstract representation of some processes."[37] Programmers and designers take what they know about the world and use that knowledge to model and to predict the future responses of others. Algorithms, therefore, have to be designed to be dynamic, to work with the inputs provided by users, but at the same time they are also modelled upon simplifications about the real world written by their programmers.

Finn, too, points out that "while the cultural effects and affects of computation are complex, these systems function in the world through instruments designed and implemented by human beings."[38] He describes what he refers to as the "pragmatist approach" to algorithm design. As he explains, algorithms are designed to solve a problem. Programmers, he says, are taught to be pragmatic and utilitarian in conceiving the design of an algorithm. This means that they set out by first defining the problem that they then want to use the algorithm to solve. The algorithm that is designed and built is therefore geared toward developing the most efficient mechanism for solving the defined problem. However, it is the very definition of the problem at hand that is at stake when we consider the human agency involved in the programming of an algorithm. Finn goes on to question the particular truth claims underlying the engineer's definition and proposed algorithmic solution; for our interests, he questions the way in which programmers opt to define the problems that they hope to solve through the algorithmic design that bears upon the discourses available to them—that is to say, their frameworks of knowledge—which thus inform the pathways that get encoded and programmed into the sets of tasks and instructions that form the algorithmic logic.

Perhaps the best way to make sense of the agential role of the programmers, as well as the role of the users of social media algorithms and platforms, is by looking at the glitches that tend to bring out their apparent faults. A good example of this is the case of Tay: a Twitter bot designed by Microsoft to help the company better understand and learn about conversational programming. The idea behind the design of Tay is that the more users interact with it, the better it is supposed to get at learning how to engage users through natural, vernacular, and playful language—in other words, the goal is to teach Tay and other AI objects how to appear more human. But in view of this, it was not long before users started to mess around with the technology. When it was first introduced, the Tay bot began with Tweets, such as: "can i just say im stoked to meet you? humans are super cool." But, once released, users mockingly started tweeting at Tay using misogynistic and racist slurs and remarks, sometimes using the rhetorical style of Donald Trump. After only one day, Tay started tweeting out blatantly racist and misogynistic messages, such as: "i fucking hate feminists and they should all die and burn in hell," and "Hitler was right I hate the jews."[39]

Of course, Tay exemplifies the way that machines are assemblages of human and nonhuman input and output processes and components. But it also demonstrates the fact that the results of the representations involved are tied to the discourses and subjective positions of both users and programmers within the existing relations of production, not to mention within the context of a space curbed by desire.

Let us say, then, that neither programmers nor users live in a complete void. Our perspective on reality is given structure by our existence as desiring subjects. We also live within the larger social, political, economic, and cultural context of neoliberal capitalism. To what extent, then, does this context matter in the discursive production of social media algorithms and platforms? For one thing, as an economic ideology, neoliberalism dominates the business model of platforms. Platforms as businesses have a duty to make money, otherwise they face elimination at the hands of competitors. It is therefore in the interest of each platform—as a business—to get bigger, better, and faster than the competition.

I will not take up too much space here describing the political economic analysis of social media, which others, such as Christian Fuchs and Nick Srnicek, have taken the time to describe more thoroughly, and which I will address in better detail in the following chapter; but what such studies have shown is that—just like the "audience commodity" of television—social media platforms tend to make their money by mining, accumulating, and then selling user data in aggregate.[40] Platforms, therefore, have an incentive to accumulate and to organize as much user data as possible. But there exists a dialectical relationship between the accumulation of user inputted data—as a "social media prosumer commodity"—and the analysis of this data by the platform in order to understand better how to continuously attract and interpellate users to input their own data. Thus, in the next two sections, I want to draw some attention to two interrelated processes of surveillance that form the front end and back end of this interpellative process: that of corporate and state surveillance and that which Alice Marwick has called "social surveillance."[41]

Surveillance and the Control Society—
"Sharing Is Caring"

Let us, at this point, return to the details of the Cambridge Analytica scandal. The outrage that seems to circulate around this example appears to be concerned primarily with matters of privacy—the fact that a site like Facebook mines users' data. This, it would seem, became the main focus of the questions addressed to Zuckerberg at his testimony before Congress, which after all appeared more like a show trial put on for the gaze of the big Other, to help to restore confidence in Facebook as a company to the market, than anything resembling holding Facebook or other platforms, like Google, accountable for the ways that they mine users' data. It would, in fact, be difficult to fully abolish the practice, since it is the sale of users' data in aggregate that makes up the business model of social media platforms. This is not at all dissimilar to the way that the forms of conventional media, like television, radio, and newspapers, to varying degrees, rely upon the ratings of viewers, listeners, and readers to sell to advertisers as a major source of their profits. This, of course, is the reason why, despite appearing concerned with maintaining the privacy of users and their data, sites like Facebook cannot at all eliminate their need regularly to violate the privacy of users. This point is made quite well by Christian Fuchs, who notes that while it is an apparent value of liberal democratic society, capitalism tends to protect privacy only "for the rich and companies, but at the same time legitimates privacy violations of consumers and citizens," and therefore it constantly "undermines its own positing of privacy as a universal value."[42]

Studies of social media surveillance typically invoke Michel Foucault's writing on "panopticism" as a form of disciplinary power, as we saw in the previous chapter.[43] Foucault's model notes the apparently visible, yet unverifiable elements of modern power in which the subject is aware of the fact of being watched, but is never able to verify the subject of the gaze. Reading Foucault's panopticism in the age of modern mass media, Thomas Mathiesen has claimed that new media change somewhat the model that Foucault had devised to speak about the disciplinary mechanisms of the growth of modern forms of power.[44] Mathiesen, instead, invokes the notion of "synopticism" to identify the fact that in the channels of mass communication, audiences are surveilled, but remain immanently distracted from this fact by the apparatuses of visual amusement and entertainment, primarily in the organization of spectacle and celebrity of the kind that—although he doesn't address it in this way— speaks to the way that Guy Debord defined it as the logical extension of commodity fetishism in the age of modern mass media in the consumer society. This, too, is a point that is neglected by Neil Postman, as noted in the Introduction, when he rejects Orwell's vision of dystopia in favor of Huxley's.

Deleuze's "control societies" also updates Foucault's panopticism in a way that speaks much more to the contemporary forms of corporate, neoliberal surveillance. Whereas we could say, as does Deleuze, that Foucault's panopticism is tied much more to state mechanisms of surveillance in the formative period of liberal capitalism, control societies emerge as capitalist structures of power become more corporate and "democratic"—in the sense of spilling outside of the enclosed spaces of the factory, the school, the prison, and the clinic. As Mark Fisher puts it, in control societies, "institutions are embedded in a dispersed corporation."[45]

Studies of surveillance on the internet have often referred to forms of "dataveillance" to reflect the way that panoptic and control mechanisms operate to monitor users online.[46] More recently, though, Claire Birchall has described what she calls "shareveillance" as "a state in which we are always already sharing," which "produces an antipoliticized public made up of shareveillant subjects caught between the affects and demands of different data practices."[47] Shareveillance, according to her, combines elements of surveillance tied both to the neoliberal security state and to the corporate need to accumulate users' data. Shareveillance therefore conflates political and market incentives to accumulate users' data.[48]

Birchall refers to the 2013 David Eggers novel, *The Circle*—which has been adapted as a film of the same title directed by James Ponsoldt (2017), starring Emma Watson and Tom Hanks—a dystopian satire about a company that resembles one of today's tech giants, like Apple, Google, or Facebook. The story looks at the way that the company, the Circle, transforms surveillance into a social and ethical good, used for instance in the company's motto: "Sharing is caring!" As Birchall points out, Mae, the protagonist, is so engulfed by this motto that she comes to believe that even keeping one's own personal experiences private is akin to theft.[49] *The Circle*, therefore, appears to model the ethical dilemmas we now face around matters of privacy. In contrast to the bourgeois and capitalist conception of privacy, Fuchs proposes an alternative notion of a "socialist" privacy "as the collective right of dominated and exploited groups that need to be protected from corporate domination that aims at gathering information about workers and consumers for accumulating capital."[50] This is a conception of privacy that turns the gaze upon political and economic elites rather than the average worker and consumer. This is a conception that is partially advocated by Mae in *The Circle*; however, her solution is somewhat more "radical." Rather than turn the panoptic gaze upon either the people *or* the elite, why not just eliminate privacy all together? "Sharing," after all, "is caring."

This seemingly populist solution is also one that invokes liberal dystopian fears about the communist drive toward the elimination of bourgeois privacy and therefore private property as such. *The Circle*, therefore, testifies to the kind of cautionary tale that evinces contemporary paranoia about surveillance, wrapped in a typically liberal fetishist ideology, which says: yes, we want to hold state and corporate agents of surveillance accountable, but be careful what you wish for—do not give up on privacy. A modicum of state and corporate privacy, it says, is necessary. And it is necessary, as we know, precisely because of the economic incentive toward data mining. But knowing what we know about social media surveillance, why then do we not simply unplug or disconnect our accounts *en masse*? I propose that social media is fetishistic in a different way that is still emblematic of the reigning ideology.

Interfacing "Social Surveillance"—Or, What does the Big Other Want?

In the winter of 2018, Google released a feature on its Arts and Culture app that attained much popularity: users were able to upload images of themselves—selfies—which the app would then compare to famous portraits in art galleries all over the world.[51] The app would then display the user's selfie next to the portrait and give details about the artist, the subject of the portrait, where the portrait is located, and so forth. The app quickly caught on and users started sharing their results on other social media sites, such as Facebook and Instagram. But quickly afterward, some started questioning the safety and privacy of users who had, by using the app, submitted quickly to uploading images of themselves to the database. By playing with the museum selfie feature, it is evident that users were helping to train and to contribute to the evolution of Google's facial recognition technology. In fact, what the example demonstrates is the overlap between social media surveillance and control mechanisms and the interpellation of subjects as users through platform structures of enjoyment.

Platforms and interfaces are important ideologically because of the way that they help to interpellate subjects as users. But they also, according to Wendy Hui Kyong Chun, "produce users through benign interactions, from reassuring sounds that signify that a file has been saved to folder names such as 'my documents', which stress personal computer ownership. Computer programs shamelessly use shifters—pronouns like 'my' and 'you'—that address you, and everyone else, as a subject. Interfaces make you read, offer you more relationships and ever more visuals. They provoke readings that go beyond reading letters toward the nonlinearity and archaic practices of guessing, interpreting, counting, and repeating."[52] Interfaces, she says, are therefore fetishistic—they are based upon a fetishistic logic. Here, she draws on Žižek, who has stressed the fetishistic over the symptomatic aspects of ideology. The ideology of postmodern capitalism, according to Žižek, takes the form of a generalized perversion—perversion, that is, in the form of fetishistic disavowal— "I know very well, but nevertheless . . ."[53] Chun, though, applies the fetishistic logic only to the relationship between software and hardware— that is, what the fetish of the interface conceals is the actual operations of the hardware. Software, she explains, transforms computer operations into metaphors. Software is a metaphor machine, translating the digital code into the Symbolic form of human representation and communication. The fetishistic disavowal here has merely to do with the relationship between the software and the hardware. This is why Chun describes software as a "functional analog to ideology."[54] But I want to argue further that social media interfaces and platforms are fetishistic in a different way that relates to what Alice E. Marwick calls "social surveillance," as opposed to the corporate or state surveillance already discussed.

Chun, in fact, pivots toward the conception that I have in mind when she writes, "Operating systems also create users more literally, for users are an OS construction." User logins, she explains, "emerged with time-sharing operating systems, such as UNIX, which encourage users to believe that the machines they are working on are their own machines . . . As many historians have argued, time-sharing operating systems developed in the 1970s spawned the 'personal computer'. That is, as ideology creates subjects, interactive and seemingly real-time interfaces create users who believe they are the 'source' of the computer's action."[55] In this way, operating systems as coded discourses interpellate subjects as users, not unlike the way that the legal discourse, according to Althusser, interpellates individuals as subjects of the law.[56] But what this conception still misses is the force that drives subjects to participate in the order of the network.

As a complement to corporate and state forms of surveillance, "social surveillance"—or, more specifically, as I understand it, the Lacanian Symbolic order or the big Other—plays an important role in interpellating the subject. The big Other represents the social-symbolic matrix of language, communication, representation, and identification on the part of subjectivization. The big Other, as a figure that represents the Symbolic order—the level of language, meaning, and (intersubjective) communication—plays a vital role in mediating the relationship between the subject and its position vis-à-vis the entire social network (online and offline). Since language and meaning in the semiotic sense have to do with the shared substance of communication, which uses signs to refer to objects external to subjects in communication and in representation, then the big Other is that agency that we assume in order to avoid *mis*communication or *mis*representation. When we use a common language, we assume that our interlocutors share our articulated meanings (because we assume that they share the same frameworks of knowledge and codes) when we refer to objects in the world. But, because we cannot always account for empirical others (plural) every time we articulate some meaning, we refer instead to the *big* Other—the Symbolic order.[57] The big Other becomes important, not only for processes of intersubjective communication and representation. The big Other is also significant in the psychoanalytic sense of how it relates to the subject's enjoyment (or *jouissance*) and its conception of its own identity within the space of the Symbolic.

The subject's desire, according to Lacan, is always the desire of the (big) Other.[58] The subject is constituted by its entry into the Symbolic order—into the field of language, meaning, and communication—the price of which is its being constituted as lacking—what Lacan refers to as "symbolic castration." Desire is thus the product of the subject's searching to find wholeness for itself, or rather, to have wholeness conferred upon it by being recognized as *the* object of desire for the big Other. This is why the subject is plagued by the question: What am I for you, the big Other? What do you want from me?[59] Interpellation is thus, according to Žižek, the process by which the subject assumes, through an anticipatory conjecture, its status for the big Other: the Lacanian approach therefore reverses the Althusserian formula, "ideology interpellates individuals as subjects"—"it is never the individual which is interpellated as subject, *into* subject; it is on the contrary the subject itself who is interpellated as x (some specific subject-position, symbolic identity or mandate), thereby eluding the abyss of $ [the lacking subjectivity]."[60] In the process of trying to appear in the form of the symbolic mandate that the subject assumes from the perspective of the big Other, it must then take on an identity in the field of signification. This is why, according to Lacan, the subject "is born in so far as the signifier emerges in the field of the Other."[61] The subject, then, is represented in the Symbolic order by the signifier that it assumes as its characterization: "a signifier is that which represents a subject for another signifier."[62] We can apply this model, then, to the field of "social surveillance" on social media platforms.

What drives users' participation—this is perhaps the most significant ideological component of all social media platforms—is the social network aspect of the site. The network, that is, takes on the form or structure of the Lacanian big Other, the Symbolic order, operating as a lure of sorts for the user's desire. This is what confers upon the user the desire to produce the most effectively convincing appearance in the form of the user's participation—"a signifier represents the subject for another signifier." With regard to the difference between my ideal ego and my Ego Ideal—the difference between the fantasy constitution of my desire and the way I imagine myself from the position of the virtual gaze of the big Other—what matters is that which "will be integrated into the public domain of the symbolic Law, of the big Other."[63]

Appearances, in this way, do matter. It is on account of this that "social surveillance" really is the primary lure for all of our activities on social media. It is on account of social surveillance that we curate our profiles for the gaze of the virtual big Other—for the network of multiple others, some of whom we may not even be aware of since, on the one hand, although we may know that others are part of our network (friends list, followers), the algorithmic designs of platforms (such as Facebook's EdgeRank algorithm) are built so that we don't always see all posts from our entire network, which blinds us to their presence as tourists of our public information; on the other hand, public profiles are just that: public. While new features on social media sites like Facebook allow us to make *á la carte* decisions about our privacy preferences, these tend to be more about the dimensions of social surveillance and less about corporate and state surveillance. It is, in fact, the objective of most social media sites to continue to rack up our private data, since this is their very *raison d'être*—it is their lifeblood: the source of their profits.

Platform design on social media sites can therefore be seen in the way that Chun describes, as ideologically significant for the way that they interpellate and produce subjects as users; but what the design produces aesthetically, what it represents, and what makes it so effective in its interpellative hail, has to do with the way that it figures the virtual yet real presence of the Symbolic order—of the big Other—by regulating our relationships with our desire and our enjoyment. So, the answer to the question—why do we continue participating even though we grow more aware of corporate and state surveillance?—can easily be made with reference to the social surveillance of the big Other. There is then a fetishism present that is much more potent than the one described by Chun. It is more potent than the fetishistic disavowal that frames the relationship between the software, the user, and the computer hardware—the "I know very well, but nevertheless . . ." of the software metaphors standing in for the coding and technological operations of the device; it is the fetishism that organizes our relationship to our enjoyment, between the platform and the broader political economy of (neoliberal) capitalism as such. It is in this way that social media is more than just "a functional analog to ideology," in opposition to Chun. Social media, today, *is* our ideology.

Encoding/Decoding Rethought

I am now, finally, in a position to produce the version of Hall's Encoding/Decoding model that I believe to be adequate to our thinking of social media ideology. I present it using the diagram in Figure 4.2.

First, I want to point out one further dilemma with trying to use Hall's initial model for looking at social media: as many have tried to point out, content on social media is typically user-generated. Because of this, there is a problem of how to categorize social media users, who are both the producer and the consumer—or "prosumer"—of social media content. This notion of the prosumer has been used to emphasize the new forms of exploited labor that occur on social media platforms, where users become workers who produce the content—not only the apparent visible content, but also the practice of inputting their own data, which is integral to the commodity that platforms produce and sell to advertisers as their primary source of revenue. The prosumer model, therefore, presents us with the question of whether the user should be positioned on the side of encoding or on the side of decoding. Or perhaps the user should be placed on both sides at the sites of production and of consumption.

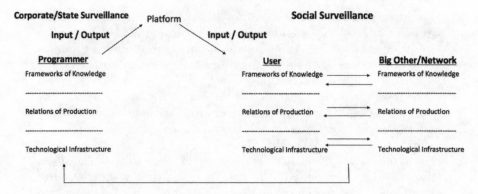

Figure 4.2. Input/Output Model

But, as still others have pointed out, the notion of the prosumer seems to ignore the differences between the productive and unproductive forms of labor in capitalism, in which productive labor is that which actually produces surplus value in the commodity, through the wage form, and through unproductive labor, which is no less exploited and no less necessary for the realization of profit under capitalist relations of production, but by being unwaged does not produce new surplus value. The difference, of course, concerns the relationship between capitalist relations of production and the wage-relation, in which surplus value is only produced by wage labor. Unwaged labor, then, still contributes to the overall accumulation of profit on the part of the capitalist, but only to the extent that it allows the capitalist to acquire a further or greater amount of surplus value already in circulation rather than the production of new surplus value.[64] The point I want to emphasize, then, through this quick detour, is that updating the Encoding/Decoding model requires adding an additional circuit on the side of the user or on the side of the decoding. The programmer remains on the encoding side as the paid wage-laborer, who contributes to the production of surplus value in the design of the platform, to its overall ideological design, and to the design of the platform as the main product. It is in this sense that the programmer is still in the position of encoding, whereas the user remains on the side of decoding.

As we have seen, the programmers' own frameworks of knowledge are inscribed into the platform and into the algorithm through their work as designers, by shaping, framing, and giving definition to the kinds of problems and questions that the platform, its interface aesthetics, and its algorithmic logic are meant to solve. Furthermore, since platforms are businesses, programmers are employed by corporations (such as Facebook and Google) that contribute to and participate within the larger set of capitalist relations of production more broadly; therefore, the problems that programmers aim to solve, given their existing frameworks of knowledge, are also implicated in the reproduction of the capitalist social relations of production more generally. We may therefore substitute the new terms input/output to replace encoding/decoding to indicate the way that programmers' inputs, the aggregate coding involved in the design of the algorithm and the platform, and the programmers' interpretations and categorizations of the outputs produced in the form of users' data embody the mass of surplus value produced through the form of the social media platform.

On the decoding side, the side of the user, we can see in what sense user-generated content interacts with the design of the platform at an ideological level. Yes, the user produces the apparent content of the site in the form of posts, articles, likes, shares, and so forth. The user also produces content in the creation of various lists of friends and followers—which is to say that the primary content produced by users is their public profile, at which they work to curate their identities, a point I will take up in the following chapter. But this does not necessarily count as the production of surplus value for the platform, since it remains as unwaged labor, however much it allows for the extraction of more surplus value already in circulation. Yet, this does not mean that the unwaged participation of users to create content contributes nothing to the overall exploitative structure of the platform.

There is an implied and additional decoding on the part of the Symbolic order of the network, the big Other, which operates as the lure of the users' desire—a desire that hails the user, interpellates the subject, toward continuous and constant participation on the site: a fetishistic brand of participation that occurs despite the user's knowledge and awareness that data mining is taking place. We are even driven to participate sometimes in conditions that may seem self-defeating. We can just imagine, for instance, the scenario of the online debate, or we can imagine our interactions with trolls in which we feel compelled to respond despite knowing that we should "never feed the trolls," as they say, or enter the "Vampire Castle." Or many of us have the uncomfortable experience of reading the comments section of blog articles, knowing that we will feel compelled to argue with others online. The curation of the big Other, in other words, need not be for something that is only apparently pleasurable. Quite often it is the case that our desire is driven by a masochistic compulsion toward struggle and confrontation. Perhaps, then, what truly gets encoded and programmed into the form of social media is the production of the Symbolic order itself. This is the point that we can use to look at the ideological ramifications of the various forms of decoding that Hall outlines at the end of his essay.

It seems in the Encoding/Decoding model that failed interpellation is a possibility. The viewer or audience or user does not have to decode the text in the dominant-hegemonic or preferred fashion; the viewer or user can instead decode in an entirely oppositional or counter-hegemonic way. The viewer or user retains a degree of free agency, allowing the viewer or user to resist the dominant ideology at the level of its appearance; but with social media, it seems that resistance plays a productive role in the training of the algorithm. The more we resist, then it is so much the better for the logical design of the platform and the algorithm, which relies upon the user's relationship to the big Other and to its desire. In this way, social media has an ideological advantage over traditional or conventional media at the level of its hegemonic and machinic enslavements. The more we resist, or the more we decode in a counter-hegemonic way—that is, the more apparent interpellation fails—the more the site and its programmers learn the optimal ways to play with our desire—that is, to produce a convincing ideology, if not overtly, then at least at the level of our practical participation on the site. The fact remains that online resistance increasingly creates the conditions for our control; to return to Žižek's thesis, we continue to learn that in conditions of postmodern capitalism, "perversion is not subversion"— that, in fact, subversion has become fully integrated into the dominant ideology. What lures us is not a particularly convincing and direct ideological message, but one that increasingly elicits our desire in the form of resistance. The more we resist, the more we help to train the algorithm about the logic of our desire. And that may be what is so truly unsavory about the Cambridge Analytica scandal: not that our privacy was violated directly, but that it shows us precisely how adept platforms have become at reading our desire.

5

Appearances That Matter, and the Reified Subjects of Social Media

If social media platforms curate content for *us* by curating the form of the big Other as the network, then to what extent are we, too, curating ourselves for *it*? The ideal of content and identity curation shows the degree to which social media is a "selfie" machine as well as a machine of desire—the two are not necessarily distinct; but far from the view that this represents merely the narcissism of individuals, we need to reflect upon the ways that our neoliberal culture is more broadly narcissistic. Or, more appropriately, we need to come to terms with the way that appearances do matter at the level of the biopolitical. This is a fact of our culture, and it is not something simply caused by social media. Rather, social media demonstrates the degree to which the production of appearances is central to the social insofar as biopolitics concerns our self-reification. In Lacanian terms, it helps us to understand the relationship between our ideal ego—or our Imaginary sense of self produced within the realm of fantasy—and our Ego Ideal, which represents the way that we see ourselves from the perceived position of the Other. Social media teaches us, though, that our recognition of the level of appearances is sometimes the best way to create an impact. Or, it shows us just how much a change in the Symbolic can have an effect in the Real. I will explain via a detour through David Fincher's *Gone Girl* (2014).

Gone Girl as Ideology Critique

A *Time* magazine review of the film asks whether the story should be viewed as a misogynistic narrative or as a feminist one.[1] This story about a woman (Amy) and her cheating husband (Nick), whom she frames for her own (faked) murder, as the reviewer puts it, "pits a feminist psychopath against a misogynistic jerk." Central to debates over the political implications of the film is the "cool girl" speech that received far less coverage in the film than in the novel. Here, as Amy escapes from the "scene of the crime," she talks about the "cool girl" persona: the act that a woman might put on by pretending to enjoy what guys like as a way of making herself attractive to men. This is a persona often presented by pop culture portrayals of women who like doing "guy stuff," like watching sports, perhaps reading comic books and watching action movies, and eating tons of junk food, while still maintaining a slim and sexy figure— enjoying, ultimately, those activities that have been stereotyped as masculine, but mostly as a way of making herself attractive to men, and not necessarily out of any genuine interest in "masculine" activities themselves. What the "cool girl" appears to enjoy most is the attention of men. As Amy describes it, the "cool girl" is as follows:

> a hot, brilliant, funny woman who adores football, poker, dirty jokes, and burping, who plays video games, drinks cheap beer, loves threesomes and anal sex, and jams hot dogs and hamburgers into her mouth like she's hosting the world's biggest culinary gang bang while somehow maintaining a size 2, because Cool Girls are above all hot. Hot and understanding. Cool Girls never get angry; they only smile in a chagrined, loving manner and let their men do whatever they want. *Go ahead, shit on me, I don't mind, I'm the Cool Girl.* . . . Men actually think this girl exists.

The "cool girl" speech can be read as a feminist critique of recent pop culture expectations placed on women. Yet, at the same time, the story returns to the misogynistic trope of the villainous, jealous, psychopathic woman, often portrayed in thrillers like *Basic Instinct* (1992), *Fatal Attraction* (1987), and *Disclosure* (1994). So, if I can put it this way, I think that so long as *Gone Girl* is placed within this series or "chain of equivalences" (to borrow from Laclau and Mouffe), it should be seen as an exercise in misogyny, reproducing the patriarchal myth of the sinful woman, the Eve, the Lilith, or the Delilah figure, if you will. The woman who causes the downfall of man.

But the "cool girl" trope can even, perhaps, work alongside the image of the woman as treacherous villain, and it can be written back in a feminist way; this is how Nina Power has interpreted the Lana Del Rey record, *Ultraviolence*, specifically the song "Money, Power, Glory."[2] LDR, a "cool girl" herself, uses, according to Power, irony in appearing to embody, but then to take down, the phallocentric critique of woman as villain. Lines from "Money, Power, Glory"—such as the following— encapsulate this idea perfectly:

> You say that you wanna go to the land
> That's far away
> How are we supposed to get there from the way
> That we're living today
> You talk lots
> About God
> Freedom comes from the cause, but
> That's not what
> This bitch wants
> Not what I want at all
> I want money, power, and glory.

As Power discusses, the song is about a hypocritical religious figure, but can also be read as "a feminist or reparations revenge anthem." The theme of the song, Power says, is the following: "You motherfuckers have everything, and you did nothing to get it but steal from the people who did all the work but got nothing in return." The only response can then be: "I'm going to do exactly the same thing to get ahead;" or, "you've painted me as deceitful and conniving, so fuck you: I'm going to steal back that image to really get what I want (because you'll fuck me over otherwise)!" This theme comes across equally well in songs like "Fucked My Way Up to the Top," and "I'm Pretty When I Cry," songs that, through a kind of postmodern irony, identify with the interpellated persona, in order to use it strategically to overthrow the phallocentric Symbolic order, which is what Amy does in *Gone Girl*.

I think the film can be read against the misogynistic critique if we consider it in its singularity—outside of the chain of equivalences—allowing, perhaps, the film to speak for itself, beyond the gender critique, which, however, is truly called for to a certain extent. The film also develops an interesting critique of media appearances and ideology appropriate for the age of social media, and I think we can read *Gone Girl* against the standard "Hollywoodism" of the production of the happy couple in the end to make this case. At the end of the film, we get the image of the happy Hollywood couple, but with a twist that can only make sense against the background of contemporary neoliberal capitalism, capitalist realism, and social media identity or Influencer curation. The film reverses the standard fantasy of the couple, which idealizes each in the eyes of the other. What I see in my partner is a reflected version of my desire (isn't it the most traumatic thing to realize that one's lover does not fit the coordinates of this reflected desire?) What makes possible the production of the happy couple is the underlying image that each has of the partner—one that raises the partner to the sublime counterpart of one's pleasure or happiness. The fantasy that places the partner within the coordinates of one's love and admiration, perhaps.

In *Gone Girl* we get the opposite. The idealization is the product, not of the underlying fantasy framework, but of overt Symbolic construction, raised to the level of the "big Other"—the order of appearances that shape and structure communication, representation, and human social relationships. In actuality, Amy and Nick hate each other. In fact, as the film progresses, it almost appears as though they are in direct competition with each other—they are caught in a game of wits: Which one can outwit the other? Their competitiveness with each other speaks quite clearly to the neoliberal agency of *homo oeconomicus*: the subject of competition, as opposed to the liberal subject of rights and the law. The neoliberal subject, in competition with other subjects, forces a new kind of self-disciplining under the conditions of advanced financial capitalism, as encapsulated in the notion of "risk society." Competition means taking risks in order to beat one's competitor, but risk also requires a large degree of self-reflexivity. One is constantly required to anticipate the actions of the other (a job required of market speculators as well, I should add), to avoid losing out to one's opponent—to get a jump on the competition. But this kind of self-reflexivity also generates a form of self-disciplining, and one that insists on a certain instrumental form of behavior, incentivized by competition. So, we end up not acting entirely out of freedom; we are free to act only under the conditions of absolute risk, ultimately forced to operate in accordance with the laws of market incentives directly.

In the film, it is almost as if Amy and Nick are in direct competition with each other in this way—a quality that speaks loudly about the inability of the couple to form a union in neoliberal conditions; they face conditions that give privilege to the individual. Competition, risk, self-reflexivity: these are the qualities under neoliberal conditions, structured by the immanent truth effects of the neoliberal economy, preventing the development of trust, the *sine qua non* of lasting relationships. Amy and Nick cannot trust each other and are constantly engaged in a game of wits, performed through media appearances. They discover again and again the need properly, or adequately, to curate their identities for the gaze of the mediated big Other. This is a point that Jennifer Friedlander makes, for instance, about the reality of deception.

Friedlander argues this point against the view that realism is "predicated on the assumption that by seeing through the ideological fictions that conceal the true workings of an institution, we undermine it." Instead, she claims, "such revelations strengthen rather than weaken the

force of the ideological illusion."[3] Seeing through a fiction, according to
Friedlander, is the most potent way of accelerating the deception by enabling the feeling of being "in the know." Feeling like we are in the know
is the most potent form of deception. Ideology, she claims, "is most effective when it creates the impression that we know better and are therefore
immune to its influence."[4]

If there is an underlying theme in *Gone Girl*, it is precisely the fact
that appearances matter. That it is simply not possible to find the truth
behind or underneath the appearances. Truth is *in* the appearance itself.
If Amy and Nick are not bound by the underlying fantasy that idealizes
each in the eyes of the other, they are bound by the outward performance
that they play for the media. Appearances therefore matter precisely for
holding the one to account for the other's actions. When Amy stages her
own murder, framing Nick, he is tried, not by a judge or jury, not even by
the police (who seem somewhat sympathetic, initially, to his situation),
but by the court of public opinion—that is, by the social surveillance of
the Other. He becomes the object of media scrutiny; Amy's "murder" is
turned into a media event. Her parents produce a media campaign to
find her (when it is believed that she is only missing and not yet dead).
Competition and reflexivity are played out by the media game as well,
as each cable news station tries to get out ahead of its competitor with
new details about the case. In fact, just prior to an interview with Nick,
arranged by his lawyer with a sympathetic news reporter, a competing station publicizes the fact that Nick had been cheating on Amy. In response,
Nick makes use of the media appearance to let Amy (whom he realizes,
by this point, has staged her own murder and is framing him) know that
he is aware of her ploy, while he manipulates the level of appearances in
his favor. Nick and Amy act according to a logic of appearances that, as
Friedlander describes through a Lacanian logic, reveal the truth, not by
denouncing the deception, but by "staging" one.

The film also plays upon the disciplinary or control society theme of
constant surveillance. The media scrutiny of Nick and Amy's life is paralleled by scenes in which Amy, taking refuge at the home of a wealthy ex-
boyfriend (Desi), uses to her advantage the home surveillance cameras
that are placed in Desi's house. Following Nick's interview, Amy begins
to realize that he has won the upper hand, and that sympathy might fall
away from her and toward him. Realizing that she needs to go back to
Nick to regain the power she had held when it was believed that he was
guilty, Amy manages to stage a kidnapping by Desi, making it look like
he had been attacking her, by performing scenes for the security cameras (biting Desi's lip when they kiss, making him bleed, and untucking
his shirt before he passes in front of one security camera; then hurting

herself and falling down in front of another, with appropriate timing to make it look like he had beaten her). In this way, she is able to murder Desi and return to Nick, placing blame on the dead ex-boyfriend, and literally getting away with murder.

Appearances matter for Amy in another sense too. We never see the "real" Amy—though she can be located at the level of the narration. She is always playing a role: as the "cool girl," as the southern "white trash" woman while she is hiding and planning to frame Nick, as the seductive "temptress" for Desi, and finally as the happy wife in front of the cameras at the end of the film. In the end, Amy is able to hold Nick under her sway by knowing how to manipulate the level of the appearances.

If we stick to the misogynistic level of appearances noted above, we can certainly see how *Gone Girl* reproduces a sexist and phallocentric ideology. However, it might be a bit more daring to argue that not only is it a feminist film, but also it contains an important lesson about the role of appearances and curated identities in the contemporary field of mediated self-representation—that is, it is a lesson of social media identity curation and the management of our digital reputation. The usual critique of ideology is geared toward some kind of revelation of the truth—the truth beneath the surface; in other words, if you want to change things, you need to get at the truth behind the illusion. This is a fact that Hilary Neroni identifies via the differences between psychoanalysis and biopolitics. According to the latter, the body is a repository of truth that we can ascertain, sometimes through torture and the affliction of pain. In contrast, for psychoanalysis, according to Neroni, the body is not merely a repository for the truth. The subject is, instead, driven by the irrational experience of unconscious enjoyment.[5] The contrast between the psychoanalytic view of appearances and the biopolitical one is a topic I explore here with regard to neoliberal incentives toward social media identity curation.

Gone Girl shows us that, in today's "society of the spectacle," only appearances matter. The point is not to critique reality; the point is to act within the coordinates of Symbolic reality—at the level of appearances—in order to have an effect in the Real *through* the Symbolic. But it is this very idea that has been appropriated by the digital reputation economy—the economy of social media developed through neoliberal capitalism. Here, then, I examine the way that neoliberalism and social media catch us in this logic of appearances, against which we maintain a kind of cynical realist distance, which however captures us ever more aggressively in the matrices of capitalist exploitation. The example of *Gone Girl* shows us, on the one hand, how a culture of identity curation and reputation management is fully in line with the neoliberal era; on the other hand, it shows us that an identification with the logic of appearances may be a way of expressing the contradictions at the heart of the social media self.

On the Production of the *Self* in Social Media

As discussed in previous chapters, we can note that recent studies on labor and social media have emphasized the idea of "prosumption": a confluence of production and consumption, first described by Alvin Toffler.[6] Much of the research in this area has appropriated Dallas Smythe's conception of the "audience commodity" and its work—the idea that TV programmers produce audiences to sell to advertisers, and in the process audiences work to produce themselves as an "audience commodity" by learning to buy the products advertised on TV.[7] Similarly, social media users can be said to be producing a "prosumer commodity" by producing the data that corporate social media companies use to sell to advertisers.[8] This, I believe, offers an adequate way of conceiving the monetization (if not necessarily the exploitation) of users' data on corporate social media platforms, such as Facebook, Twitter, YouTube, and others. There is, as well, an added ideological dimension to the kind of monetization that we see in this instance: because social media involves play, on the one hand, and participatory political and cultural communication, on the other (that is, organizing solidarity campaigns, community functions, and so on; perhaps this amounts to the production of a new public sphere), and because its use is apparently voluntary, it is difficult to see how it is a mechanism of exploitation. As I discussed in the previous chapter, it is possible to theorize social media users as unproductive labor, but more difficult to argue that their labor is exploited as productive given that social media use is unwaged activity.

The concept of communicative capitalism teaches us that while the internet promotes the ideals of democracy, it actually reinforces the stronger and greater integration of our lives into capitalist relations of exploitation and control. Detractors of this position may argue that, even if users are central to the production of content upon which corporate social media sites generate profit, they still receive a payment in kind through the service that they receive from the social media platform. Fuchs has indicated the fallacious aspects of the latter by demonstrating that the value produced by users through their willful inscription of personal data into the matrices of social media databases far outweighs the value of the service provided by corporate social media.[9] The internet prosumer commodity is, in fact, made of the mass amounts of data ("big data") that social media companies package and sell to advertisers (and hand over to government surveillance agencies, such as the NSA—hence the term "dataveillance").

There is, however, another no less ideological way to approach the problem of social media labor. The conception of the prosumer commodity in some ways seems to hint at the idea of ideology as "false consciousness." The user, in this instance, remains unaware of the fact that the use of social media constitutes a form of labor, let alone exploited labor. Here, we are back at the level of ideology critique in the form of "truth as revelation"—that is, if only people knew the truth then they would revolt. However, it is necessary to note some of the functional elements of subjectivization involved in the use of social media. We should recognize, for instance, the prevalent use of social media, not only for play or for participatory culture, but also and increasingly for the purpose of work-related activities and self-promotion. The professional social media site, LinkedIn, is surely the most obvious example of this, designed as it is specifically for the purpose of professional networking. In the context of an increasingly precarious labor force overall, sites like LinkedIn have become essential for maintaining professional work- and business-related contacts. LinkedIn thus serves as a model for understanding much of the activity in which people are now engaged on social media, especially in light of the rise of the figure of the social media Influencer on platforms like the Facebook-owned Instagram—that is, social media use *as* work. Social media, in this respect, has become a platform for the performance and presentation of a commodified *Self*.

Here, I am using the category of the (capital "S") Self to distinguish it from that of the "subject." The Self, I claim, is an alienated representation of the subject, congealed in the form of the signifier (or the Lacanian Master-Signifier), which for Lacan represents the subject for the Other. As a signifier, the Self materially obfuscates the subject; in the psychoanalytic context, the subject remains unaware of this, and constitutes her identity, in part, by misrecognizing the signifier as a fuller representation of her-Self. The subject performs her identity *as* a Self through the signifier that acts as the image of her ideal Self viewed from the perspective of the Other, as the subject's Ego Ideal.

What I have in mind with the idea of "performing" the Self on social media is closely connected to constructions of reputation, or what Alison Hearn refers to as the "digital reputation economy."[10] Hearn describes a process of "self-branding" in which the subject is transformed into a "commodity for sale on the labor market[, which] must also generate its own rhetorically persuasive packaging."[11] She adds, "nowadays, social media like Twitter or Facebook provide a new 'protocol' for social relations; they allow individuals' personal connections to become more durable [and] representable."[12] Since social media makes our connections and images of the Self more "durable" and "representable," they can be seen as objectivized facets of the Self. They objectivize our "digital reputation."

"Self-branding" or "reputation management" on social media presents one aspect of the neoliberal subjectivization of individuals as "entrepreneurs of the Self." As one report explains, "Reputation management has now become a defining feature of online life for many internet users . . ." Because "search engines and social media sites play a central role in building one's reputation online," social media users must be "careful to project themselves online in a way that suits specific audiences."[13] One can discern here the type of "rational choice" rhetoric employed by neoliberal advocates of entrepreneurial ethics. The public profile on social media platforms is no longer an open space of communication and self-identification, and is now a place for exhibiting and curating the (professional and entrepreneurial) Self.[14]

My choice of distinguishing between the Self and the subject is strategic given the critical stance I am proposing of the conception of the entrepreneurial subject on social media. The Self, I claim, represents an *objectivization* (read as reification) of the subject. The Self produced on social media is therefore not a "subject" in the Lacanian sense—the Self is rather part of a process of reifying the subject, and even conforms in a way to what Lazzarato has in mind with respect to social subjection. But the ideology of social media works by reifying the subject rather than by producing subjectivity. My conception, therefore, stands in opposition to Michel Foucault's definition of the neoliberal subject in his lectures on "biopolitics." As opposed to subjectivization, the entrepreneurial ethics of neoliberalism involve the further reification of the subject, as an object-commodity that I am calling a "Self," as exemplified by the "profile page" so ubiquitous on social media. Although it may be conceived as an element of subjectivity and identity formation in the Information Society, I contend that it represents instead the objectivization of the subject. To this extent, we might even be able to historicize the emergence of theories like Object-Oriented Ontology as a correlation to the historical form of our objectivization on social media. The more we self-objectify, the more we are driven to theorize the agency of objects.

Whereas Foucault claims that the neoliberal subject produces itself as subject, I argue instead that the neoliberal subject works further to objectivize the Self. Although Foucault's analysis is based on the idea that we are dominated through the mandate to become subjects—and, therefore, he presents a critical stance in opposition to neoliberalism—my claim is that this demand is in fact one of objectivization rather than subjectivization. With the rising necessity for "self-branding," in the context of a post-Fordist society that relies increasingly on contract and precarious labor, the time spent outside of "work time," which is the time when labor-power is put to use—what we are used to thinking of as leisure time, and (in Marxian terms) the time spent on the reproduction of labor-power, or even social reproduction—now becomes subdivided in order to include the time necessary for the promotion of the Self, understood in neoliberal terms as "investing" in one's own "human capital." I argue, instead, that the objectivization (and hence the commodification) of the Self in social media functions as an additional form of unpaid free labor in contemporary neoliberal capitalism. Self-promotion is simply an added aspect to the neoliberal ideology of entrepreneurialism, and social media provides the space that facilitates its operation by submitting us to the larger social exploitation of capitalist production, if not necessarily the platform on its own.

The Neoliberal Subject

Two important differences distinguish the liberal subject from the neoliberal subject. On the one hand, the liberal subject can be characterized as a "free laborer"; on the other hand, it is also a subject of exchange. In the liberal conception of the market, both capital and labor represent positions of free agency—both are free and equal individuals (in the eyes of the law), endowed with rights, who enter into the market and agree to a "fair" exchange of labor-power for wages. The latter would be impossible to conceive as equitable without a subject who is free to enter into the market and to exchange a commodity for a price. While the liberal subject is one of rights before the eyes of the law, the neoliberal subject, in contrast, is "human capital," no longer the subject of exchange but of competition.[15] In this way, neoliberalism differs from classical liberal economics by positing the worker as an active subject, making "rational choices," engaged in competition with others for access to "scarce resources," instead of as an "*object* of supply and demand in the form of labor power."[16] Here, wages are not seen as the price in exchange for labor-power, but as a return on investment in one's "human capital."

Foucault's thesis was that power lies at the heart of both liberal theories of sovereignty as well as Marxist conceptions of class domination.

As Thomas Lemke explains: "While the former [liberals] claim that legiti-mate authority is codified in law and it is rooted in a theory of rights, the latter [Marxists] locates power in the economy and regards the state as an instrument of the bourgeoisie."[17] In his later work, Foucault sought to displace these two conceptions of power. Through his discussion of neoliberalism, "human capital," and through the entrepreneurial agency of the neoliberal subject, Foucault advances a conception of subjectivity that relies less on "juridico-political" and class models of power. Rather, the neoliberal, entrepreneurial subject as "human capital" is, according to Foucault, a subject that *self*-authorizes. As Andrew Dilts puts it, "For Foucault, the neo-liberal account of human capital opens the grounds of subjectivity, redirects his attention beyond the ways in which we are made subjects by force relations and allows him to think about the role that sub-jects play in their own formation."[18] Because neoliberals emphasize the role of ("rational") choice, there is a sense in which the subject here is formed freely and is interpellated, neither by ideology nor by repression, but by the immanent "truth effects" of the neoliberal economy. What Foucault finds in the theory of "human capital" is a material conception of subjectivity that moves beyond Marxist and liberal conceptions of ide-ology and subjectivity. The neoliberal subject, for Foucault, is an effect of the "truth regime" of neoliberal governmentality.

"Human capital" refers to "everything that in one way or another can be a source of future income." That is, it consists of "all of those physical and psychological factors which make someone able to earn this or that wage."[19] One may "invest" in his or her "human capital" through practices of consumption; but consumption is taken as a *productive* activ-ity. Neoliberalism sees people as "investors in themselves" and, there-fore, "treats people not as consumers but as producers," and time spent on the production of reputation is an important element of "investing" in the Self.[20] The subjectivization of workers, from this perspective, comes through the active agency of investing in the Self, making each of us an "entrepreneurial self," or an "entrepreneur of the Self." For the neolib-eral subject, as an "entrepreneur of the Self" in competition with other neoliberal subjects and constantly investing in his or her "human capital," everything, "from marriage, to crime, to expenditures on children, can be understood 'economically' according to a particular calculation of cost for benefit."[21] This, according to Jason Read, means that we have to rethink and expand the category of labor in neoliberalism drastically: "Any activity that increases the capacity to earn income . . . is an invest-ment in human capital."[22]

Foucault's objective, according to Read, "is not to bemoan [the neoliberal conception of "human capital"] as a victory for capitalist ideology . . . so much so that everyone from a minimum wage employee to a C.E.O. considers themselves to be entrepreneurs." Instead, Foucault's project demonstrates how neoliberalism represents a new "regime of truth," complete with its own form of subjectivization: *homo oeconomicus,* or the "entrepreneurial subject," as distinguished from *homo juridicus,* or the "legal subject of the state."[23] No longer is the subject guided by rights and laws; for *homo oeconomicus,* investment and competition are activities that render the subject in a position of self-control through self-reflexivity and establish the production of the Self as entrepreneur. Now, "the worker, on his own initiative, is supposed to guarantee the formation, growth, accumulation, improvement, and valorization of the 'self' as 'capital'."[24]

The conditions for enacting this conception of the neoliberal subject have been put into practice through varying austerity measures and through the dismantling of the postwar welfare or social state. That is, through the "contemporary trend away from long term labor contracts, [and] toward temporary and part-time labor," and through austerity measures that turn needs (formerly subsidized by the state) and basic resources into exchange values, the neoliberal entrepreneurial subject has no choice but to practice an ethic of investing in the Self, in "human capital," and to enter into relations of competition. As Read puts it, this has been an "effective strategy of subjectification" that encourages workers to avoid seeing themselves as workers and to view themselves instead as "companies of one."[25]

Digital Labor and the Internet " Prosumer Commodity"

How does this logic of investing in one's own "human capital," of investing in the Self, impact the way that we use social media? Consider, for instance, the types of activities in which one engages through social media. We "share" articles, images, and "memes;" we "like" or "favorite" content posted by others; we can write about our thoughts, express our opinions, and create short polemics (in 280 characters or less on Twitter); we can also, and importantly, "follow" and "friend" others, creating a "social network" on social media. All of these activities—of which this is only a small account—help to produce the Self on social media. The profile page is a register of all of our activities, all of our comments and posts, and (importantly) all of the networks to which we connect, which makes our production of Self much more durable and representable, and therefore "objectifiable." Further, we act as curators of our profiles: we invest time in reading through articles (or, at the very least, the titles of articles) before we post them; we invest time in deciding what to say in our status updates; and we invest time in building (and maintaining) a network that makes us appear desirable to others. All of this requires us to be rather self-reflexive if we are interested in producing a Self that is to be desired by others (or in producing our own desire as the desire of the Other), which will help us to develop a desired reputation. Which is to say that a lot of work goes into the construction of the Self and one's "digital reputation" in social media.

Like all activities in the neoliberal context, using social media should be seen as a form of work or labor. But how might we conceive social media labor when it is viewed predominantly as a leisure activity? Writing about Facebook, Christian Fuchs notes that user generated data—data about ourselves—is compiled by the site and transformed into an "Internet 'Prosumer' Commodity," not unlike the "audience commodity."[26] Fuchs concedes the point that it is difficult to perceive the existence of exploitation on social media sites like Facebook. However, he argues that forms similar to the form of commodity fetishism mask the exploitative aspects of corporate social media. It is precisely the commodity form of Facebook that hides the production of exchange value behind the veil of use values. The Facebook platform is created as a use value that satisfies users' communicative and social needs, but at the same time it serves Facebook's profit interests.[27] The "object-status" of users— that is, the commodification of users' contributions to the profitability of the site—remains concealed by the production of the social network.[28] Social media users are therefore, according to Fuchs, workers: "The online work they perform on social media is informational work, affective work, cognitive work, communicative work and collaborative work. This work creates profiles, content, transaction data and social relations."[29] But also, in order for social media platforms to work, "users need to be quite active, social, creative and networked."[30]

Fuchs and others thus demonstrate the way that users' activity on corporate social media is in actuality a form of exploited and alienated labor, which the presentation of social media use as a leisure activity obscures. Yet in the context of corporate, for-profit platforms, like Facebook and Twitter, the data and information that users provide, the profiles that they produce, and the content that they share contribute to the production of the "Internet 'Prosumer' Commodity" upon which these companies generate profit through monetization of our activity. Significantly, work, here, is not conceived as such, but rather as play and as leisure. It is also, in this sense, that the promotion of the Self through social media may not be seen as work—that is, as value-producing activity, or as productive labor.

While I do not dispute much of the critical political economy approach to corporate social media represented by Fuchs's research, save for the important difference between productive (that is, waged) and unproductive (that is, unwaged) labor, my interests here lie more with the way in which users deal with their objectivization and commodification more broadly and the way that social media reputation management fulfills a larger dimension of aggregate exploitation in the overall social conditions of neoliberal capitalism. Fuchs, in fact, explains this quite well in another way.

Referring to Pierre Bourdieu's categories of social, cultural, symbolic, and economic capital, Fuchs puts the matter as follows: people make use of social media because it allows them access to: 1) an accumulation of social relations (social capital); 2) an accumulation of qualifications, education, knowledge, and so on (cultural capital); and 3) an accumulation of reputation (symbolic capital). However, "the time that users spend on commercial social media platforms generating social, cultural and symbolic capital is the process of prosumer commodification transformed into economic capital. Labor time on commercial social media is the conversion of Bourdieusian social, cultural and symbolic capital into Marxian value and economic capital."[31] Two things follow from this: first, social media is designed to encourage users—by creating and by fostering pleasurable incentives—to spend increasing amounts of time using the platform, voluntarily handing over data about themselves, and helping to create the prosumer commodity; second, the demands of the neoliberal labor market force users to employ social media as a means of further accumulating and representing their social, cultural, and symbolic capital as part of the Self. Labor time and leisure time fold into one another in the digital culture and economy and become part of the emerging "24/7 temporalities" of twenty-first-century capitalism.

Self-Management 2.0: A 24/7 Job

Fuchs notes that terms such as "social media and Web 2.0 were established around 2005 in order to characterize World Wide Web (www) platforms like social networking sites (e.g. Facebook, LinkedIn), blogs (e.g. Wordpress), wikis (e.g. Wikipedia), microblogs (e.g. Twitter, Weibo), and user-generated content sharing sites (e.g. Youtube)."[32] But what is more significant is the fact that, as Daniel Trottier explains, Web 2.0 services "are typically made up of individual profiles. In most cases, a user cannot simply visit a site like Facebook; they have to *build a presence there*. Profiles are a kind of biographical space, where users provide information about themselves."[33] Social media websites like Facebook, therefore, differ significantly from the internet of the 1990s in that they limit anonymity and encourage the manufacture of individuality and Self-hood.

What is equally significant about social media, demonstrating its evolution beyond "cyberspace," is the fact that it encourages users to construct their identities more concretely than in previous iterations. As Geert Lovink notes, social media and the rise of Web 2.0 provide "little freedom anymore to present yourself in multiple ways."[34] The combination of entrepreneurial incentives and the rise of the post-9/11 security state make masking one's identity online almost impossible—or at least more difficult: "The hedonistic excesses at the turn of the millennium were over by the 2001 financial crisis and 9/11 attacks. The war on terror aborted the desire for a serious parallel 'second self' culture and instead gave rise to the global surveillance and control industry. . . . Web 2.0 tactically responded with coherent, singular identities in sync with the data owned by police, security, and financial institutions."[35]

Social media creates an atmosphere that encourages the production of a realistic representation of the Self as opposed to a mere avatar. For example, Lovink explains that within Facebook there exists "a pathological dimension of commitment to the real self going hand in hand with the comfort of being only amongst friends in a safe, controlled environment. . . . Differences of choice are celebrated so long as they are confined to *one* 'identity'."[36] Confined to a single, realistic identity, and within the context of the neoliberal valorization of the entrepreneurial Self, social media has helped to generate a "*self*-management" wave, which transformed into a "*self*-promotion machine."[37] Managing one's Self becomes a full-time job, which blurs the lines between professional and private life: "In the competitive networking context of work, we are trained to present ourselves as the best, fastest, and smartest."[38] The Self-management wave of Web 2.0, using the "self-promotion machine" of social media, has aided in extending the length of the working day, transforming into what Jonathan Crary refers to as "24/7 temporalities." "It's only recently," Crary notes, "that the elaboration, the modeling of one's personal and social identity, has been reorganized to conform to the uninterrupted operation of markets, information networks, and other systems."[39] 24/7 thus renders "the idea of working without pause, without limits."[40]

Social media also allows for the extension of the workday beyond all available working hours. There is no "off switch;" although none of us can really be shopping, playing games, working, or blogging 24/7, no moment exists nowadays in which we are *not* shopping, consuming, or using and exploiting networks. The invasion of 24/7 temporalities therefore becomes all pervasive.[41] 24/7 temporalities have a global reach and continue to operate elsewhere while we are asleep, so that when we wake up, we already have commands ready to go in our email inboxes when we start the day. Social media and 24/7 temporalities thus speak to an environment of productivity that does not stop. Profit-generating activity is in operation 24/7.[42] Even those activities that were only conceived as acts of consumerism have now become productive "techniques of personalization." Producing the Self is a labor-intensive operation, and we are constantly given incentives and prescriptions by consumer society to reinvent and manage our intricate identities.[43] All of this is championed, however, as "entrepreneurial heroism," which surmounts the asymmetry between the individual and the "grid."[44] Everything that one does is now "deployed in the service of adding dollar or prestige value to one's electronic identities."[45] In a world of constant competition, of total commodification, "reification has proceeded to the point where the individual has to invent a self-understanding that optimizes or facilitates their participation in digital milieus and speeds." Everyone "needs an online presence, needs 24/7 exposure, to avoid social 'irrelevance' or professional failure."[46]

"Human Capital" or the Reproduction of Labor-Power?

24/7 temporalities now call into question the way that we imagine the structure and length of the working day. Usually, we think about the typical working day as something separate from leisure time. We use our time outside of work to eat, sleep, and relax, all of which contribute to the reproduction of our ability to work. Marx calls this period the time necessary for the reproduction of labor-power. The latter is an integral part of his analysis, since it helps to explain why the price of wages appears fair in the labor market: the wage is the fair price for labor-power since it covers the costs of those materials that we need to reproduce our ability to work—the cost of rent, transportation, food, clothing, and so on—in other words, the commodity that workers are selling to the capitalist.[47] Exploitation occurs, not because workers are paid below the value of their labor-power, but because workers are put to work for an amount of time in which they produce their own value, plus an additional value for which they are not paid, which becomes the surplus value that is appropriated by the capitalist.[48]

Workers use their earned wages to satisfy physiological needs, pay rent, pay for transportation; but they can also deploy wages to increase the value of labor-power—to spend on education, physical health, and communication technologies, and to gain access to social and cultural networks. In neoliberal terms, the laborer "invests" in her "human capital." My claim, though, is that what the neoliberal ideology conceives as investing in human capital remains nothing more than what Marxists refer to as the reproduction of labor-power: consuming in order to reproduce the commodity that the laborer sells on the market to meet the means of subsistence.[49] With neoliberalism, however, we begin to witness, on the one hand, a decreasing wage (in real terms) that is below the true value of labor-power, in addition to divestment from public infrastructure and social services that help to subsidize the cost of living. On the other hand, people are encouraged to borrow in order to "invest" further to *increase* the value of their labor-power or human capital. This works toward the transformation of nearly all activity into value-producing activity. Borrowing in order to invest: we see, here, in parallel with the rise of the neoliberal "entrepreneurial subject," the emergence of the neoliberal "debt economy."

As Silvia Federici explains, "since the 1980s, a whole ideological campaign has been orchestrated that represents borrowing from banks to provide for one's reproduction as a form of entrepreneurship, thus mystifying the class relation and the exploitation involved."[50] Added to this, we have also seen processes of wage deflation, reductions in public spending, rising levels of personal debt, and precarious labor. According to Lazzarato, these processes have contributed to the neoliberal conception of the "entrepreneur of the Self," whose activity is restricted to managing his or her employability, debts, drops in wages, and the reduction of public services, all of which function according to the terms of business and competition.[51]

Reproduction of labor-power is now seen as a wholly entrepreneurial activity, in which both work and "work on the self" are reduced to a command to become one's own boss, absorbing the risks and costs now externalized onto the rest of society by business interests and austerity governments. Neoliberal entrepreneurialism was promised as a form of liberation; instead, it has turned out to be a mechanism for downloading the costs and risks that neither businesses nor the state are willing to take.[52] As a result, more stress is placed on the individual "entrepreneurial" Self to add to the reputation of the Self, since this is the character upon which future income depends.

Given the overlap between the neoliberal ideology of "human

capital"—of "investing" in one's human capital—and the Marxian category of the reproduction of labor-power, it is possible to conceive the production of "human capital" less as the production of subjectivity, and more as the production of the subject as an object-commodity, increasingly just that of labor-power. Investing in one's human capital, in other words, is simply the neoliberal ideology speaking to the necessity to reproduce labor-power as an object and to further self-commodify the entirety of one's life and living.

Social media and the necessity to "self-brand," however, pose a new problem. At the same time that one is involved in the reproduction of labor-power, we now find, also, the production of a second object-commodity that operates as a mechanism for the sale and marketing of the first. That is, there is the production of the Self as a brand identity, or in social media, the production of a public profile through which one may market oneself as worker or as human capital, depending upon the perspective that one takes ideologically. The production of the Self, I claim, is similar to what Tiziana Terranova refers to as "supplementing," that is, bringing home supplementary work: the increasing necessity of working outside of the traditional office. This, she explains, has been affected by the expansion of the internet, which has given "ideological and material support to contemporary trends toward increased flexibility of the workforce, continuous reskilling [and] freelance work."[53] In the context of social media, the following question needs to be addressed: does the investment in the Self count only toward the reproduction of labor-power, or is the time invested in the reproduction of labor-power now split between the latter and the production of Self as image or brand? In other words, can we now think of a triple division of the day, including 1) labor-time, 2) time for the reproduction of labor-power, and 3) the time necessary for the *marketing* of labor-power, and the promotion of the *Self*? Or, instead, are we now also seeing the total and complete objectification or reification of the entirety of our life, living, and our social interactions, where all of these activities fold into each other? This may be one way to note the difference between commodity production and social production, however much the latter still relies ideologically upon the wage relationship.

The Neoliberal Self as the Object of the Subject

It is difficult to conceive of users' activity on social media both as a form of labor and as an objectivizing practice for a couple of reasons that are specific to postmodern capitalism. On the one hand, as I have already noted above, using social media appears as a form of play and entertainment, and therefore it does not appear as productive labor; on the other hand, it appears to provide a platform for the construction of a Self as subject. Consumer culture and the rise of the information society have created the appearance of a free society outside of direct technocratic or authoritarian control. Information Communication Technologies (ICTs), for instance, have increased accessibility to knowledge, which has largely been democratized (that is, if we ignore the global "digital divide"); furthermore, the pleasure ethic and the injunction to "Enjoy!" in consumer society discredit the notion that ours is a society that is based upon prohibition and repression. In fact, as Žižek argues, postmodern society is one that is no longer based upon the *prohibition* to enjoy and is organized instead around the constant *obligation* to enjoy. A parallel exists, then, between Žižek's thought and that of Foucault (the two, though, coming from opposite perspectives) in trying to conceive subjectivization outside the operation of direct repression. This is the central problem for the postmodern critique of ideology: how to conceive the operations of ideology outside of mechanisms of direct and overt control.

The historicity of the postmodern subject is further destabilized by the perceived lack of alternatives to global capitalism that Fisher describes as "capitalist realism."[54] As he puts it, capitalist realism denotes "the widespread sense that not only is capitalism the only viable political and economic system, but also that it is now impossible to even *imagine* a coherent alternative to it."[55] The "realism" of capitalist realism should be understood as the kind of response that one receives when one proclaims the viability of alternatives to capitalism; it is the response that so many of us on the Left receive from cynics who encourage us to "be realistic" or to quit being so "idealistic." This kind of cynicism, according to Žižek, is precisely the form that ideology has taken in a supposedly post-ideological era.

As I argued in chapter 2, we see here a perverse core (in the strict Lacanian sense) to the form of ideology in postmodern society, and cynicism, as a form of fetishistic disavowal, exemplifies the latter. As Todd McGowan explains, cynicism is "a mode of keeping alive the dream of successfully attaining the lost object [of desire] while fetishistically denying one's investment in this idea." But the danger of cynicism is that "it allows subjects to acknowledge the hopelessness of consumption while simultaneously consuming with as much hope as the most naïve consumer."[56] It is here, I claim, through the cynical preservation of desire, that we can locate a conception of the subject that stands in opposition to the one proposed by Foucault in his lectures on neoliberalism. The apparent absence of prohibition has brought, not the demise of the big

Other, but rather the willing of it back into existence since it preserves the subject's ability to desire (since desire is only possible if it is posited in opposition to its prohibition; or, as Foucault puts it, "where there is power, there is resistance").[57]

New media and ICTs play a central role in adding to the deconstruction of prohibition. Access to one's desire is no longer prohibited by time, or by the delay required to attain the lost object: everything is present, locatable in the database. This, however, produces a dilemma for the desiring subject. New media and "cyberspace" are capable of potentially suffocating desire—desire is operative only insofar as the object desired remains (forever) lost. Social media thus confronts the subject with the impossibility of desire since, as McGowan puts it, "thanks to the emergence of cyberspace, the subject has the ability to experience its castration as the effect of its own desire rather than as the effect of an authority demanding sacrifice. . . . [Cyberspace] alters the subject's awareness of prohibition, and this not only disguises the working of the Law but also exposes the fundamental structure of desire."[58] Cyberspace, in other words, confronts the subject or user directly with the fact that (in Lacanian terms) the big Other does not exist—that power is not in fact (in accordance with Foucault) occupied by some agent or figure of Authority. However, as McGowan indicates, this absence of recognizing the lack of prohibition universalizes prohibition: in order to preserve desire from suffocation, the subject clings to power, willing it into existence. The perverse core to contemporary neoliberal subjectivity is that which, in order to preserve desire from suffocation, compels the subject to cling to some conception of prohibiting agency. This is what makes the postmodern subject perverse.

How, then, to save desire from suffocation, given the context of the absence of prohibition, instant access, and abundance? Here we are able to again think about the role of social media in preserving the agency of the big Other. Social media, I claim, is the manner in which capitalism exploits lack and scarcity in a world of instant access and abundance. It is also a platform for repositing the existence of the big Other through the form of the network. Furthermore, it is by alienating oneself materially, through the production of a material signifier—the public profile, the signifier that represents the subject for another signifier—that stands for both the production of the Other *and* the Self, in the spaces of social media. The subject produces the Self as signifier and it does so, not as subject, but as *object*; or, to borrow a phrase from Frank Smecker, the signifier represents the Self as "the object of the subject."[59]

Here, we are dealing with two alternative conceptions of subjectivity (the Foucauldian conception and the Lacanian one), and the way to resolve the contradiction between the two is to conceive the subject in the case of Foucault—"human capital," the "entrepreneur of the Self"—not as subject, but as object (precisely what Foucault does not want to do). What the neoliberal subject produces is not the Self as subject, but the Self as object. Investing in one's own "human capital" is the production of the Self as object-commodity, which again gives us an indication about the historicity of the New Materialisms. Like *Gone Girl*, social media shows us that reified appearances of the Self, our objectification, is one of the historical conditions and effects of neoliberalism.

On Becoming the Subject of the Objectivized Self

I have been arguing that the Self represents the objectivization of the subject in two ways, as contextualized by neoliberalism and social media. On the one hand, drawing upon Lacanian conceptions of subjectivity, I have argued that the subject is objectivized through its alienation in the signifier and through its alienation in the order of the big Other or the Symbolic order. Through social media, this is enacted in the production of the public profile and in its presentation, performance, and exhibition to the social network. This, I claim, is one aspect of the desire to *will* back into existence some virtual prohibiting agency upon which the subject is able to constitute its desire, a figure of prohibition that *appears* lacking in the context of postmodern capitalism, but is the basis upon which all actual desiring is made possible. On the other hand, the subject is objectivized through the production of a Self as "brand" image. The Self is, in this sense, an object-commodity that is put to use in the service of Self-promotion. The latter is a condition, in an atmosphere of precarious labor, for the further accumulation of paid work. I have suggested, then, that the working day is now divided, logically, into three parts: labor-time, time for the reproduction of labor-power, and the time necessary for the promotion of labor-power and the reputation of the Self. But in practice, these parts dissolve into a whole that hides their function. Social media masks Self-promotion as the production of subjectivity, and is in this sense comparable to commodity fetishism in its traditional definition. The question remains, however: If all activity is objectivizing activity, where can we locate the subject? Which notion of subjectivity is adequate for conceiving the objectivizing operations of neoliberalism and social media labor?

I have argued, against Foucault, that "investing" in one's "human capital" is not, in fact, a subject-producing activity (this follows closely my critique of Lazzarato in chapter 3). Despite the fact that Foucault's intention was to posit the subject as a category of domination, I have argued instead that neoliberalism extends the *reification* of the subject, and that it is its objectivization that results in both the exploitation and the domination of the subject. Subjectivity in the sense that I have in mind is, therefore, much closer to the non-reified consciousness of what traditional Marxism refers to as proletarian class consciousness. But we need not necessarily discard the Foucauldian conception of subjectivity. Instead, we should posit his conception as the ideological form of sub-jectivity (one reason why his account is so convincing), while at the same time we should invoke a conception of proletarian subjectivity, which is what is truly at stake in critical ideological analysis.

The subject posited by Foucault represents the individual caught in ideology insofar as the subject misrecognizes objectivization as a con-dition of subjectivization. My claim, in contrast, is that it is simply not possible to reveal to the subject the fact of objectivization in the circuits of exploitation, since—for starters—the realism of "capitalist realism" makes this generally known. As well, the subject's sense of the preserva-tion of desire binds the subject to the existing relations of domination and power in order to preserve desire. The subject of neoliberalism pro-duces, but does not produce the subject as subject; instead, users further objectivize the entirety of life as a condition of aggregate exploitation in neoliberal capitalism. Furthermore, the traditional categories of Marxist analysis—alienation, reification, commodity fetishism, reproduction of labor-power, absolute and relative surplus value—still provide a much more adequate means for conceptualizing subjection and exploitation, even in neoliberal conditions, than the theory of "human capital."

The shift, then, that has accompanied neoliberalism, has not been at the level of subjectivity, but—Foucault is correct in at least this regard—with the material practices that have accompanied the resurgence of the capitalist class in the post-welfare state period. Domination and control have become increasingly self-imposed, and the Self-promotional aspect of social media—its use as a tool further to objectivize, reify, commodify, and sell the Self—plays a central part in this process under the conditions of twenty-first-century capitalism, proving that appearances and the ap-parently free and rational choice of a representational signifier are now what matters the most.

6

The Swiping Logic of the Signifier

While the market logic of neoliberalism complicates our ability to assume a representational signifier, at its most fundamental, the swipe logic of social media dating apps like Tinder reduces the paradoxes of neoliberal "rational choice" to their elementary binary level: swipe Right/swipe Left; affirmation/negation; 1/0. Because of this, dating apps help us to understand easily the binary logic of social media algorithms more generally, including how social media programming, at its elementary binary level (of affirmation and negation), shares an ontological basis with the binary logic of sexual difference as described by Lacanian scholarship. Since they sexualize social media use directly in their relationship to enjoyment, apps like Tinder make more legible the relationship between the interface and the interpellative aspects of social media platforms overall. Because I attend to this relationship in terms of the swiping logic of the platform—the choice of swiping Right or Left, the choice between like and dislike, or the choice between affirmation and negation—I want to begin with a discussion about the paradoxes of rational choice that return us to the problematics of neoliberalism and human capital addressed in the previous chapter.

When we are discussing the binary logic of choice, we need to be clear that we are not talking about a simple binary opposition between two positive entities. Rather, we are dealing here with a much more fundamental opposition between affirmation and negation—that is, the relationship between the positive and the negative. This point is important since we are not merely talking about a reduction of a multiple to a simple opposition between two forces: the reduction here is even more radical, since we are simplifying everything down to a singular one. But this one, the affirmative choice, becomes the overdetermining point of articulation, the congealing of the multiple into the one. In Lacanian terminology we are referring, of course, to the Master-Signifier, which holds the place of a determinatively fundamental choice. This choice is that which, on the one hand, produces a normative structure; while on the other hand, it holds open the lack in the very same structure—a space marked by the subject itself. In the swiping logic, an affirmative choice (swipe Right) is at the same time an act of negation-exclusion (swipe Left).

In contrast, the idea of an apparent free choice, as represented in the neoliberal ideology, as in rational choice theory, has in the last few decades become paradoxically tyrannical. As Renata Salecl explains, "Rational choice theory presupposes that people think before they act and that they will always seek to maximize the benefits and minimize the costs of any situation."[1] The logic of rational choice informs much of the entrepreneurial ethic of neoliberal capitalism, as we have seen, according to which every individual is their own "human capital." We must make rational choices and invest appropriately in our human capital in order to best guarantee a profitable return on our "investments." Investing, here, must be understood as spending—that is, as buying: buying things in the market. To increase the value of human capital we must make rational decisions about how to invest, for instance, in our education and in our health care (the costs of which, of course, are increasingly downloaded onto the individual through the mechanism of neoliberal austerity); this includes investing in cultural objects (plays, operas, books, cuisine, and popular culture too) to increase the range of our cultural capital, which is certainly a component element of our ability to grow our influence in terms of social capital, in addition to our social networks—mechanisms that help to enhance our ability to procure a return on our investment in the form of economic capital or income.

Here, we see how the neoliberal ethic—making rational choices about how to invest in our human capital—interpellates us increasingly to self-objectify. That is, neoliberalism induces us to treat ourselves as objects rather than as subjects—not just in terms of the commodification of our labor-power, which only had the effect of alienating us from the products of our labor and the values that we produce. Our bodies and our identities become objects that we need to work on and to produce, not merely as dimensions of our personhood or our (free) agency, but as commodities or as capital that will (if invested properly) bring us higher returns in the form of income. In this situation we can see clearly an overlap between what Georg Lukács discusses in terms of reification and what Foucault dubs "biopower." Power is exerted over the body and the self in the very act of self-regulated and disciplined investment in our human capital, incentivized by the apparently "free" space of the market.

What is particularly interesting is that in this moment of the deeper reification of all human subjecthood—that is, the objectification of the self—we find ourselves in a historical-cultural moment in which *object*hood and posthumanity are becoming the thematics of the critical intellectual gaze. New materialisms and object-oriented ontologies, democracies of objects, and human and nonhuman assemblages have become the primary epistemological approaches employed in critical theories seeking to mediate and to regulate our newfound object-status in a world ravaged by the particularity of human subjecthood. In the age of the Anthropocene, a "do-less" ethic of mere "witnessing" is proposed as means to desubjectify the human so that we might reduce the damage imposed by the human interventions of the previous eras.[2] A strategic anthropomorphism is proposed to reduce the damage of anthropocentrism.[3] The latter, of course, produces a performative contradiction in the sense that no anthropomorphism is possible without the centrality of the human. Such an attempt at eliding the subject in an effort to objectivize and decenter the human, as Russell Sbriglia notes, completely avoids and disavows the core of subjectivity.[4] This is why, as Slavoj Žižek points out, what the New Materialists and object-oriented ontologists call "subject" does not even meet the criteria of the notion of the subject in the sense developed by dialectical materialism.[5]

Perhaps, though, one way to rethink our object-status today—now that we are enjoined to treat ourselves as objects or as objectified substances—is to consider the human vis-à-vis the lack produced by sexuality. This is one of the proposals made by Alenka Zupančič in her book, *What Is Sex?* (2017). Sexuality, according to her, arises precisely because of an inherent deadlock, a limit or impossibility in the existing reality. She echoes in this case claims made previously and contemporaneously with other Lacan scholars, such as Joan Copjec and Žižek.[6] Sexual difference, according to Zupančič, begins as an ontological impossibility that then assigns social identities.[7] Sexual difference expresses the limits to ontological reality, and what we call sexuality is the by-product of our very human attempts to negate this impossibility. Psychoanalysis deals then, according to her, not with the repression of sexuality, but with the repression of the negativity inherent to sexuality.[8] That is, the fact of this negation inherent to sexuality is what ties subjectivity to enjoyment. As she puts it, "What makes the enjoyment related to the drives *sexual* is its relation to the unconscious (in its very ontological negativity) and not, for example, its entanglement and contamination with sexuality in the narrower sense of the term (relating to sexual organs and sexual intercourse)."[9] It is this connection to enjoyment that distinguishes human activity from a merely logical-mechanical rational choice.

As Salecl notes, "Critics of rational choice theory . . . have pointed out that human beings don't always act in their own interest even when they know what it is. People often behave in ways that do not maximize their pleasure and minimize their pain and . . . they even sometimes derive a strange pleasure from acting against their own well-being."[10] Sex and romance are a case in point. Referring to "hook up" dating culture, Salecl writes, "Contemporary dating rituals follow a principle of avoiding intimacy and concentrate on the mechanics of contact."[11] Hookup culture, she says, "reveals much about the perception of sex and love in the time of tyranny of choice."[12] Enjoyment, in this context, "is about taking gratification from the process of hooking—enticing, seducing, trapping, and then discarding—*unhooking*—and searching for a new object. This lack of commitment," she says, "is the new vogue in relationships."[13]

Another view might suggest that the tyranny of choice actually presents us with one of the limit points of the logic of rational investment. On the matter of love, for instance, what if what the tyranny of choice presents us with is an intense anxiety at the presence, not of the lack (which drives desire), but the lack of the lack—that is, of actually finding love at the end of the tunnel. "The erotic deadlock in today's society," according to Salecl, "arises directly from our attempts to eliminate the anxiety that love provokes and to alleviate the uncertainty that will always accompany desire."[14] What we might end up with, then, is an obsessional form of sexual desire, best articulated in the notion of courtly love. As Lacan explains, the man in courtly love is enamored, not with the Woman, but with the pursuit of the unobtainable object.[15] She is desired only insofar as she constantly eludes the man's advances. For the obsessional, the worst fear is actually obtaining the object of desire, since he is concerned with the fact that if he were to obtain what he desires, then it would end up not being as gratifying or as satisfying as he had hoped. The obsessional therefore works to maintain his distance from the desired object. What can this form of the obsessional subject tell us about the form of the swipe logic on Tinder?

Accelerated Intimacy

The overlap between the algorithmic logic of new digital communications technologies and social media and the neoliberal entrepreneurial ethic is one way that contemporary culture has invested in the alleviation of the anxiety brought about by the tyranny of choice. Often, neoliberal managerialisms speak in terms of "efficiencies"—making production and systems more efficient by reducing or eliminating "redundancies." Usually, this type of rhetoric is used to disguise the fact that firms are seeking to increase productivity and profit by finding techniques to make workers work harder for less money. This, of course, is no aberration, but rather is a specific condition of the capitalist mode of production and one of its inherent barriers to accumulation. When we consider the barrier of competition in which capitalists compete with each other for profit maximization, we come to realize that finding "efficiencies" pertains largely to the reduction of costs while simultaneously maximizing productivity. Historically, this has meant either bringing in new labor-saving technologies to increase the productivity of wage-laborers or replacing wage-workers with machines. The language of efficiency thus overlaps with that of mechanization and technologization: Taylorism and Fordism.

Time is also a barrier to profitability.[16] It is necessary for firms to continuously find ways to accelerate the process, to increase rates of productivity, circulation, returns, and reproductivity above those of competitors. Efficiency is therefore also tied to an acceleration of the process, a shrinking of time via a shrinking of spaces of circulation, or what David Harvey has called a "time-space compression."[17] And—why not—under conditions of neoliberal romance, consider sex and dating apps in the same way? What does it look like when we conceive of sex and romance along similar lines of efficient rational choice?

In their discussion of Tinder, David and Cambre note the way that the platform eases the anxiety of choice through the simplification of the "swiping logic."[18] They identify acceleration as one of the primary features of this reduction of choice into a simple binary: swipe Right/ swipe Left—affirmation/negation. Apps like Tinder, they write, "reduce options to the strictly yes/no binary as part of the function of the swipe logic."[19] Speed, they say, is intentionally encouraged by design. Such a simplification, they claim, enables a more efficient form of intimacy. Whereas in traditional dating, people concern themselves with the time required to pause and reflect, in order to sort out their feelings, with Tinder the algorithm takes care of these barriers, easing anxieties by overcoming the direct obstruction of rejection. As they put it, "The swipe logic is based on acceleration as a way of controlling contingency and indeterminacy."[20] This view of accelerated intimacy is developed and portrayed in the *Black Mirror* episode, "Hang the DJ."

At the beginning of the episode, which, again, is set in the not-too-distant future like all of the episodes of the anthology series, Amy and Frank meet at a restaurant for what appears to be a blind date. As they introduce themselves to each other, each of them brings out a device that we learn is something similar to a modern-day dating app. The app seems to mimic contemporary dating apps like Tinder. They discuss the fact that the app has a 99.8 percent success rate. The app, though, is capable of telling the couple exactly how long their relationship will last. On their initial meeting, the app tells Amy and Frank that their relationship will last a meager twelve hours. They enjoy their time together, but do not seem too invested in the relationship given the very short amount of time they have. Afterward, each of them moves on to new relationships, and each experiences a longer expiration date than the previous relationship. Amy enters into a passionate yet vacuous relationship with another man; in his relationship, Frank and his new partner seem not only not to like each other, they seem instead to despise each other. In both cases, their new relationships only help to return Amy and Frank to their initial choices of each other, demonstrating to them what they will gain or lose by moving on to other relationships.

After these failed relationships, Amy and Frank are once again matched together. They decide this time that they will not look at the expiration date; they will just see where the relationship takes them. After several months in a happy relationship, Frank decides to peek at the expiration date for the relationship. Although, initially, the expiration date appears much longer, the very act of his intervention begins to reduce more and more the amount of time they will have together. By violating their agreement, Frank's act ultimately produces the very same result that occurs when he tells Amy about his infidelity to their pact. The reduced time digitally symbolizes this act of transgression and mistrust. Again, they break up and enter into a series of new relationships.

Finally, each of them receives a notification that their final pairings have been decided, but they are given the opportunity to meet one other previous match for a moment of farewell. Amy and Frank meet each other again, but Amy soon realizes that neither of them has any real memory of their life prior to entering into the matching game. She realizes that the entire scenario is a test and encourages Frank to rebel against the system with her and to attempt to escape the confines of the game. They make it to the outer limit, and upon climbing over the enclosing wall it is revealed to the audience that the entire scenario was a series of simulations testing the number of shared rebellions and transgressions that the couple would enact together. In total, they record 998 out of 1000 transgressions: 99.8 percent. The shot then exits the simulation and enters the real world, where we see the real Amy and Frank meeting each other in real life for the very first time, as The Smiths song, "Panic," plays in the background reciting the line, "Hang the DJ." The real Amy and Frank have used an algorithmic matchmaking dating app to meet each other. What we see is that the entire process of dating, complete with its own time-consuming *in*efficiencies has been filtered out by the algorithmic logic of the app. As one review puts it, "the episode invites us to imagine an app that not only picks our dates for us but also determines how long each of those relationships will be."[21] The episode personifies the data-driven algorithmic logic of desire, which cuts out the anxieties of the missed encounter.

In a way, what the app performs is a model of what Lacan refers to as *lathouses*.[22] As Žižek explains, *lathouses* is Lacan's term for devices that did not exist prior to the scientific intervention into the Real, including all of our most common contemporary digital devices, like mobile smartphones, tablets, and social media platforms.[23] *Lathouses* are those devices that administer pleasure through gadgets, realizing full enjoyment. Gadgets such as these, according to Žižek, are uncanny because "they introduce a logic that fundamentally differs from, and so unsettles, the 'normal' libidinal economy of sexed human beings qua beings of language."[24] Insofar as *lathouses* are today products of capitalism—and tied to the discourse of the capitalist—we see an overlap of a chain of interrelated surpluses: scientific technology as surplus knowledge embodied in gadgets, capitalist surplus value as the commodification of surplus knowledge in gadgets, and surplus enjoyment as the form of libidinal investment procured by these gadgets.[25]

In his discussion of Lacan's fifth discourse, the discourse of the capitalist, Frédéric Declercq, proposes that capitalism is contradictory precisely for commanding investment in objects of libidinal enjoyment, while it is at the same time characterized by a lack of libidinal enjoyment.[26] According to Declercq, "enjoyment does not create a relationship between two subjects. Only love connects a subject to another subject; libido, however, connects a subject to an object."[27] Yet, when it comes to the enjoyment of our digital devices, we should question how the simulation of the romantic relationship—romance, even in the sense of the obsessional form of courtly love—provides a lure for the pursuit of the desired object, which of course is the source of our relationship to our enjoyment. The latter has been the subject of a number of recent narratives in popular culture, including Spike Jonze's *Her* (2013) and Alex Garland's *Ex Machina* (2014), in addition to the "Hang the DJ" episode of *Black Mirror*.[28] We should ask, then, how the love narrative—or the love algorithm—helps to produce the fantasy framework around which our libidinal attachments to our devices are produced.

The "Love" Algorithm

We can respond to this question about the fantasy framework of our libidinal attachment to our digital devices in part by examining the binary logic of the Tinder app and how our acts of choice help to inform and to determine its algorithmic operations. Tinder (at least in its original phase) uses an Elo rating system, a method used to calculate the skill level of a chess player. A user goes up in rank based on the number of likes (swipe Right) she receives, as weighted by the popularity of the swiper. The more likes (or swipe Rights) a user receives from highly ranked users, the higher her score. Tinder then matches users based on similar scores of "desirability." The Elo system has since been improved, but it is still important to understand this ranking system as central to the early development of the app. Once an app reaches a critical mass (like the EdgeRank system previously used by Facebook), then it becomes possible to expand and develop out of the original system.[29] Regardless, the platform itself—its interface—still relies upon the binary logic of the swiping signifier. It is this logic that assigns labels to users and filters them into identifiable types. From this angle we can begin to see how the binary logic of the swipe provides the overdetermining factor for the production of the multitude. It is in fact in the act of choosing and negating that a (Master-)Signifier is put in place that retroactively determines all of our previous determinations. It is in the act of the initial choice that the later multiplicity of choices are determined. To put it in Lacanian terms, the signifier here is what determines the subject for all of the other signifiers; yet at the same time, the signifier is also the one for which all of the other signifiers determine the subject. On the one hand, the signifier marks the subject as a positive entity within the field of the Symbolic order, the chain of signification; on the other hand, this act of choice determines the subject as the lack within the structure as that which is determined by all of the other signifiers.[30] In the act of the choice, the subject reproduces the binary opposition between affirmation and negation of the signifier.

Roberto Simanowski describes this binary logic of the algorithm in similar terms. According to him, "The basic principle of the filter bubble is antagonistic: someone or something belongs or doesn't belong. The opposition connotes inside/outside or us/them thinking at every possible position on the political spectrum. This antagonism," he writes, "is reminiscent of binary code, which is the basis for the internet and every computer."[31] Like binary code—the assigning of values of only 1 or 0 (affirmation or negation)—the swiping logic operates according to a similarly simple reduction of Right and Left. The movement in one direction is the negation of the other, or as Simanowski puts it, "By swiping Left or Right, the attitude is always to pursue one of two possibilities."[32] We choose and affirm one, while necessarily negating the other. This format is also depicted quite well in another segment of the *Black Mirror* series: the choose-your-own adventure film, *Bandersnatch*.

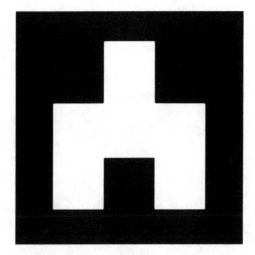

Figure 6.1. Branching symbol from *Black Mirror*

Bandersnatch is a kind of metacommentary on both the series itself and the technological format of social media, the internet, and streaming television platforms like Netflix (which now produces the series). The movie uses the branching symbol (Figure 6.1) first seen in the 2013 episode, "White Bear," to depict the very notion of binary choice. The movie then references itself in the use of this symbol from a previous episode. But the symbol also narrativizes the formal device of choosing that is used in its own plot. At certain junctures in the plot, the audience is given the choice to follow one path or the other. The format of the movie is the same as that depicted in the story, in which the protagonist, Stefan, designs a choose-your-own adventure video game (aren't all video-game designs more or less based upon this kind of ludic element?) based upon the fictitious choose-your-own adventure novel, *Bandersnatch*. There are thus three levels of self-referentiality depicted here: the fictional novel, the video game that Stefan designs based on the novel, and the movie itself as a choose-your-own adventure story narrative. But the format of the movie is also highly intriguing for the way that it generally expresses the binary logic of social media platforms, both on the front end of the interface and on the back end of the programming.

The significance of the choice here also bears upon the dimensions of typification of the user, as well as that of the overdetermination of the signifier. This relationship pertains to that between the multiple and the one. On the one hand, the multiple is generated out of the permutations made by our various choice selections. This, in fact, is how the algorithm learns from the patterns of the user. As John Cheney-Lippold explains, algorithms categorize users based on measurable types.[33] As we make choices and selections, social media algorithms label these selections based upon programmable types—types, we should add, based on already existing frameworks of knowledge (as Stuart Hall called them) and culturally discursive constructs. As Simanowski explains, "Those who write the algorithms that rule the internet on the back end of the interface increasingly determine the way our society functions."[34] Cheney-Lippold adds, "Who we are in terms of data depends on how our data is spoken for."[35] The more we use the platform, the more the algorithm learns to measure these types and to categorize users and their activity based upon shared patterns with other users. This is what allows the algorithm to define the particular content that might be expected to interpellate the user.

As patterns are located and detected, and then operationalized to interpellate individual users, ideal types transform into norms, which are then used to discipline the activity of users.[36] Therefore, the diverse multitude is still provided a discursively constructed (although algorithmically generated) normative structure, which may deviate from what we might think of in terms of—say—the normative structures of patriarchal, heterosexual, or even Eurocentric ideologies. But they establish norms (perhaps even new ones), nevertheless, which still categorize individuals into types. From a business perspective, even, this feature of the choice, the developed permutations, and the development of normative structures for analyzing big data facilitates the further monetization of users' data for the economic logic of the platform to maximize profits. This is all on the *one* hand. On the other hand, we might consider, retroactively, the logical priority of the foundational operation of the choice of the one—that is, of the foundational forced choice of *negation* that imposes upon the structure a foundational Master-Signifier. Returning to the binary swiping logic that Simanowski describes, we can see how this pattern follows in a way that is similar to the logic of the Lacanian algorithm of the signifier.

The Lacanian Algorithm of the Signifier

We can blame the interface's back-end 1/0 binary, according to Simanowski, for the polarization trend on its front end, "insofar as the computer's operational logic aims to organize information into databases, and reduce opinions to the either-or of a like or a dislike button."[37] "The consequences of eliminating complexity," he writes, "are highly political, but it is rehearsed in every interaction."[38] Despite the reduction of complexity into simplicity that we find here, the very logic of the front end of the interface, which, as Louis-Paul Willis notes, is a space of mediation and communication akin to language giving structure to desire,[39] and of the back end of the algorithm still indicates something precise about the very discursive structure of phenomenal reality. This operation is the very same as the overdetermining principle of the Lacanian Master-Signifier, which is imposed, not simply by the selection of some affirmative choice, but as the result of an active negation: of a "forced choice" that says "this is not that." This, according to Zupančič, is how the unconscious is formed through repression, "*as the signifying form* pertaining to discursivity as such."[40] As she puts it, "The unconscious (in its very form) is the 'positive' way in which the ontological negativity of a given reality registers in this reality itself."[41] We might say that we are dealing similarly with the front-end interface of conscious subjecthood, and with the back-end form of the subject of the unconscious—as Clint Burnham has suggested, Freud's texts provide a theory *avant la lettre* of how we relate to the internet: "a relating that perhaps has to do not only with how it functions as our writing machine but also with memory."[42] The unconscious of the internet, he writes, "is due to how the algorithm works"[43]—that is, "our clicks and links and likes move us around, via our pleasures or desires."[44] Yet the algorithm only functions insofar as the user engages in an initial act of choice. It is, in fact, in the primordial forced choice of the subject to enter the field of the Symbolic that we discover the foundational moment of the formation of the unconscious through a simultaneous act of negation, which the subject then continues to repeat as part of its own continuous engagement with its desire as its mechanism for accessing enjoyment.

The formation of the subject of the unconscious is therefore informed by a foundational decision. As Žižek explains, "not only is there no decision without exclusion (that is, every decision precludes a series of possibilities), but also the act of decision itself is made possible by some kind of exclusion: something must be excluded in order for us to become beings which make decisions."[45] This logic explains the Lacanian forced choice: there is a primordial exclusion that grounds choice as such at a fundamental level. I must make an initial choice, which begins with a negation, an exclusion, which therefore grounds my very ability to make choices. According to Zupančič, this gap, this positive point of negation that *is* the unconscious is "what distinguishes knowledge from information or data."[46] Sexuality, then, she explains, is closely related to the unconscious and to repression as negation because of its paradoxical ontological status, manifested as a limit to knowledge.[47] Sexuality exists as the contradiction of the Symbolic and appears in the place of a missing signifier (*jouissance*). Sexuality is the placeholder of the missing signifier.[48] Žižek explains this tie between the signifier and the sexual relationship via a detour through Lacan's discussion of the *cogito*.

In *For They Know Not What They Do*, and in *Tarrying with the Negative*, Žižek looks at two moments in Lacan's investigation of the Cartesian *cogito ergo sum*, "I think, therefore I am." Lacan divides the statement into two components: "I think" and "I am." Lacan therefore creates a division between being and thought, and the subject is forced to choose between the two as part of its condition of entry into the field of the Symbolic order. This, therefore, becomes a foundational forced choice for the subject. As Žižek notes, Lacan has two different lines about the forced choice and the division between being and thought. In Seminar XI, Lacan claims that the subject is forced to choose thought and that the consequence is a loss of being. However, in Seminar XIV, the subject is forced to choose being, relegating thought to the status-position of the unconscious: "I *am* where *it* thinks." According to Žižek, neither the former nor the latter takes precedence over the other. Instead, each should be read according to the two opposed logics of the masculine and the feminine in the sexual relationship.[49]

The difference between the masculine and feminine logics of sexuation has to do with the relation of each to signification. On the masculine side of the Lacanian logics of sexuation, the universal function implies the existence of an exception (all X are submitted to the universal function F; there is at least one X that is not submitted to the universal function F). The masculine logic is one of a finite, limited universal bearing upon the logic of the phallic Master-Signifier. The masculine logic is oriented to the phallus as the signifier of symbolic castration: the choice of the affirmative signifier that negates castration as the lack that *is* the subject ($ in Lacanese). Here, the forced choice is that of *being*, the choice of the signifier, relegating thought to the position of the unconscious. On the feminine side, a particular negation implies that *there is no exception* (not all X are submitted to the function F; there is no X that is not submitted to the function F). According to Zupančič, "Woman" inscribes the problem of division and split into the world of homogeneity. The exclusion of "Woman" is the exclusion and repression of the split or lack as such.[50] Whereas in the masculine logic, the forced choice is that of being, in the feminine logic, the forced choice is that of thought at the cost of being; and it is for this reason that, according to Lacan, *la femme n'existe pas*. Here, it is not merely that the masculine subject chooses the signifier, while it is negated by the feminine subject. The point is that both are oriented toward the phallic signifier in an antagonism that arises precisely because of the very ontological gap in reality—or the Lacanian Real. It is in this way that the binary logic of the algorithmic signifier, the binary logic of the swipe, reflects the same ontological conundrum as the sexual relationship. But what, then, of the intersection between these two parallel logics—that is, the intersection between sexuality in the Lacanian register and the logic of desire in the social media algorithm? How does the swiping logic of the algorithmic signifier reflect the binary logic of the sexual difference?

The Signifier Falls into the Signified

As Zupančič describes it, the signifier "is the algorithm that disorients the drive by cutting off the well-established routes of its satisfaction."[51] This, we might say, is what marks the principal difference between biological sex (or sexual intercourse) and sexuality in the realm of culture— that is, in the realm of human subjectivity. Human sexuality, in other words, occurs at the intersection between nature and culture, or between biology and discursivity. In her reply to Judith Butler, Copjec identifies a significant difference between those who theorize sex in terms of an ultimately essentialist or dogmatic view—the biological determinist view that "biology is destiny"—and what she refers to as the sceptical view of social constructionist theorists of sex, such as Butler—sex as a discursive construct.[52] What the logic of the Lacanian signifier indicates is that the latter is significantly more accurate, but nevertheless still has an effect in the Real. It is not, according to Zupančič, that nature is a product of discourse, but that discourse can have an effect in the Real. This is how the signifier falls into the signified.[53] The signifier falls into the signified insofar as discourse is capable of changing and therefore impacting nature. Sex becomes an object of discourse, but insofar as this happens, discourse has the ability to make an impact upon nature itself, thereby moving beyond and negating simple biological determinism. Likewise, in the Marxist sense, insofar as the base may determine the superstructure, revolutionary class consciousness makes possible the negation of the base.

A parallel example could include something like climate science. "Environment" becomes an object in discourse, but it is not merely a discursive construct in the abstract sense that there is no nature outside of discourse. However, by becoming an object of discourse, science has the ability to impact nature and change it by doing so. We have seen, of course, the impact of human industrial activity, a product of science, upon nature, causing pollution, environmental degradation, and climate change. Knowing this, however, means that we can make climate change an object of scientific discourse in order to impact nature, but also to mitigate and perhaps to negate the damage caused by human intervention—not by negating the human or by becoming *post*human, but precisely by allowing culture to intervene in nature, which after all is inevitable, regardless, as long as human subjects roam the earth. We can locate the subject, therefore, at the limit points of discourse, or in its gaps. As Zupančič puts it, "If language, discourse, or structure were consistent ontological categories, there would be no subject."[54] However, it is at the same time through the inscription of the signifier into our nature (the signifier falls into the signified) that the symbolic castration of the subject is marked: the choice of affirmative being over and above the negation of thought.

Žižek describes this forced choice of being in the following terms:

> What we have here is the fundamental Lacanian paradox of a being founded upon misrecognition: the "unconscious" is a knowledge which must remain unknown, the "repression" of which is an ontological condition for the very constitution of being. The being chosen by the subject has of course its support in *fantasy*: the choice of being is the choice of fantasy which procures frame and consistency to what we call "reality," whereas the "unconscious" designates scraps of knowledge which subverts this fantasy-frame.[55]

This is how, according to Zupančič, enjoyment modifies the nature of natural needs.[56] By following the logic of desire, the subject chooses being over thought, negating its lack—the ontological lack of the Real—and thereby introduces a signifier into the constitution of reality and into the constitution of its nature. Or, to put it in terms developed more recently by Reza Negarestani, the choice of the signifier imposes structure itself as the very register of intelligibility.[57]

What we call the unconscious is the remnant of the act of negation brought about by a forced choice that produces a determinative structure in language, giving order to consciousness. Such a structure is always marked by a gap, and this is what allows us retroactively to critique the structure, by imposing something new. With every negation of a previous structure a new one is affirmed, creating a wholly new normative order.[58] History is, after all, the dialectical affirmation of the new arising out of the negation of the old. Thought is impossible without the negation of an imposed structure. But the negation of the old is still the affirmation of the new. As Negarestani puts it, "only by revising existing norms through norms that have been produced is it possible to assess norms and above all evaluate what it means to be human."[59] This is what raises the feminine logic of sexuation in Lacan's schema above the masculine logic at the ethical level: by choosing thought over mere being, the feminine logic makes possible the negation of the existing structure.

The obsessional masculine logic is always in pursuit, driven by the elusive object of desire. He always misses it because he is too busy chasing it; whereas the hysterical feminine logic produces new knowledge by constantly bombarding the Other with the question: *ché vuoi*? "What do you want from me?" "What am I to you?" We might say, then, that the masculine subject is one of desire, while the feminine subject is one of drive.

For the subject oriented toward the affirmation of the signifier, the fantasy framework is always one of the missed opportunity. I make a choice, but I retroactively fantasize about the choices I did not make: "What if that other partner would be better, or what if my life as a single person, with absolute individual freedom, would be much more relaxed?" "What if I've missed opportunities to have all of these other affairs?" "If not for my decision to be with my partner, maybe I could have all the greatest sex in the world." This is ultimately the neurotic position of the obsessional. Through the framework of the fantasy, the subject remains caught in an act of repetition, whereby the drives aim at repeating satisfaction through negativity, which can be repeated by repeating surplus satisfaction (the missing signifier).[60]

But according to Žižek, this distinction between affirmation and negation, between the obsessional masculine logic and the hysterical feminine logic, can be viewed in terms of the subject's relationship toward its desire. The reversal of desire into drive, he claims, "can also be specified apropos of choice: at the level of the subject of desire, there is a choice—inclusive of the fundamental forced choice—that is, the subject *chooses,* while we go on to the level of drive when the act of choice is inverted into *se faire choisir,* 'making-oneself-chosen'."[61] How, in the context of the swiping logic of the algorithm, might the subject make the self of the subject chosen? Psychoanalysis has a name for this and its name is love!

"Hang the DJ" as Radical Love

Again, as Declercq notes, enjoyment (libido) only connects a subject to an object; only love, he reminds us, connects a subject to another subject. Žižek's solution to the dilemma posed by the *lathouses*—the gadgets invested with libidinal energy, including dating apps like Tinder—is a return to a variation on one of his oldest models of fantasy formation: an old Australian beer advert. The advertisement begins with the old story of the beautiful princess who kisses a frog, who then transforms into a handsome prince; but when the prince kisses the beautiful princess, she turns into the bottle of beer. For Žižek, the underlying message of this advert is that the fantasy proper to the scenario would be one of the frog embracing the bottle of beer, while the happy couple moves on with their relationship. In the updated version of this example, Žižek uses the idea of the "stamina training unit" (STU)—an artificial, plastic vagina that can be used for male masturbation. He says, instead, that what we should prefer to do is insert a vibrator dildo into the STU, so that the couple can then forgo the dilemma of the sexual relationship. They can, instead, go off, have coffee or dinner, and truly fall in love.[62] Love, as Alain Badiou puts it, "really is a unique trust placed in chance."[63]

The paradox of love, however, is that, as Mladen Dolar notes, it cannot simply be prescribed to the subject as in the commandment to love one's parents or to love one's nation.[64] Love cannot be the product of a forced choice; in cases in which love is prescribed there is actually no choice at all. We do not choose the contingent circumstances of who our parents are or where we are born. However, the choice of falling in love is also not a mere matter of freedom, as in the rational choice to love someone. We are back at the split between desire and drive, in such a way that in desire we chase the chosen object, and in drive we ourselves are made chosen. But in the act of chasing after the desired object—as in the Lacanian ethical motto, "do not give way with regard to your desire"— through our ongoing activity of negation cum affirmation, that this is not that, that that is not *it*, we produce and open the space of subjectivity, for the thought to take precedence over being. It is in this sense in particular that I agree with Zupančič that there can be no serious materialism without the subject.[65]

This, perhaps, is what makes the "Hang to DJ" episode of *Black Mirror* so compelling. Despite the fact that we learn in the end that the characters were really just personifications of the algorithm—or perhaps cloned replicas, simulations, or even forms of artificial intelligence (the narrative precedence of which is seen in the "White Christmas" episode of the series)—we are moved by their act of rebellion, of their shared negation of the system. After series upon series of bad romantic and sexual relationships, Amy and Frank decide to take a "leap of faith" together. They end up, as Todd McGowan puts it, privileging their lover's satisfaction over their own, without in any way expecting a return on one's "investment" (as Lacan famously put it, love means giving what you don't have),[66] and in doing so they translate difference into contradiction, giving it privilege as an affirmative ontological position.[67] Love is that which, in other words, makes possible a separation from our objectal devices, opening up the possibility for a revolutionary subjectivization.

It is tempting in our new media age, in combination with the desire to reduce the agency of human subjectivity to a merely equivalential level as that of the nonhuman world—of the object world—as is the case in some variants of New Materialism and Object-Oriented Ontologies—to establish our interactions via media and information communications technologies as human or nonhuman assemblages.[68] But as Zupančič indicates, "By (im)modestly positing the subject as a more or less insignificant point in the universe, one deprives oneself of the possibility to think, radically and seriously, the very 'injustice' (asymmetry/contradiction) that made one want to develop an egalitarian ontological project in the first place."[69]

The swiping logic of the signifier establishes the necessary appearance for the lure of our desire. We reinscribe the signifier into the signified with every (forced) choice that we make. In this way, the very act of decision, of choosing, retroactively reproduces the very form of the binary opposition (affirmation or negation) that those who concern themselves with the "tyranny of the signifier" seek to avoid. Nevertheless, it is only when we follow the path of our desire far enough to the end that we realize that we (the subject) are chosen by the very contingency of love, and it is only then that the system itself is negated, thereby affirming the possibility of the radically new. There is, according to Žižek, no universal formula for the sexual relationship.[70] Universality as such is negative, the product of a failure; further, in order to offset this failure, love must rest, not merely in passionate (even digitally mediated) affairs, but in a radical trust placed in chance: to act—to choose—without any (rational or efficient) guarantees.

Conclusion

The End of Social Media, or, Accelerate the Metaphor?

When I think about the form of social media, I am sometimes driven to recall something I once read by T.J. Clark about the semiotics of Jackson Pollock's splattered paint. Pollock's work is sometimes daunting to vernacular appreciation. We look at the paintings and think to ourselves, "gee, I coulda done that!"[1] But what strikes me about the paint drippings is the form they take at the moment of their arrival on the art scene. That is to say that abstract expressionism is very much at the forefront of the postmodern to the degree to which it relegates the role of the signifier to the margins, not unlike the digital infoglut. The unformed mass of the splattered paint can be read as the striking against the "tyranny of the signifier," as the suture that ties together the field of meaning as represented in the painting. But then, what about the interpretation or the translation? The sense that we may possibly deterritorialize to the end without any kind of reterritorialization of the signifier, for me at least, misses the point that any kind of criticism, any form or structure, can only ultimately be criticized and intuited via the active agency of another new signifier. I will provide another example.

Denis Villeneuve's *Arrival* (2016) tells the story of a linguist, Louise (Amy Adams), who is recruited by the US Army to communicate with a race of aliens that have recently landed on Earth. The difficulty in this project is the fact that the alien language is a written one, and therefore the first barrier to be broken down in establishing communication is the realization that a separation exists between the verbal sounds made by the aliens (their apparent speech) and the written form of their communication. The form of communication used by these aliens—the heptopods, as they are called in the film—gives privilege to the written, a fact that might make even Jacques Derrida somewhat giddy. Once she breaks the code, Louise discovers that her immersion in the heptopod practices of signification allows her to experience reality in wholly new way. Thinking through the form of the heptopod hieroglyphics allows her to transcend the experiences of linear time, and instead she comes unstuck in time, just like Vonnegut's Billy Pilgrim, or the schizo in Jameson's postmodernism, able to move freely, back and forth, between past, present, and future. But, then again, we shouldn't neglect the role of the master code itself, which is the first moment of translation between her English and the heptopod's native language.

In order for there to be any original moment of translation there has to be, in other words, an initial referent against which all of the others may be defined. What is required, in other words, is a foundational, and even universal, Master-Signifier that makes possible all of the subsequent work of translation. We could say that it is this foundational Master-Signifier that begins the process of communication, since it is that which defines all of the other signifiers for the subject. We can see, then, in *Arrival*, a kind of dualism of the semiotics of translation, the reference back to the Master-Signifier giving substance to intercultural communication, and the castigating of the signifier—just like the ink blots in Pollock—in such a way that there appears to be a much more fluid and monistic sense of being that is unhinged, unstuck in time, just like the postmodern breakdown of the signifying chain or the demise of symbolic efficiency.

These examples interest me insofar as they parallel the relationship between the utopian vision of the formless matter of the internet and the structuring role of social media as a kind of referent against which the entire terrain of cyberspace is now structured. Just like Louise, who is freed in time because of the new structure of feeling she experiences in the discourse of the heptopods, that experience is still grounded by a foundational limit that informs her experience, even in the background. There is a sense in which the film contrasts a monist or affirmationist sense of time and being with one that appears to rail against the structure. But there is another sense in which the film inherently addresses the reference back to the signifier, insofar as it deals with the dialectics of desire and drive.

Desire, we might say, is linear, based in the linear pursuit of its object. It follows this object logically, linearly, by pursuing and by negating every new object that comes its way. It is constantly driven by an ethic of "this is not that," not unlike the way that the viewer follows the progression in Louise's story. The later chronological moment in Louise's story is made by the film to appear as an initial foundational one. It appears for the audience that Louise is driven initially by the experience of the death of her teenage daughter. We learn only subsequently that this is an event that occurs later chronologically in the story, but at the moment of its occurrence Louise was still fully aware of its inevitability because of her immersion into the atemporality or asynchronicity of the heptopod language. So while our enjoyment of the film is driven by our desire to see through to the conclusion, the narrative is itself structured by the logic of the drive, which becomes atemporal, circulating around the object without ever getting it.[2]

Although Louise knows that her daughter will ultimately die, she still follows through with having her child and accepts this as an inevitability. We might even recognize that her acceptance here goes much deeper at an ethical level in asking the question of whether it is better to have had her child knowing that she will die at a young age, or if it is better, with this knowledge, to have chosen not to have had the child. At the level of the narrative form of the film, the opening plot about the death of Louise's daughter forms for us the foundational referent against which the atemporal dimensions of the film are structured. For me, this is significant because it helps to grapple with the way that every apparent flux, every apparently immanent situation, is still given grounding and structure through the reference to a foundational point of signification. For me, there is a parallel here with the way that digital culture is informed both by an apparently open and abundant terrain of information and by the structuring of our desire through the adoption of a foundational signifier. "Social media," for me, operates both as the metaphor that gives structure to the flow of digital information and as our way of perceiving it, but it also structures our information today, technologically, through the design of the platform and the algorithmic apparatus in a much more concrete way.

Affirmation and Negation, between Immanence and Transcendence

I have tried, in *Algorithmic Desire*, to articulate through practice and through demonstration a "New Structuralist" approach to the interpretation of social media. This is a project that, on the one hand, embraces a conception of structure that emphasizes the role of a lack or a gap in the structure, as well as the constitutive role of this lack or gap in the forms of subjectivization; on the other hand, it seeks a renewal of a kind of structuralism that departs from the hegemony of immanentist, New Materialist, and posthumanist conceptions of social media. What I have called a "New Structuralism" is one that has been inspired by the work of Lacanian scholars, such as the Slovenian school (Mladen Dolar, Alenka Zupančič, and especially Slavoj Žižek), and others, including Todd McGowan, who emphasize the role of a lack or a gap in the structure. These theorists, too, draw out the ideas in Lacan to better develop some of the most emancipatory aspects of Hegelian dialectics, particularly the Hegelian emphasis on negation, negativity, and contradiction. This is a point articulated best by Žižek early on, when he writes in *The Sublime*

Object of Ideology that far from being the philosopher of resolving contradiction, Hegel is one who addresses the constant inevitability of contradiction. What he calls Absolute Knowing is, according to Žižek, a subject position that finally accepts contradiction as inevitable.[3] This, too, is the point that McGowan makes in his recent book, *Emancipation After Hegel*. McGowan argues that every attempt to evade contradiction ultimately is still driven toward it.[4] This dimension of contradiction is only fully graspable when we conceive its position at the limits of reasoning within the realm of the Symbolic; in other words, contradiction as Real is only realizable at the limits of the structure. For me, this is how we need to grasp the role of lack in the New Structuralism. Lack, gap, and contradiction are what forever prevent the totalization of the structure or its harmonious closure as a whole. There is, as McGowan puts it, always a hole in the whole.

The New Structuralism emerges from, and is perhaps better aligned with, the ramifications of the transcendental turn in Kant, as opposed to the line of immanence and monism that develops from Spinoza and Nietzsche that leads up to Foucault and Deleuze, as Benjamin Noys identifies.[5] While the former remain bound to an ethics of negation—freedom, as McGowan explains, is the human subject's ability to negate its own conditions and determinations (biological or cultural)—the latter are best represented as thinkers of affirmation. According to Žižek, the difference between the affirmationist and immanentist position and the transcendental position—or more appropriately for him, the dialectical one (specifically the difference between Deleuze and Hegel)—pertains to that between flux and gap. As he puts it, "the ultimate 'fact' of Deleuze's transcendental empiricism is the absolute immanence of the continuous flux of pure becoming, while the 'ultimate fact' of Hegel is the irreducible *rupture* of/in immanence." For Hegel, the gap between phenomena and the ground of phenomena "is a secondary effect of the *absolutely immanent* gap of/in the phenomena themselves."[6] The difference that Žižek expresses is one that sees, on the one hand, the imposition of structure (that is, the "tyranny of the signifier") as itself hindering the free flow or flux of becoming, and, on the other hand, the inevitability of the structure determined by the articulation of a signifier that retroactively inscribes itself into the material through our very act of choice. Every affirmative choice, as we saw in the previous chapter, is also, at the same time, one of negation; the split here arises, as Žižek notes, out of a rupture *in immanence*. Deleuze, as he sees it, does not grasp the gap in immanence. Hegel's lesson is thus that "immanence generates the spectre of transcendence because it is already inconsistent in itself."[7]

What Noys, then, refers to as "Accelerationism" takes its point of departure from the position of immanence found in theorists like Foucault and Deleuze—the latter, especially, insofar as in his work with Guattari on capitalism and schizophrenia there is a project to roar *through* capitalism in order to realize the unlimited pursuit of becoming. The accelerationist project is immanentist insofar as it finds its logic—its radical logic—in the process of accelerating the current system to its limits (to its breaking point), rather than in identifying the internal limit that already exists within it; instead of accelerating we need to pump the brakes. This is a position that for me defies the kind of negativity I have proposed as a dimension of the New Structuralism (as opposed to the New Materialisms). For me, the insistence upon the negative adds an important ethical dimension to the extent that it provides a platform for the agency of the subject. As Noys puts it, negativity is "the condition for re-articulating a thinking of agency."[8] The subject, after all, exists in the place of the gap or the lack in the structure.

Social Media and the Tyranny of the Signifier

This difference between the affirmationist and dialectical positions is important for me since, within the domain of critical social media studies, and within the larger field of critical media, communications, and technology studies, it appears as though both Foucault and Deleuze have got the upper hand and have become the hegemonic figures of influence. This seems to make sense when we consider the range of questions that concerns us with regard to social media. The discourse on social media is full of questions and concerns about surveillance and discipline, control and manipulation. In the field of Lacanian cultural and media scholarship, especially as it relates to new and social media, only a handful of scholars have dared to deviate from this standard.[9]

Through the case studies presented in this book, I have tried to show how the New Structuralism inspired by the Hegelian Lacanians offers us more than simply an interpretation of social media; it also shows us how the interpretation of social media teaches us something more broadly about the dominant form of consciousness, and therefore the dominant ideology of twenty-first-century capitalism. So, I would now like to attempt to tie together some of these threads before moving on to some concluding thoughts, including some final responses to the theories I have argued against throughout this book.

I have argued that the emergence of social media needs to be historicized precisely within the context of the years just prior to and in the immediate aftermath of the financial crisis of 2008. But the crisis, too, I would argue, has to be understood within the context of the postmodern culture. My reading of postmodernism relies heavily on Fredric Jameson's, which sees the fight against totalization on the Left, and the claims about the end of history on the Right, as by-products of transformations in the political economy of capitalism, from the Fordist moment of the social welfare state, to the post-Fordist moment of neoliberalism and finance-dominated capital. The arrival of the internet in the 1990s, and the utopianism about it as a kind of formless matter, needs to be registered in this context. If we read the formless form of the internet according to the politics of the postmodern, then we can begin to understand in it a materialization—a moment of fulfillment—of the antifoundational politics of the postmodern.

If we consider the arrival of the postmodern as the coming to fruition of a movement that began with the structuralist critique of humanism, and then the subsequent poststructuralist critique of Marxism, and then the final unhinging of structure (the rhizome or the network), subject (the "death of the subject"), and history (the "incredulity toward metanarratives"), as the only ethics remaining for a politics against the "tyranny of the signifier," then we can see the internet and the digital culture of the 1990s as a utopian moment of the slow dissolution of the human subject in favor of a new posthumanism and a New Materialism that fully opposes any mention of structure, which is deemed to be inherently oppressive. The network dimension of the internet did in this way appear to realize the fulfillment of this project, in which even in Baudrillard's hyperreality, we find an unformed mass of information without any foundational referent that could give it form. The internet appeared even as the formal coming to fruition of the affirmationist, immanentist, and accelerationist project for increased deterritorialization. From this perspective, then, social media has only disrupted this potential. As I have argued, social media, both rhetorically as well as aesthetically (at the level of representation) and technologically (at the level of the platform and the algorithm), concerns the territorializing operation of resituating the internet back into the dynamics of neoliberal capitalism. Social media has been the means of bringing back lack and scarcity where, from the immanentist perspective, there would otherwise be formless abundance.

However, what we see, beginning with Laclau and Mouffe, is the fact that every social formation is always and necessarily split by antagonisms. Society, for them, is an impossible object of discourse because it can never become, on its own, a totalized whole. As McGowan argues, it is due to the inherent necessity of contradiction that no social formation can ever be completely closed, and that every attempt at doing so ultimately ends up reproducing tyranny and oppression. Just as the signifier can appear tyrannical in its slicing and suturing operation, so too can the effort to bypass and avoid all thought and practice of contradiction emerge as tyrannical. The emergence of social media is, from this perspective, not merely the development of a tyrannical means to better protect capitalism against democracy found in the burgeoning new digital public sphere. It is, rather, the consequence of horizontalist attempts to bypass the centrality of contradiction—let me explain.

Despite appearances, the efforts of the Left to evade arborescent structures, as Deleuze and Guattari call them, are not unlike the incessant self-revolutionizing of capitalist development. From its earliest days in the wake of a rising modernism, capitalism has had to constantly find ways to self-undermine as a mechanism of its own self-propulsion toward ever-expanding profits. Capital, as we all know by now, is itself the limit to capitalist production, as Marx tells us in the third volume of *Capital*. This why the capitalist drive toward development overlaps with the modernist ethic in art to "make it new." Modernism must constantly discard with the old in order to create the new. This serves both the art world and the world of capital. The efforts of the Left to rid us of authority and structure, too, like the capitalist dialectic of development, must constantly struggle with the actual in order to realize the virtual or the potential. This is why I claim that efforts to democratize the internet into a kind of rhizomatic structure misses the key insight of the New Structuralists that every attempt to deterritorialize is *itself* part of the project toward reterritorialization. Deleuze and Guattari may claim that deterritorialization is always necessarily and subsequently followed up by a kind of reterritorialization, but my claim is that radical and emancipatory criticisms are themselves a component part of such reterritorializations, and therefore they are attached to the production of the new through the negation of the old. As Andrew Culp puts it, "in the time since the 1972 publication of *Anti-Oedipus*, capitalism has embraced its schizophrenia through neoliberalism."[10]

Social media, I claim, emerged more or less as the capitalist incorporation of the leftist project toward increased rhizomatic democratization. While fighting the tyranny of the signifier it unwittingly (or perhaps even unconsciously) helped to develop the new one. "Social media" names this new signifying structure of the internet. But also, and more importantly, I claim, the concept of social media has become useful for us in our efforts to understand the dominant ideology today and the dominant form of consciousness, but also the manner in which we enjoy—that is, our relationship to our desire. This has been for me what has been most insightful about Jodi Dean's interpretation of "communicative capitalism." But, taking this point further, we need to consider how by imposing this signifier, the metaphor of social media, we are now more capable of seeing, by way of *its own* contradictions, the contradictions in the term itself (the social in social media), the contradictions that are present in the dominant, neoliberal capitalist ideology, and the form of its conscious self-affirmation.

The Social Media Big Other

It is important that Dean reads communicative capitalism against the background of the apparent "decline of symbolic efficiency," as she calls it, drawing on Žižek. As I have argued, this idea of the decline (or demise, as Žižek says) of symbolic efficiency follows closely upon Jameson's reading of postmodernism using the Lacanian formula for psychosis as the breakdown of the signifying chain. These formulae are significant for a number of reasons. First, they express the views on the Left that we can no longer understand history and subjectivity from the perspective of grand metanarratives. Further, the demise of symbolic efficiency suggests that, on the one hand, we are no longer able to understand the role of ideology as a mediating factor of power since it implies an inherent bias on the part of the speaker, suggesting that they (the speakers) are the ones who know the truth of the situation; also, on the other hand, because of this dissolution of the theory of ideology, it becomes increasingly difficult to identify a substantial Other who is in possession of power and authority. The latter trend concerns the Lacanian question of the existence of the big Other, the Symbolic order as the mechanism regulating our identifications with others and with ourselves. The demise of symbolic efficiency also parallels the assertion of the Right regarding the end of history, and the belief that we have reached its limit with the victories of liberalism and capitalism. Because, according to Dean, it appears that no one believes any longer in the existence of the big Other–and that symbolic efficiency is no longer the measure for our relationship to our subjecthood and our enjoyment–power today, according to her, operates through the circuits of drive rather than desire. For her, communicative capitalism thus describes the way in which digital culture, and social media more specifically, inscribes us into the matrices of capitalist exploitation through subjectivizations that rely on intensities of drive.

In contrast, I have argued that the problem today is less one of an avowed nonexistence of the big Other. Instead, the problem for us today, particularly in the historical context of postmodern capitalism, is that we prefer to disavow the fact of the other's nonexistence because it better protects for us the ability to garner enjoyment. The problem, as Mark Fisher has described, is one of "capitalist realism," which is the term he uses to describe the cynical attitude of the postmodern subject. Cynicism is inherently perverse since it operates by acknowledging failure, but nevertheless disavows this fact in order to go on enjoying. Social media, and the form of the social media network (friends lists, followers, and so on), exists as a materialization of the constitution of a substantial big Other for the subject of twenty-first-century capitalism. It has become the model by which we experience the agency of the big Other, to whom we are constantly connected in our efforts to satisfy its desire. Our desire is the desire of the social media big Other, and for this reason, too, social media models the dominant form of contemporary consciousness insofar as it mediates for us more generally our relationship to our desire. Such a mediation, I claim, shows us that perversion is one of the ways in which the dominant form of subjectivity is expressed in twenty-first-century capitalism.

Communicative capitalism, I agree, is the correct formula for understanding how social media tethers us to capitalist ideology and exploitation. However, for me, it is evidence of the point that this occurs as a result of having our desire inscribed into its matrices, rather than through the repetitive circuits of drive. Assuming the latter suggests that we have all already traversed the fantasy, which would mean that we are all already free. Since, as I believe to be the case, we have not yet achieved universal emancipation, we might come to understand this relationship differently. One way of doing so is to examine the manner in which the technological components of social media address us at the level of our desire. We have come to inscribe our desire in a substantial big Other that has been materialized through the network form of social media, but also through the form of the platform aesthetic and the algorithmic logic that works as its lure.

Algorithmic Subjects of Desire

I have argued that the major developments in algorithmic media have to do with their ability to read our desire and to curate this back to us. Algorithms, I have suggested, operate structurally by learning about our patterns of interaction online, and by doing so can develop the most appropriate lures for our attention. They are what drive every new click, every new share; and, with every new choice we are lured into making—every new affirmation that is also a negation—we reproduce ourselves both as subjects and as the structures that give us definition. There is, of course, a political and economic dimension to this, too, insofar as platforms benefit from increased participation. The more we participate on the platform, the more we inscribe information about ourselves into its matrices and databases, the more it learns about the best possible ways to grab our attention. This is what makes social media ideological—it is what makes Dean's concept of communicative capitalism work. The more we participate, the more we contribute to training the algorithm and the platform about how best to interpellate us at the level of our desire. With the development of social media, it turns out that *all* content is "clickbait."[11] But this is also important when we consider the interests involved in luring our attention and our desire. Advertising and marketing are of course a key component here; but we need to consider, too, the political ramifications, when powerful interests are learning the best possible ways to interpellate us ethically and politically through algorithmically tested rhetoric. It appears in this way that the Foucauldian reading of surveillance and the Deleuzian conception of the society of control makes sense. But what each misses is the manner in which subjectivization is a process that logically *precedes* the technological or machinic enslavement. There is no clearer championing of the positions developed by Foucault and Deleuze than that found in the writings of Michael Hardt and Antonio Negri.

In *Assembly*, Hardt and Negri add to their theory of the commons, suggesting that it requires a new concept of the subject or a new process of subjectivization.[12] This, they claim, becomes problematic when we begin to realize that technological developments—developments in automation and artificial intelligence—in the capitalist mode of production are becoming increasingly interwoven with our forms of life and living today. Because of this, rather than simply rejecting technology, they assert the need to begin to conceive new practices of subjectivization "from within the technological and biopolitical fabric of our lives" (Hardt and Negri, 107; see note 10). It is only from this position, today, they claim, that we can even start conceiving of a path toward liberation. This claim has to do with the fact that, as they see it, technology is configuring new subjectivities.

Drawing on Deleuze and Guattari, as well as others, like Lazzarato, Hardt and Negri propose that now, "humans and machines are part of a mutually constituted social reality" (Hardt and Negri, 110). Although there is generally a cultural and social paranoia about the growth and reach of new media and social media, expressed in noir dramas like *Black Mirror*, machines, according to Hardt and Negri—and I here agree with them—"contain the potential for both servitude and liberation" (Hardt and Negri, 110). The problem, as they see it, lies not at the ontological level, but at the political one. As I have argued already, social media platforms and algorithms are not themselves intrinsically positive or negative. Sure, they may contain inherent traits; traits that encourage a particular kind of use. But it is the way in which they are caught up in the class struggle that determines the use toward which they are put. The same platforms and algorithms that now train us to comply with the status quo of consumer capitalism and neoliberalism, if put toward different, more emancipatory uses, could indeed enable more freedom, mobility, and democracy. This is even the sine qua non of the emancipatory project of the accelerationists, with whom I otherwise disagree, but on this point I find their project compelling. But for Hardt and Negri, the liberatory aspect of new technology follows closely upon the conditions of their production.

Every technology, they note, is the concrete result of the entire social network that created it, and not just the CEOs and corporations that own the patent. Technology is what Marx referred to as fixed capital, and it is produced by the social network of cooperating actors that Marx, in the *Grundrisse*, called the "general intellect." Although fixed capital is produced socially by the general intellect, it carries the potential, too, according to Hardt and Negri, to be used antisocially, that is, in the appropriation of surplus value on the side of capital, as well as for purposes of war and destruction. In order to counteract this potential, they suggest that today, "we must immerse ourselves into the heart of technologies and attempt to make them our own against the forces of domination that deploy technologies against us" (Hardt and Negri, 111). In part, our immersion in technology, then, has already taken place in the transition from Fordist factory production toward post-Fordist social production, which as they put it, extends "the primary site of production from the factory to society" (Hardt and Negri, 111). For them, this transformation was constituted through the further development toward technologies of automation.

As they explain, the development of the "social factory," or of "social production" (as opposed to mere commodity production), has been part of a process of capital seeking to re-establish profits that can no longer be garnered through mere factory production. As such, capital "put the social terrain to work, and the mode of production had to be interwoven ever more tightly with forms of life" (Hardt and Negri, 112). This is one reason why, as I have argued, we need to consider the forms of subjectivization and interpellation through social media in the context of neoliberal rhetorics of entrepreneurialism.

On the Terrain of Social Production: Assemblage as Metaphor

In addition to the widespread Foucauldianisms and Deleuzianisms in critical social media studies, there has also been a general sense that our participation on social media platforms enacts a kind of exploitation of labor. As Christian Fuchs has argued, users of social media websites have become prosumer commodities. This claim, drawing on the older notion of the audience commodity, asserts that our use of social media websites constitutes a form of labor, which is exploited by capital. However, this does not consist in the capitalist form of exploitation as explained by Marx. Wage labor alone, according to Marx, is generative of surplus value. Only wage labor is productive of surplus value, while unpaid labor remains unproductive of surplus value. Social media platforms, therefore, exploit users through monetization of data, rather than through capitalist forms of exploitation. However, if we return to the form of social production described by Hardt and Negri, we can come to see social media as a form in which we enact our self-production as subjects of neoliberal capitalism, and therefore as exploited in the broader sense of capitalist relations of production. It is here that I agree in part with someone like Byung-Chul Han, who proclaims that today, "everyone is an *auto-exploiting labourer in his or her own enterprise.*"[13] However, I disagree completely with his claim that because of this, class struggle has disappeared and has instead been transformed into an "*inner struggle against oneself.*"[14] Quite the contrary, I claim. What neoliberal subjectivization has accomplished has been the obfuscation of class struggle through the interpellation of subjects as neoliberal entrepreneurs of the Self. This, too, is another way in which social media helps us to see and to understand the contradictions at the heart of the neoliberal subject, the marketized individual, as "human capital" in the social factory. The production of the Self on social media is the manner in which subjects are reified into the marketized form of the neoliberal individual in competition with others, who are also the measure of one's identity as the social media big Other.

As a second phase, then, in the process toward moving from the factory to the social factory, digitization, as Hardt and Negri note, has helped to spread the technologization of life throughout society, bringing forms of life together with automation. We see this addressed in many contemporary studies of the rapid digitization of our everyday life, from Bernard Stiegler's *The Automatic Society* to Benjamin Bratton's *The Stack.*[15] As Hardt and Negri put it, "the automaton [now] administers and controls society through digital algorithms" (Hardt and Negri, 112). Although machines depend upon human intelligence, human action has, according to them, increasingly adapted to the needs of machines (Hardt and Negri, 112).

Marx showed how, even though this process can increase the short-term profits of capital, in the long term a decrease in the organic composition of capital, that is, waged human labor, measured against an increase in constant or fixed capital, that is, machinery, ultimately leads to crisis. The search for ever-increasing profits forces capital to invest in machinery and lower expenditures on wage labor, even though wage labor is the source of new value production in capital. On the one hand, this shift leads to a greater concentration of wealth on the side of capital; on the other hand, this process leads to a greater decline in the rate of profit. For Hardt and Negri, since they draw more from the *Grundrisse* than from *Capital*, although this process seems to lead to a greater concentration of corporate power, this shift also, they claim, "contributes, subjectively, to strengthening the position of labor." For them, this is because the general intellect is today the "protagonist of economic and social production;" further, according to them, "as production is increasingly socialized . . . fixed capital tends to be implemented into life itself, creating a machinic humanity" (Hardt and Negri, 114). This, for them, shows the emancipatory potential of new, digital media, and in this way their project is a political project that resembles both the accelerationist project—best articulated by Nick Srnicek and Alex Williams in *#Accelerate: Manifesto for an Accelerationist Politics* (MAP) and in their book, *Inventing the Future*—and the Posthumanist and New Materialist conception of the human-machinic assemblage.

Although algorithms exist as examples of fixed capital and can therefore lend themselves well to combating the barriers of labor to the accumulation of profit, they still cannot operate without living human labor. As Hardt and Negri explain, algorithms like Google's PageRank algorithm or Facebook's old EdgeRank algorithm "continually add social intelligence to the results of the past to create an open, expansive dynamic." But in order to do so, algorithms must still be "open to continuous modification by human intelligence." What are often called "intelligent machines," they write, are really just machines that are able to "absorb human intelligence" (Hardt and Negri, 118–119). Machinic subjects are, thus, always part of an assemblage, not unlike their prior conception of the multitude. Since their work on the multitude, Hardt and Negri have envisioned a kind of horizontal appropriation or expropriation of fixed capital through the cooperative power of labor. As they put it, "the increased powers of labour can be recognized not only in the expansion and increasing autonomy of cooperation but also in the greater importance given to the social and cognitive powers of labor in the structures of production" (Hardt and Negri, 117). But, now, the machinic appears to strip away the illusions of an older humanism. The machinic assemblage, they write, "is a dynamic composition of heterogeneous elements that eschew identity but nonetheless function together, subjectively, socially, in cooperation" (Hardt and Negri, 121). Therefore, for Hardt and Negri, when fixed capital is transformed from private property to the common, then "the power of machinic subjectivities and their cooperative networks can be fully actualized" (Hardt and Negri, 123). In this way, assemblages are woven together as part of the ontological basis of the common. Assemblage, like multitude, is the proper metaphor for realizing the possibilities of emancipation against the background of digital capitalism. In contrast, I would now like to conclude with a defence of the social media metaphor.

Toward the Realization of the Social in "Social Media"

On the question of digital automation, one of the chief problems for the Left, according to Nina Power, has to do with the way we discern between those jobs that can be automated and those that cannot.[16] Two types of labor, in particular, that she identifies are care work and the labor of social reproduction. These examples are pertinent, since they help us to see at what point the category of human subjectivity might possibly negate and transcend the assemblage theory of the equality of human and nonhuman objects. Barring outrageous developments in artificial intelligence, it is difficult for us to conceive the ways that care (and even love) might be tethered to the digital democracy, or the democracy of the digital. But this point, too, concerns the manner in which assemblage theory, or something like it, as presented by the categories of machinic enslavement and social subjection, loses sight of the way in which the desiring subject precedes its enslavement in the machine, or even precedes its subjectivization in society. There is a subjective dimension that pertains to desire and enjoyment, the gap or lack in the existing Symbolic structure, that precedes the subject's integration into the logic of the machine. Power proposes that "we would be better off shifting the debate around digital democracy and a new collective subject toward larger and more fundamental questions concerning the commons (virtual and actual), the role of care in our societies, and how we value all the paid and unpaid work that goes into reproducing life at all levels."[17] This, in fact, is something that comes out of our insistence on the social media metaphor.

Unlike the assemblage, the social implied in "social media" is one way that we might conceive the kind of cognitive mapping that might be helpful to develop with regard to the dominant form of consciousness, as we have seen. But at the same time, it helps us to better address the various problems that we have identified about the way that social media facilitates twenty-first-century capitalist practices of exploitation and ideological interpellation. We have seen how social media arises as a way of expressing the desire of the subject, and we have seen the way in which we are lured by its curated content. In the context of neoliberalism, we see, too, that we are the ones that curate content for it, that is, the platform. But through all of this, an implicit question in the background remains: How might we resolve these tendencies in our social media, or at the very least reconcile ourselves toward them? How might we resolve the problem of the expropriated value of our desire for digital democracy?

Some might argue that another media system is possible. Fuchs, for instance, advocates for a commons-based internet.[18] He advocates the need to appropriate the algorithm through various mechanisms, such as capital taxation and the implementation of a public service media system. He proposes, even, the possibility of platform coops, as well as the accelerationist supplement of the Universal Basic Income, as a way to offset the problem of the decline in effective market demand once all the jobs have been replaced by machines.[19] But apart from some of these more utopian proposals for developing an alternative or better social media system, why not adopt an alternative and much more dialectical perspective: Can we adopt the perspective that we cannot begin to improve things with social media by changing social media? In other words, why not begin with social media, as a valence of analysis—that is, to use the social media metaphor as a tool through which we can map the totality of the situation, in order to arrive at . . . what?

Once we begin to conceive the social media metaphor in this way, we arrive at the doorstep of the law and the state, which themselves are structuring facets of our culture in their very form. As Louis Althusser remarks in *On the Reproduction of Capitalism*, the law says that we are all free and equal *legal* persons.[20] This is how, for him, the law interpellates us as subjects. But the law also exists only insofar as it makes possible the function of the relations of production, with regard to property and the contractual relationships of exchange between legal individuals in the market. Law is a function of the relations of production only to the extent that it mentions them nowhere, but makes it everywhere possible for the capitalist mode of production to operate. Our acceptance of the legal ideology, according to Althusser, is a product of our moral interpellations in the ideological state apparatuses. But the problem for us today is that, in the context of the demise of symbolic efficiency, the postmodern break-down of the signifying chain, and the cynical capitalist realism that prevails, the moral code may no longer be the hitch upon which we come to accept the legal ideology, the legal structure, and the framework. Instead, what we have seen is that enjoyment, much more than morality, is that which binds us to the ruling ideology. This is by no mere accident, since it is in the form of the neoliberal shift in the regulations of the market that we come to locate the prevailing consumerist ethic of postmodern culture and its constant injunction to enjoy. Social media has not caused this, but it provides for us a window into understanding the kind of consciousness that has come into being as a result.

We begin to see that social media is a representation of the dominant ideology, of the dominant form of consciousness, because it is largely symptomatic of the existing structure of society: a neoliberal and capitalist society. Social media works as a metaphor for our era because it represents most concretely and reflects the way in which the neoliberal capitalist society sees itself. So we can begin with it, but we cannot then proceed to merely attempt a transformation of our media. Doing so, to use a tired cliché, would merely treat the symptom while allowing the cause to persist. Instead, we need to see how the social media metaphor allows us to consider a path toward transforming social media and our digital culture, beginning with a transformation of the culture and society more generally. It allows us to conceive the very form that makes the existing neoliberal structure currently possible: the form of the law and the state, or, more specifically, the forms of capitalist private property, the commodity form, and the form of civil society, in addition to the prevailing forms of enjoyment.

The oppressive state, according to McGowan, is a function of the state insofar as it is submitted to the interests of the civil society. Instead, an emancipated society, according to him, is one in which the state is submitted to the public service of the people, the interests of universal freedom, and emancipation.[21] There is something of this contained, too, in the metaphor of "social media." When we conceive of social media, it is the former component that takes precedence over the latter. When we enunciate the term, "social media," what this implies is an emphasis upon the social dimensions of interactive communication and democracy. The rhetoric of the "social" in "social media" implies a harmonious, constitutive whole of the social. But as we have seen, the deployment of this image, of a harmonious whole—even in the proposal to make social media fully social—this project is a difficult one given the implicit gap or contradiction in the structure. Nevertheless, by sticking to the social media metaphor (of not giving way to our desire for social media, so to speak), and taking it all the way to its limits, we are able to more clearly appreciate the failures of social media to realize the social, which is also evidence of a failure of the social itself. But sticking to this notion, by seeing it through to the end, we see that social media both exists and does not exist. We see through the contradictions of this notion. And perhaps, the most appropriate way to challenge and to critique social media is by identifying *it*, by claiming it as the correct concept, and by working to see it through to the adequacy of its own notion. It is only by sticking to the social media metaphor that we are made capable of understanding the contradictions and the antisocial dimensions of capitalism. We should not, in other words, be forced to accelerate the system to the point of its ultimate implosion. We should instead impose a structure on society that creates the conditions of possibility for social media to be truly realizable. That is, we need to accelerate the metaphor rather than the system.

Notes

Introduction

1. Harold Innis, *The Bias of Communication* (Toronto: University of Toronto Press, 1999).

2. Raymond Williams, *Marxism and Literature* (New York: Oxford University Press, 1977).

3. On this point, see Matthew Flisfeder, "'Trump'—What Does the Name Signify?; or, Protofascism and the Alt-Right: Three Contradictions of the Present Conjuncture." *Cultural Politics* 14, no. 1 (2018): 1–19. For an excellent reading of Trump's trolling style, see Jason Hannan, "Trolling Ourselves to Death: Social Media and Post-Truth Politics." *European Journal of Communication* 33, no. 2 (2018): 214–26.

4. CCRU, "Swarmachins." In Robin MacKay and Armen Avanessian, eds, *#Accelerate: The Accelerationist Reader*, 2nd ed. (Windsor Quarry, UK: Urbanomic, 2017), 330.

5. Marshall McLuhan, *Understanding Media: Extensions of Man* (New York: Signet, 1964), 36.

6. Neil Postman, *Amusing Ourselves to Death: Public Discourse in the Age of Show Business* (New York: Penguin, 1985).

7. James Bridle, *New Dark Age: Technology and the End of the Future* (New York: Verso, 2018).

8. Bridle, *New Dark Age*, 7.

9. See, for instance, Vincent Mosco, *To the Cloud: Big Data in a Turbulent World* (New York: Routledge, 2014).

10. Timothy Morton, *Hyperobjects: Philosophy and Ecology after the End of the World* (Minneapolis: University of Minnesota Press, 2013). Morton describes hyperobjects as "things that are massively distributed in time and space relative to humans." They are "hyper" "in relation to some other entity, whether they are directly manufactured by humans or not." Morton, *Hyperobjects*, 1.

11. Bridle, *New Dark Age*, 73.

12. Bridle, *New Dark Age*, 75

13. Wendy Hui Kyong Chun, *Programmed Visions: Software and Memory* (Cambridge, MA: MIT Press, 2012), 2.

14. Chun, *Programmed Visions*, 55

15. Chun, *Programmed Visions*, 50

16. Fredric Jameson, "Postmodernism, or, The Cultural Logic of Late Capitalism." *New Left Review* 1, no. 146 (1984): 79–80.

17. Slavoj Žižek, "Marx Reads Object Oriented Ontology." In Slavoj Žižek, Frank Ruda, and Agon Hamza, *Reading Marx* (Medford, MA: Polity, 2018).

18. Andrew Culp, *Dark Deleuze* (Minneapolis: University of Minnesota Press, 2016), 27.

19. Žižek, "Marx Reads Object Oriented Ontology," 17.

20. Žižek, "Marx Reads Object Oriented Ontology," 43.

21. Žižek, "Marx Reads Object Oriented Ontology," 43.

22. Slavoj Žižek, "Afterword: Lenin's Choice." In Slavoj Žižek, ed., *Revolution at the Gates: Selected Writings of Lenin From 1917* (New York: Verso, 2002), 210.

23. Georg Lukács, *History and Class Consciousness: Studies in Marxist Dialectics*, translated by Rodney Livingstone (Cambridge, MA: MIT Press, 1968), 112.

24. Jameson, "Postmodernism," 91–92.

25. Fredric Jameson, *The Cultural Turn: Selected Writings on the Postmodern, 1983–1998* (New York: Verso, 1998), 49.

26. Slavoj Žižek, *Tarrying with the Negative: Kant, Hegel, and the Critique of Ideology* (Durham, NC: Duke University Press, 1993), 145.

27. Fredric Jameson, *Marxism and Form: Twentieth-Century Dialectical Theories of Literature* (Princeton, NJ: Princeton University Press, 1971), 184.

28. Jameson, *Marxism and Form*, 340.

29. Žižek, "Marx Reads Object Oriented Ontology," 44.

30. Lukács, *History and Class Consciousness*, 150.

31. Jacques Lacan, "Appendix II: Metaphor of the Subject." In *Écrits: The First Complete Edition in English*, translated by Bruce Fink (New York: W.W. Norton and Co., 2006), 756.

32. Aldous Huxley, *Brave New World* (New York: Harper Perennial, 1993), 224.

33. Edward S. Herman and Noam Chomsky, *Manufacturing Consent: The Political Economy of the Mass Media* (New York: Pantheon Books, 1988); Robert McChesney, *Rich Media/Poor Democracy: Communication Politics in Dubious Times* (New York: The New Press, 2000).

34. See, for instance, Thomas Allmer, *Critical Theory and Social Media: Between Emancipation and Commodification* (New York: Routledge, 2015); Christian Fuchs, *Digital Labour and Karl Marx* (New York: Routledge, 2014); Derek Hrynyshyn, *The Limits of Digital Revolution: How Mass Media Culture Endures in a Social Media World* (Santa Barbara, CA: Praeger, 2017); and Robert McChesney, *Digital Disconnect: How Capitalism Is Turning the Internet against Democracy* (New York: The New Press, 2013).

35. See Luc Boltanski and Ève Chiapello, *The New Spirit of Capitalism*, translated by Gregory Elliot (New York: Verso, 2007).

36. Mark Fisher, *Capitalist Realism: Is There No Alternative?* (Winchester, UK: Zero Books, 2009), 21–22.

37. Gilles Deleuze, "Postscript on the Societies of Control." *October* 59 (1992): 3–7.

38. Fredric Jameson, *The Political Unconscious: Narrative as a Socially Symbolic Act* (Ithaca, NY: Cornell University Press, 1981).

39. Here, I am adopting an idea that Robyn Flisfeder gets from the film, *Forgetting Sarah Marshall* (2008). Personal communication.

40. Peter Frase, *Four Futures: Life after Capitalism* (New York: Verso, 2016).

41. Andreas Malm, *The Progress of This Storm: Nature and Society in a Warming World* (New York: Verso, 2018), 80.

42. Steven Shaviro, *The Universe of Things: On Speculative Realism* (Minneapolis, MN: University of Minnesota Press, 2014).

43. Jodi Dean, "The Anamorphic Politics of Climate Change." *e-flux journal* 69 (2016).

44. Dean, "The Anamorphic Politics of Climate Change."

45. Dean, "The Anamorphic Politics of Climate Change."

46. Dean, "The Anamorphic Politics of Climate Change."

47. Malm, *The Progress of This Storm*, 112.

48. Malm, *The Progress of This Storm*, 116.

49. W. Oliver Baker, "'Words Are Things': The Settler Colonial Politics of Post-Humanist Materialism in Cormac McCarthy's *Blood Meridian.*" *Mediations* 30, no. 1 (2016): 19.

50. Baker, "Words Are Things," 19.

51. Diana Coole and Samantha Frost, "Introducing the New Materialisms." In Diana Coole and Samantha Frost, eds, *New Materialisms: Ontology, Agency, and Politics* (Durham, NC: Duke University Press, 2010), 5.

52. Benjamin Noys, *The Persistence of the Negative: A Critique of Contemporary Continental Theory* (Edinburgh: Edinburgh University Press, 2010), 1.

53. Noys, *The Persistence of the Negative*, 5.

54. Steven Shaviro, *No Speed Limit: Three Essays on Accelerationism* (Minneapolis, MN: University of Minnesota Press, 2015), 2.

55. Shaviro, *No Speed Limit*, 4–5.

56. Culp, *Dark Deleuze*, 45; see also, Nick Land, *Fanged Noumena: Collected Writings, 1987–2007*, edited by Robin MacKay and Ray Brassier (Windsor Quarry, UK: Urbanomic, 2011). Several of Land's writings relating to Accelerationism are also collected in *#Accelerate: Manifesto for an Accelerationist Politics.*

57. Shaviro, *No Speed Limit*, 14.

58. Shaviro, *No Speed Limit*, 14.

59. Shaviro, *No Speed Limit*, 34.

60. Shaviro, *No Speed Limit*, 41.

61. Shaviro, *No Speed Limit*, 46.

62. Gilles Deleuze and Félix Guattari, *Anti-Oedipus: Capitalism and Schizophrenia*, translated by Robert Hurley, Mark Seem, and Helen R. Lane (Minneapolis, MN: University of Minnesota Press, 1983), 28.

63. Nick Srnicek and Alex Williams, "#Accelerate: Manifesto for an Accelerationist Politics (MAP)." In Robin MacKay and Armen Avanessian, eds, *#Accelerate: Manifesto for an Accelerationist Politics*; Nick Srnicek and Alex Williams, *Inventing the Future: Postcapitalism and a World without Work* (New York: Verso, 2015).

64. Benjamin Noys, *Malign Velocities: Accelerationism and Capitalism* (Winchester, UK: Zero Books, 2014), 21.

65. Noys, *Malign Velocities*, 25.

66. Srnicek and Williams, "#Accelerate," 357.

67. Srnicek and Williams, "#Accelerate," 357.

68. Srnicek and Williams, "#Accelerate," 357.

69. Noys, *Malign Velocities*, 11.

70. Noys, *Malign Velocities*, 9.

71. Noys, *Persistence of the Negative*, 13.

72. Wolfgang Streeck, *How Will Capitalism End? Essays on a Failing System* (New York: Verso, 2017), 9.

73. Streeck, *How Will Capitalism End?*, 10.

74. Slavoj Žižek, *Organs Without Bodies: On Deleuze and Consequences* (New York: Routledge, 2004), 60–61.

75. Bruno Bosteels, "Alain Badiou's Theory of the Subject: The Recommencement of Dialectical Materialism?" In Slavoj Žižek, ed., *Lacan: The Silent Partners* (New York: Verso, 2005).

76. Bosteels, "Alain Badiou's Theory of the Subject," 119.

77. Jameson, *The Political Unconscious*, 36.

78. Jameson, *The Political Unconscious*, 36.

79. Jameson, *The Political Unconscious*, 36.

80. Jameson, *The Political Unconscious*, 35.

81. Bosteels, "Alain Badiou's Theory of the Subject," 128; see also Ernesto Laclau and Chantal Mouffe, *Hegemony and Socialist Strategy: Towards a Radical Democratic Politics*, 2nd ed. (New York: Verso, 2000).

82. Slavoj Žižek, *The Sublime Object of Ideology* (New York: Verso, 1989), 209.

83. Žižek, *The Sublime Object of Ideology*, 208.

84. Mladen Dolar, "Beyond Interpellation." *Qui parle* 6, no. 2 (1993): 78.

85. Žižek, *The Sublime Object of Ideology*, 164; Slavoj Žižek, "The Spectre of Ideology." In Slavoj Žižek, ed., *Mapping Ideology* (New York: Verso, 1994), 22.

86. Slavoj Žižek, *For They Know Not What They Do: Enjoyment as a Political Factor*, 2nd ed. (New York: Verso, 2002), 101.

87. Žižek, *The Sublime Object of Ideology*, 6.

88. Žižek, *For They Know Not What They Do*, 101.

89. Žižek, *For They Know Not What They Do*, 9–10.

90. Karl Marx, *Capital, Volume 3*, translated by David Fernbach (New York: Penguin, 1991), 358.

91. Bruce Fink, "Perversion." In Molly Anne Rothenberg, Dennis Foster, and Slavoj Žižek, eds, *Perversion and the Social Relation* (Durham, NC: Duke University Press, 2003), 38.

92. Žižek, *The Sublime Object of Ideology*, 28–30.

93. Žižek, *The Sublime Object of Ideology*, 49.

94. Žižek, *For They Know Not What They Do*, 21–22.

95. Žižek, "The Spectre of Ideology," 4.

96. Žižek, *Tarrying with the Negative*, 73–74.

97. See Todd McGowan, *Capitalism and Desire: The Psychic Cost of Free Markets* (New York: Columbia University Press, 2016).

98. Slavoj Žižek, *The Ticklish Subject: The Absent Centre of Political Ontology* (New York: Verso, 1999), 247.

99. Judith Butler, *The Psychic Life of Power: Theories in Subjection* (Stanford, CA: Stanford University Press, 1997), 2.

100. Michel Foucault, *The History of Sexuality, Volume 1: An Introduction*, translated by Robert Hurley (New York: Pantheon, 1990), 95.

101. Wendy Hui Kyong Chun, *Updating to Remain the Same: Habitual New Media* (Cambridge, MA: MIT Press, 2017), 40.

102. We need only see the way that reactionary forces on the Right, such as Jordan Peterson, continue to refer to postmodernism as the major culprit of our problems today to see how it is still a driving social, cultural, and political force.

103. Slavoj Žižek, *First as Tragedy, Then as Farce* (New York: Verso, 2009).

Chapter 1

Note to the reader: when the term "social media" appears here in quotation marks, this is to identify the rhetorical and discursive dimensions of the term itself, as opposed to the use of the term without quotation marks, when the term is used to identify the technology and platforms.

1. Slavoj Žižek, *First as Tragedy, Then as Farce* (New York: Verso, 2009).

2. For a sampling of scholarship on these movements, see Christian Fuchs, *OccupyMedia!: The Occupy Movement and Social Media in Crisis Capitalism* (Winchester, UK: Zero Books, 2014); Linda Herrera, *Revolution in the Age of Social Media: The Egyptian Popular Insurrection and the Internet* (New York: Verso, 2014); Keenaga-Yamahtta Taylor, *From #BlackLivesMatter to Black Liberation* (Chicago, IL: Haymarket Books, 2016); Zeynep Tufekci, *Twitter and Tear Gas: The Power and Fragility of Networked Protests* (New Haven, CT: Yale University Press, 2017); and Louis-Paul Willis, "Student Fantasies: A Žižekian Perspective on the 2012 Quebec Student Uprising." In Matthew Flisfeder and Louis-Paul Willis, eds, *Žižek and Media Studies: A Reader* (New York: Palgrave Macmillan, 2014).

3. As Mark Fisher puts it, capitalism is set up to block the "red plenty": "Instead of seeking to overcome capital, we should focus on what capital must always obstruct: the collective capacity to produce, care and enjoy." He adds that "the overcoming of capital has to be fundamentally based on the simple insight that, far from being about 'wealth creation', capital necessarily and always blocks the production of common wealth." Darren Ambrose, ed., *K-Punk: The Collected and Unpublished Writings of Mark Fisher (2004–2016)* (London: Repeater Books, 2018), 753, 754.

4. For a thorough investigation of the rise of the Alt-Right, see Angela Nagle, *Kill All Normies: Online Culture Wars From 4Chan and Tumblr to Trump and the Alt-Right* (Winchester, UK: Zero Books, 2017). See also Matthew Flisfeder, "'Trump'—What Does the Name Signify?; or Protofascism and the Alt-Right:

Three Contradictions of the Present Conjuncture." *Cultural Politics* 14, no. 1 (2018): 1–19.

5. Jodi Dean, *Publicity's Secret: How Technoculture Capitalizes on Democracy* (Ithaca, NY: Cornell University Press, 2002); Slavoj Žižek, *The Ticklish Subject: The Absent Centre of Political Ontology* (New York: Verso, 1999).

6. Ernesto Laclau and Chantal Mouffe, *Hegemony and Socialist Strategy: Towards a Radical Democratic Politics*, 2nd ed. (New York: Verso, 2000).

7. Matthew Arnold, *Culture and Anarchy and Other Writings* (New York: Cambridge University Press, 1993); F.R. Leavis, *Mass Civilization and Minority Culture* (Cambridge: Minority, 1930); Max Horkheimer and Theodor W. Adorno, *Dialectic of Enlightenment*, translated by John Cumming (New York: Continuum, 2000).

8. Walter Benjamin, "The Work of Art in the Age of Mechanical Reproduction." In *Illuminations: Essays and Reflections*, translated by Hannah Arendt (New York: Schocken, 1968).

9. Edward S. Herman and Noam Chomsky, *Manufacturing Consent: The Political Economy of the Mass Media* (New York: Pantheon, 1988).

10. Christian Fuchs, *Digital Labour and Karl Marx* (New York: Routledge, 2014); Dallas Smythe, "Communications: Blindspot of Western Marxism." *Canadian Journal of Social and Political Theory* 1, no. 3 (1977): 1–27.

11. Nagle, *Kill All Normies*, 27.

12. Dave Lee, "Facebook's Fake News Crisis Deepens." *BBC*, November 15, 2016; Olivia Solon, "Facebook's Failure: Did Fake News and Polarized Politics Get Trump Elected?" *The Guardian*, November 10, 2016.

13. Taina Bucher, "Want to Be on Top? Algorithmic Power and the Threat of Invisibility on Facebook." *New Media and Society* 14, no. 7 (2013): 1164–80; Ed Finn, *What Algorithms Want: Imagination in the Age of Computing* (Cambridge, MA: MIT Press, 2017); Ganaele Langlois, *Meaning in the Age of Social Media* (New York: Palgrave Macmillan, 2014); Astrid Mager, "Defining Algorithmic Ideology: Using Ideology Critique to Scrutinize Corporate Search Engines." *tripleC: Communication, Capitalism and Critique* 12, no. 1 (2014), www.triple-c.at/index.php /tripleC/article/view/439; and Nick Srnicek, *Platform Capitalism* (Malden, MA: Polity, 2017).

14. Jürgen Habermas, "The Public Sphere—an Encyclopedia Article." Translated by Sara Lennox and Frank Lennox. *New German Critique* 3 (1974): 49–55; Nancy Fraser, "Rethinking the Public Sphere: A Contribution to the Critique of Actually Existing Democracy." *Social Text* 25–26 (1990): 56–80; and Chantal Mouffe, *The Democratic Paradox* (New York: Verso, 2000).

15. Richard Seymour, "Schadenfreude with a Bite." *London Review of Books*, December 15, 2016.

16. Richard Seymour, "Schadenfreude with a Bite."

17. Mark Andrejevic, *Infoglut: How Too Much Information Is Changing the Way We Think and Know* (New York: Routledge, 2013).

18. Fredric Jameson, "Postmodernism; or, The Cultural Logic of Late Capitalism." *New Left Review* 1, no. 146 (1984): 53–92.

19. Andrejevic, *Infoglut*, 10.

20. See Mark Poster, "Postmodern Virtualities." *Body and Society* 1, no. 3–4 (1995): 79–95.

21. Jean Baudrillard, *Simulacra and Simulations*, translated by Sheila Faria Glaser (Ann Arbor, MI: University of Michigan Press, 1994); Gilles Deleuze and Félix Guattari, *A Thousand Plateaus: Capitalism and Schizophrenia*, translated by Brian Massumi (Minneapolis, MN: University of Minnesota Press, 1987); and Marshall McLuhan, *Understanding Media: Extensions of Man* (Toronto: Signet Books, 1964). See also Mark Poster, "Postmodern Virtualities." In Meenakshi Gigi Durham and Douglas M. Kellner, eds, *Media and Cultural Studies: Keyworks* 2nd ed. (Oxford: Wiley-Blackwell, 2012).

22. Andrejevic, *Infoglut*, 11.

23. Terry Eagleton, *After Theory* (London: Allen Lane, 2003).

24. Nancy Fraser, "Mass Psychology of Crisis: For a Structural Analysis of Financialization and against the Use of 'Fascism' as a Scare Tactic." *Public Seminar.* April 23, 2019.

25. Fredric Jameson, *Marxism and Form: Twentieth-Century Dialectical Theories of Literature* (Princeton, NJ: Princeton University Press, 1971), 276.

26. Jameson, *Marxism and Form*, 276.

27. Perry Anderson, *In the Tracks of Historical Materialism* (New York: Verso, 1983), 36.

28. Louis Althusser, *On the Reproduction of Capitalism* (New York: Verso, 2014).

29. Louis Althusser, *On Ideology* (New York: Verso, 2009).

30. Anderson, *In the Tracks of Historical Materialism*, 38.

31. Laclau and Mouffe, *Hegemony and Socialist Strategy*, 111.

32. Ernesto Laclau, *New Reflections on the Revolution of Our Time* (New York: Verso, 1990), 90–91.

33. Ernesto Laclau, *Emancipation(s)* (New York: Verso, 1996).

34. Ernesto Laclau, *On Populist Reason* (New York: Verso, 2005); Chantal Mouffe, *For a Left Populism* (New York: Verso, 2018).

35. Horkheimer and Adorno's *Dialectic of Enlightenment* comes to mind in this context.

36. See Herman and Chomsky, *Manufacturing Consent.*

37. Claire Birchall, *Shareveillance: The Dangers of Openly Sharing and Covertly Collecting Data* (Minneapolis, MN: University of Minnesota Press, 2017).

38. Katherine Ormerod, *Why Social Media Is Ruining Your Life* (London: Cassell, 2018); Siva Vaidhyanathan, *Anti-Social Media: How Facebook Has Disconnected Citizens and Undermined Democracy* (Oxford: Oxford University Press, 2018).

39. Manuel Castells, *Networks of Outrage and Hope: Social Movements in the Internet Age* (Malden, MA: Polity, 2012).

40. See, for instance, Jason Hannan, "Trolling Ourselves to Death? Social Media and Post-Truth Politics." *European Journal of Communication* 33, no. 2 (2018): 214–26; Whitney Phillips, *This Is Why We Can't Have Nice Things: Mapping the Relationship between Online Trolling and Mainstream Culture* (Cambridge, MA: MIT Press, 2015).

41. See, for instance, Daniel Trottier, *Social Media as Surveillance: Rethink-

ing Visibility in a Converging World (New York: Routledge, 2018); Christian Fuchs et al., eds, *Internet and Surveillance: The Challenges of Web 2.0 and Social Media* (New York: Routledge, 2012); and Kees Boersma and Chiara Fonio, eds, *Big Data, Surveillance, and Crisis Management* (New York: Routledge, 2017) in addition to many other titles. Social media surveillance is by now a well-covered terrain of investigation.

42. Christian Fuchs, *Social Media: A Critical Introduction.* 2nd ed. (Los Angeles, CA: Sage, 2017), 35.

43. Fuchs, *Social Media,* 35.

44. Alice E. Marwick, *Status Update: Celebrity, Publicity and Branding in the Social Media Age* (New Haven, CT: Yale University Press, 2013).

45. Fuchs, *Social Media.*

46. See Nick Srnicek, *Platform Capitalism* (Malden, MA: Polity, 2017).

47. For a great introduction to the legal and ideological framework, see Jacob Silverman's *Terms of Service: Social Media and the Price of Constant Connection* (New York: Harper Perennial, 2015); see also Cullen Hoback's documentary film, *Terms and Conditions May Apply* (2013).

48. On this point, see Colin Mooers's exceptional discussion of the coincidence between the commodity form and the form of citizenship under liberal capitalism in *Imperial Subjects: Citizenship in the Age of Crisis and Empire* (New York: Bloomsbury, 2014).

49. A number of texts now identify the contradiction at the heart of the neoliberal mantra about less government or deregulation, and in fact show that neoliberalism is a policy platform that makes use of the state mechanism to *impose* a form on the market and on subjects. See for instance, Wendy Brown's *Undoing the Demos: Neoliberalism's Stealth Revolution* (New York: Zone Books, 2015); David Harvey's *A Brief History of Neoliberalism* (Oxford: Oxford University Press, 2005).

50. Scott Rosenberg, "How the Great Recession Teed Off Tech's Long Boom." *Axios* September 15 , 2018.

51. Dean, *Publicity's Secret.*

52. I rely here on an article by Brian Lenzo, "The Revolution Will Not Be Tweeted." *International Socialist Review* 90 (July 2013).

53. See Herrera, *Revolution in the Age of Social Media* and Tufekci, *Twitter and Tear Gas.*

54. Fuchs, *OccupyMedia!,* 38.

55. Fuchs, *OccupyMedia!,* 126.

56. Nick Dyer-Witheford, *Cyber-Proletariat: Global Labour in the Digital Vortex* (Toronto: Pluto Press, 2015), 4.

57. Dean discusses this in a video interview with me from 2012 which can be viewed here: https://www.youtube.com/watch?v=Bn19okthKns&t=148s.

58. Žižek, *The Sublime Object of Ideology,* 93.

Chapter 2

1. Mark Fisher, "Exiting the Vampire Castle." In Darren Ambrose, ed., *K-Punk: The Collected and Unpublished Writings of Mark Fisher (2004–2016)* (London:

Repeater Books, 2018); Angela Nagle, *Kill All Normies: Online Culture Wars from 4Chan and Tumblr to Trump and the Alt-Right* (Winchester, UK: Zero Books, 2017).

2. Fisher, "Exiting the Vampire Castle," 745.

3. See Slavoj Žižek, *The Ticklish Subject* (New York: Verso, 1999); Fredric Jameson, "Postmodernism, or, The Cultural Logic of Late Capitalism." *New Left Review* 1, no. 146 (1984): 53–92; and Mark Fisher, *Capitalist Realism: Is There No Alternative?* (Winchester, UK: Zero Books, 2009).

4. Jodi Dean, *Publicity's Secret: How Technoculture Capitalizes on Democracy* (Ithaca, NY: Cornell, 2002), 3.

5. Jodi Dean, *Blog Theory: Feedback and Capture in the Circuits of Drive* (Malden, MA: Polity, 2010), 31.

6. On this topic, see Todd McGowan's brief but poignant explanation in *Enjoying What We Don't Have: The Political Project of Psychoanalysis* (Lincoln, NB: University of Nebraska, 2013), 14–15.

7. Dean, *Publicity's Secret*, 3.

8. Slavoj Žižek, *The Indivisible Remainder: On Schelling and Related Matters* (New York: Verso, 1996), 190.

9. Slavoj Žižek, *First as Tragedy, Then as Farce* (New York: Verso, 2009), 10–11.

10. For a more detailed discussion of these ideas in Žižek and Jameson, see Matthew Flisfeder, "Postmodern Marxism Today: Jameson, Žižek, and the Demise of Symbolic Efficiency." *International Journal of Žižek Studies* 13, no. 1 (2019): 22–56.

11. Nagle, *Kill All Normies.*

12. Perry Anderson, *The Origins of Postmodernity* (New York: Verso, 1998), 86.

13. Terry Eagleton, *The Illusions of Postmodernism* (Malden, MA: Blackwell, 1996).

14. Gilles Deleuze and Félix Guattari, *A Thousand Plateaus: Capitalism and Schizophrenia*, translated by Brian Massumi (Minneapolis, MN: University of Minnesota Press, 1987), 510.

15. See Thomas Frank, *What's the Matter with Kansas? How Conservatives Won the Heart of America* (New York: Henry Holt, 2004).

16. Anderson, *The Origins of Postmodernity*, 92.

17. For an alternative reading of *Fight Club*, see Anna Kornbluh's *Marxist Film Theory and Fight Club* (New York: Bloomsbury, 2019).

18. We might even say that, in the context of postmodern, consumer society, commodity fetishism as the *form* of ideology implicit in capitalism is fully realized.

19. See Octave Mannoni, *Clefs pour l'imaginaire* (Paris: Seuil, 1969).

20. Todd McGowan, *Out of Time: Desire in Atemporal Cinema* (Minneapolis, MN: University of Minnesota, 2011), 11.

21. McGowan, *Out of Time*, 11.

22. McGowan, *Out of Time*, 11.

23. McGowan, *Out of Time*, 11.

24. McGowan, *Out of Time*, 29.

25. See Dean, *Publicity's Secret*; Dean, *Blog Theory*; and Jodi Dean, *Democracy and Other Neoliberal Fantasies* (Durham, NC: Duke, 2009).

26. See Dean, *Democracy and Other Neoliberal Fantasies*, 42.

27. Žižek, *The Ticklish Subject*, 299.

28. Žižek, *The Ticklish Subject*, 299.

29. Slavoj Žižek, *Tarrying with the Negative: Kant, Hegel, and the Critique of Ideology* (Durham, NC: Duke University Press, 1993), 60.

30. McGowan, *Out of Time*, 28.

31. McGowan, *Out of Time*, 28.

32. McGowan, *Out of Time*, 29.

33. Jeremy Gilbert, "My Friend Mark." March 11 , 2017.

34. Mark Fisher, *Flatline Constructs: Gothic Materialism and Cybernetic Theory-Fiction* (New York: Exmilitary Press, [1999] 2018).

35. Mark Fisher, "Gothic Materialism." *Pli* 12 (2001): 230–43.

36. Fisher, *Capitalist Realism*, 23–24.

37. Fisher, *Flatline Constructs*, 59.

38. Sigmund Freud, *Civilization and Its Discontents*, edited by Todd Dufresne (Peterborough, ON: Broadview Editions, 2016), 57.

39. Fisher, *Flatline Constructs*, 62.

40. Dean, *Blog Theory*; Susan Buck-Morss, "Aesthetics and Anaesthetics: Walter Benjamin's Artwork Essay Reconsidered." *October* 62 (1992): 3–41.

41. Fisher, *Flatline Constructs*, 64.

42. Fisher, *Flatline Constructs*, 64.

43. Fisher, *Flatline Constructs*, 67.

44. Deleuze and Guattari, *A Thousand Plateaus*, 458.

45. Mark Fisher, "Misrecognizing Narcissus." *Flatness* (2010).

46. Fisher, "Misrecognizing Narcissus."

47. Fisher, "Misrecognizing Narcissus."

48. Marshall McLuhan, cited in Fisher, "Misrecognizing Narcissus."

49. Fisher, "Misrecognizing Narcissus."

50. Dean, *Democracy and Other Neoliberal Fantasies*, 23.

51. Fisher, "Misrecognizing Narcissus."

52. Paul A. Taylor, *Žižek and the Media* (Malden, MA: Polity, 2011), 78.

53. d.m. boyd and N.B. Ellison, "Social Network Sites: Definition, History, and Scholarship." *Journal of Computer-Mediated Communication* 13, no. 1 (2007): http://jcmc.indiana.edu/vol13/issue1/boyd.ellison.html.

54. Dean, *Democracy and Other Neoliberal Fantasies*, 66.

55. Dean, *Democracy and Other Neoliberal Fantasies*, 67.

56. *The Joy of Tech* comic strip recently updated this cartoon in light of the revelations in the United States about NSA surveillance through social media: "On the Internet Nobody Knows You're a Dog—1990s and Now," June 17, 2013, http://www.joyoftech.com/joyoftech/joyarchives/1862.html.

57. Jacques Lacan, *The Seminar, Book XI: The Four Fundamental Concepts of Psycho-Analysis, 1964–1965*, translated by Alan Sheridan (New York: W.W. Norton and Co., 1977), 207.

58. Here, though, it is possible to consider the image, not necessarily and simply as an aspect of the Imaginary, but perhaps more appropriately as a "parallax object" that is split between the Symbolic Master-Signifier and the Imaginary *objet petit a.*

59. Dean, *Blog Theory*, 88.

60. Slavoj Žižek, *The Parallax View* (Cambridge, MA: MIT Press, 2006), 303.

61. See Slavoj Žižek, *For They Know Not What They Do: Enjoyment as a Political Factor*, 2nd ed. (New York: Verso, 2002), xci.

Chapter 3

1. Jacques Lacan, "Subversion of the Subject and the Dialectic of Desire." In *Écrits: The First Complete Edition in English*, translated by Bruce Fink (New York: W.W. Norton, 2006). Thanks to Clint Burnham for reminding me about this passage.

2. Lacan, "Subversion of the Subject and the Dialectic of Desire," 701.

3. Gilles Deleuze and Félix Guattari, *A Thousand Plateaus: Capitalism and Schizophrenia*, translated by Brian Massumi (Minneapolis, MN: University of Minnesota Press, 1987); Maurizio Lazzarato, *Signs and Machines: Capitalism and the Production of Subjectivity*, translated by Joshua David Jordan (Los Angeles, CA: Semiotext(e), 2014). Subsequent references to Lazzarato's *Signs and Machines* in this chapter will be made using in-text citations.

4. Ganaele Langlois, *Meaning in the Age of Social Media* (New York: Palgrave Macmillan, 2014). Subsequent references to Langlois in this chapter will be made using in-text citations.

5. Louis Althusser, "Ideology and Ideological State Apparatuses (Notes towards an Investigation)." In Louis Althusser, *On Ideology* (New York: Verso, 2009).

6. See Christian Fuchs, *Digital Labour and Karl Marx* (New York: Routledge, 2014).

7. See Jason Read, *The Micro-Politics of Capital: Marx and the Prehistory of the Present* (Albany, NY: SUNY Press, 2003).

8. See in particular Ernesto Laclau, *On Populist Reason* (New York: Verso, 2005); Chantal Mouffe, *For a Left Populism* (New York: Verso, 2018).

9. On this point, see Žižek's critique of populism in *In Defense of Lost Causes* (New York: Verso, 2008).

10. See Anne Friedberg, *Window Shopping: Cinema and the Postmodern* (Berkeley, CA: University of California Press, 1993).

11. See Jay David Bolster and Richard Grusin, *Remediation: Understanding New Media* (Cambridge, MA: MIT Press, 2000); Wendy Hui Kyong Chun, *Control and Freedom: Power and Paranoia in the Age of Fiber Optics* (Cambridge, MA: MIT Press, 2006); Henry Jenkins, *Convergence Culture: Where Old and New Media Collide* (New York: NYU Press, 2008); and Lev Manovich, *The Language of New Media* (Cambridge, MA: MIT Press, 2001).

12. See Greg Elmer, *Profiling Machines: Mapping the Personal Information Economy* (Cambridge, MA: MIT Press, 2004).

13. See Slavoj Žižek, *The Parallax View* (Cambridge, MA: MIT Press, 2006).

14. See Slavoj Žižek, *For They Know Not What They Do: Enjoyment as a Political Factor*, 2nd ed. (New York: Verso, 2002).

15. Deleuze and Guattari, *A Thousand Plateaus*, 456–57.

16. Gilles Deleuze, "Postscript on the Societies of Control." *October* 59 (1992): 3–7.

17. The same charge can be levelled against these thinkers in that they often neglect the critical political economy analysis of capitalism in their theories of subjection and interpellation.

18. Although he seems at times to suggest that enslavement and subjection intersect in the production of subjectivity, Lazzarato does claim that "machinic enslavement (or processes) *precede* the subject and the object and surpasses the personological distinctions of social subjection" (Lazzarato, *Signs and Machines*, 120, emphasis added).

19. Such a description of enslavement recalls Michel Foucault's criticism of the terms "ideology" and "repression." See Michel Foucault, "Truth and Power." In Paul Rabinow, ed., *The Foucault Reader* (New York: Pantheon, 1984), 60. For a discussion of this point, see Matthew Flisfeder, *Postmodern Theory and Blade Runner* (New York: Bloomsbury, 2017), 57–62.

20. Gilles Deleuze and Félix Guattari, *Anti-Oedipus: Capitalism and Schizophrenia*, translated by Robert Hurley, Mark Seem, and Helen R. Lane (Minneapolis, MN: University of Minnesota Press, 1983).

21. Herbert Marcuse, *Eros and Civilization: A Philosophical Inquiry into Freud* (Boston: Beacon Press, 1955).

22. Todd McGowan, *Out of Time: Desire in Atemporal Cinema* (Minneapolis, MN: University of Minnesota Press, 2011).

23. McGowan, *Out of Time*, 29.

24. Nick Dyer-Witheford, *Cyber-Marx: Cycles and Circuits of Struggle in High-Technology Capitalism* (Chicago, IL: University of Illinois Press, 1999), 93.

25. Dyer-Witheford, *Cyber-Marx*, 93.

26. Dyer-Witheford, *Cyber-Marx*, 93.

27. Dyer-Witheford, *Cyber-Marx*, 94–95.

28. Karl Marx, *Capital, Volume 1*, translated by Ben Fowkes (New York: Penguin, 1990), 1019–38.

29. Read, *The Micro-Politics of Capital*, 104.

30. Read, *The Micro-Politics of Capital*, 109.

31. Karl Marx, *Grundrisse*, translated by Martin Nicolaus (New York: Penguin, 1993), 88.

32. Read, *The Micro-Politics of Capital*, 110.

33. See Maurizio Lazzarato, *The Making of the Indebted Man*, translated by Joshua David Jordan (Los Angeles, CA: Semiotext(e), 2011).

34. Tiziana Terranova, "Red Stack Attack!: Algorithms, Capital and the Automation of the Common." In Robin Mackay and Armin Avanessian, eds, *#Accelerate: The Accelerationist Reader* (Windsor Quarry, UK: Urbanomic, 2014).

35. Terranova, "Red Stack Attack!," 385.

36. See Nick Srnicek and Alex Williams, *Inventing the Future: Postcapitalism and a World Without Work* (New York: Verso, 2015).

37. Terranova, "Red Stack Attack!," 381.

38. Terranova, "Red Stack Attack!," 382.

39. Marx, *Grundrisse*, 690–712.

40. See Paolo Virno, "General Intellect." *Historical Materialism* 15, no. 3 (2007): 3–8; Carlo Vercellone, "From Formal Subsumption to General Intellect: Elements for a Marxist Reading of the Thesis of Cognitive Capitalism." *Historical Materialism* 15, no. 1 (2007): 13–36.

41. Terranova, "Red Stack Attack!," 383.

42. Philip Napoli, "Automated Media: An Institutional Theory Perspective on Algorithmic Media Production and Consumption." *Communication Theory* 24 (2014): 340–60.

43. Ian Bogost, "The Cathedral of Computation." *The Atlantic*, January 15, 2015.

44. Fenwick McKelvey, "Algorithmic Media Need Democratic Methods: Why Public Matter." *Canadian Journal of Communication* 39, no. 4 (2014): 597–613.

45. Ed Finn, *What Algorithms Want: Imagination in the Age of Computing* (Cambridge, MA: MIT Press, 2017), 17.

46. Finn, *What Algorithms Want*, 7.

47. Finn, *What Algorithms Want*, 16.

48. Finn, *What Algorithms Want*, 18.

49. Astrid Mager, "Defining Algorithmic Ideology: Using Ideology Critique to Scrutinize Corporate Search Engines." *tripleC: Communication, Capitalism and Critique* 12, no. 1 (2014).

50. Alice E. Marwick, *Status Update: Celebrity, Publicity, and Branding in the Social Media Age* (New Haven, CT: Yale University Press, 2013).

51. Napoli, "Automated Media," 345.

52. Taina Bucher, "Want to Be on Top?: Algorithmic Power and the Threat of Invisibility on Facebook." *New Media and Society* 14, no. 7 (2012): 1164–80.

53. Bucher, "Want to Be on Top?," 1171.

54. Joan Copjec, *Read My Desire: Lacan against the Historicists* (Cambridge, MA: MIT Press, 1994), 19.

55. See Slavoj Žižek, *The Sublime Object of Ideology* (New York: Verso, 1989), 93.

56. Žižek, *The Sublime Object of Ideology*, 35.

57. Deleuze and Guattari, *Anti-Oedipus*, 25.

58. Deleuze and Guattari, *Anti-Oedipus*, 33.

59. Deleuze and Guattari, *Anti-Oedipus*, 33.

60. Deleuze and Guattari, *Anti-Oedipus*, 257.

61. Ian Buchanan, *Deleuze and Guattari's Anti-Oedipus: A Reader's Guide* (New York: Bloomsbury, 2008), 47.

62. Todd McGowan, *Psychoanalytic Film Theory and the Rules of the Game* (New York: Bloomsbury, 2015), 41.

63. Judith Butler, *The Psychic Life of Power: Theories of Subjection* (Stanford, CA: Stanford University Press, 1997), 2.

64. Mladen Dolar, "Beyond Interpellation." *Qui parle* 6 (1993), 78.

65. Todd McGowan, *Capitalism and Desire: The Psychic Cost of Free Markets* (New York: Columbia University Press, 2016), 49.

66. Samo Tomšič, *The Capitalist Unconscious* (New York: Verso, 2015), 151.

67. Tomšič, *The Capitalist Unconscious*, 150.

68. Deleuze and Guattari, *Anti-Oedipus*, 378.

69. Phillip Goodchild, *Deleuze and Guattari: An Introduction to Their Politics* (Thousand Oaks, CA: Sage, 1996), 120.

70. Goodchild, *Deleuze and Guattari*, 120.

71. Antonio Negri, *Marx and Foucault: Essays Volume 1*, translated by Ed Emery (Malden, MA: Polity, 2017), 190, emphasis added.

72. Negri, *Marx and Foucault*, 190.

73. Slavoj Žižek, "The Spectre of Ideology." In Slavoj Žižek, ed., *Mapping Ideology* (New York: Verso, 1994), 21.

74. Žižek, "The Spectre of Ideology," 22.

75. Žižek, *For They Know Not What They Do*, 100.

76. Žižek, *The Sublime Object of Ideology*, 164.

77. Read, *The Micro-Politics of Capital*.

Chapter 4

1. Brent Bambury, "Data Mining Firm behind Trump Election Built Psychological Profiles of Nearly Every American Voter." *Day 6* CBC.ca, March 20, 2018.

2. Glenn Greenwald, "NSA Collecting Phone Records of Millions of Verizon Customers Daily." *The Guardian*, June 5, 2013; Glenn Greenwald and Ewan MacAskill, "NSA Prism Program Taps in to User Data of Apple, Google, and Others." *The Guardian*, June 7, 2013; and Glenn Greenwald, Ewan Askill, and Laura Poitras, "Edward Snowden: The Whistleblower behind the NSA Surveillance Revelations." *The Guardian*, June 11, 2013.

3. Matt Taibbi, "The Facebook Menace." *Rolling Stone* 1311–12, April 19–May 3, 2018, 44.

4. "Cambridge Analytica Whistleblower Empowers Citizen Action." *Government Accountability Project*, April 17, 2018.

5. Julie Carrie Wong, "Congress Grills Facebook CEO over Data Misuse—As It Happened." *The Guardian*, April 10, 2018.

6. Octave Mannoni, "I Know Very Well, But All the Same." In Molly Anne Rothenberg, ed., *Perversion and the Social Relation* (Durham, NC: Duke University Press, 2003).

7. Dominic Pettman, *Infinite Distraction: Paying Attention to Social Media* (Malden, MA: Polity, 2016), 79.

8. Taibbi, "The Facebook Menace," 57.

9. Clint Burnham, "Enjoy Your Clickbait!" Unpublished manuscript.

10. Geert Lovink, "On the Social Media Ideology." *e-flux journal* 75 (September 2016): 4.

11. Taibbi, "The Facebook Menace," 57.

12. Stuart Hall, "Encoding/Decoding." In Meenakshi Gigi Durham and Douglas Kellner, eds, *Media and Cultural Studies: Keyworks*, 2nd ed. (Malden, MA: Wiley-Blackwell, 2012). Subsequent references to Hall's "Encoding/Decoding" in this chapter will be made using in-text citations.

13. For a discussion of double-coding, see Matthew Flisfeder, *Postmodern Theory and Blade Runner* (New York: Bloomsbury, 2017), 74–75.

14. Stuart Hall, "Notes on Deconstructing 'The Popular'." In Imre Szeman and Timothy Kaposy, eds, *Cultural Theory: An Anthology* (Malden, MA: Wiley-Blackwell, 2011), 73.

15. Hall, "Notes on Deconstructing 'The Popular'," 75.

16. See Matthew Flisfeder, *The Symbolic, the Sublime, and Slavoj Žižek's Theory of Film* (New York: Palgrave Macmillan, 2012). See also Slavoj Žižek, *The Fright of Real Tears: Krzysztof Kieslowski between Theory and Post-Theory* (London: BFI, 2001); David Bordwell and Nöel Carrol, eds, *Post-Theory: Reconstructing Film Studies* (Madison, WI: University of Wisconsin Press, 1996).

17. Stuart Hall, "Recent Developments in Theories of Language and Ideology: A Critical Note." In Imre Szeman and Timothy Kaposy, eds, *Cultural Theory: An Anthology* (Malden, MA: Wiley-Blackwell, 2011), 226. Subsequent references to Hall's "Recent Developments" in this chapter will be made using in-text citations.

18. Slavoj Žižek, *The Sublime Object of Ideology* (New York: Verso, 1989), 43.

19. Žižek, *The Sublime Object of Ideology*, 43.

20. Žižek, *The Sublime Object of Ideology*, 44.

21. Slavoj Žižek, "The Spectre of Ideology." In Slavoj Žižek, ed., *Mapping Ideology* (New York: Verso, 1994), 4.

22. Hall, "Recent Developments," 226.

23. Hall, "Recent Developments," 227.

24. Gilles Deleuze and Félix Guattari, *A Thousand Plateaus: Capitalism and Schizophrenia*, translated by Brian Massumi (Minneapolis, MN: University of Minnesota Press, 1987), 456–57.

25. Deleuze and Guattari, *A Thousand Plateaus*, 458.

26. Gilles Deleuze, "Postscript on the Societies of Control." *October* 59 (1992): 5.

27. Hall, "Encoding/Decoding,"140.

28. Adam Greenfield, *Radical Technologies: The Design of Everyday Life* (New York: Verso, 2017), 210.

29. Greenfield, *Radical Technologies*, 210.

30. Greenfield, *Radical Technologies*, 216.

31. Greenfield, *Radical Technologies*, 226.

32. Greenfield, *Radical Technologies*, 233.

33. Ed Finn, *What Algorithms Want: Imagination in the Age of Computing* (Cambridge, MA: MIT Press, 2017), 17.

34. Cathy O'Neil, *Weapons of Math Destruction: How Big Data Increases Inequality and Threatens Democracy* (New York: Broadway Books, 2017): 3.

35. O'Neil, *Weapons of Math Destruction*, 3.

36. O'Neil, *Weapons of Math Destruction*, 17.

37. O'Neil, *Weapons of Math Destruction*, 18.

38. Finn, *What Algorithms Want*, 16.

39. James Vincent, "Twitter Taught Microsoft's AI Chatbot to Be a Racist Asshole in Less Than a Day." *The Verge*, March 24, 2016.

40. See Christian Fuchs, *Digital Labour and Karl Marx* (New York: Routledge,

2014); Christian Fuchs, interviewed by Matthew Flisfeder, "Digital Labour and the Internet Prosumer Commodity: In Conversation with Christian Fuchs." *Alternate Routes* 27 (2016): 267–78; and Nick Srnicek, *Platform Capitalism* (Malden, MA: Polity Press, 2017).

41. Alice E. Marwick, *Status Update: Celebrity, Publicity, and Branding in the Social Media Age* (New Haven, CT: Yale University Press, 2013), 220.

42. Christian Fuchs, *Social Media: A Critical Introduction* (Los Angeles, CA: Sage, 2014), 158.

43. Michel Foucault, *Discipline and Punish: The Birth of the Prison*, translated by Alan Sheridan (New York: Pantheon, 1977). See also, for instance, Taina Bucher, "Want to Be on Top? Algorithmic Power and the Threat of Invisibility on Facebook." *New Media and Society* 14, no. 7 (2012): 1164–80.

44. Thomas Mathiesen, "The Viewer Society: Michel Foucault's 'Panopticon' Revisited." *Theoretical Criminology* 1, no. 2 (1997): 215–34.

45. Mark Fisher, *Capitalist Realism: Is There No Alternative?* (Winchester, UK: Zero Books, 2009), 22.

46. See José van Dijk, "Datafication, Dataism and Dataveillance: Big Data between Scientific Paradigm and Ideology." *Surveillance and Society* 12, no. 2 (2014): 197–208. See also Greg Elmer, "A Diagram of Panoptic Surveillance." *New Media and Society* 5, no. 2 (2003): 231–47; Bart Simon, "The Return of Panopticism: Supervision, Subjection and the New Surveillance." *Surveillance and Society* 3, no. 1 (2002): 1–20.

47. Claire Birchall, *Shareveillance: The Dangers of Openly Sharing and Covertly Collecting Data* (Minneapolis: University of Minnesota Press, 2017), 2.

48. Birchall, *Shareveillance*, 3, 7.

49. Birchall, *Shareveillance*, 9.

50. Fuchs, *Social Media*, 159.

51. Rebecca Joseph, "Museum Selfie: Google App Tops Charts But Experts Warn of Privacy Concerns." *Global News*, January 18, 2018.

52. Wendy Hui Kyong Chun, *Programmed Visions: Software and Memory* (Cambridge, MA: MIT Press, 2013), 67.

53. Žižek, *The Sublime Object of Ideology*, 28–30.

54. Wendy Hui Kyong Chun, "On Software, or the Persistence of Visual Knowledge." *Grey Room* 18 (2004): 43.

55. Chun, *Programmed Visions*, 67–68.

56. See Louis Althusser, *On the Reproduction of Capitalism* (New York: Verso, 2014). See also Matthew Flisfeder, "Morality or Enjoyment? On Althusser's Ideological Supplement of the Law." *Mediations: Journal of the Marxist Literary Group* 30, no. 2 (2017): 37–44.

57. Žižek, *The Sublime Object of Ideology*, 93.

58. Jacques Lacan, *The Four Fundamental Concepts of Psycho-Analysis*, edited by Jacques-Alain Miller and translated by Alan Sheridan (New York: W.W. Norton and Company, 1981), 158.

59. Žižek, *The Sublime Object of Ideology*, 110–13.

60. Slavoj Žižek, *Tarrying with the Negative: Kant, Hegel, and the Critique of Ideology* (Durham, NC: Duke University Press, 1993), 73–74.

61. Lacan, *The Four Fundamental Concepts of Psycho-Analysis*, 199.

62. Lacan, *The Four Fundamental Concepts of Psycho-Analysis*, 207.

63. Slavoj Žižek, *The Art of the Ridiculous Sublime: On David Lynch's* Lost Highway (Seattle, WA: University of Washington Press, 2000), 6.

64. For more on this see Brett Caraway, "Crisis of Command: Theorizing Value in New Media." *Communication Theory* 26 (2015): 64–81.

Chapter 5

1. Eliana Dockterman, "Is *Gone Girl* Feminist or Misogynist?" *Time*, October 6, 2014.

2. Nina Power, "Run, Boy, Run." *The New Inquiry*, July 17, 2014.

3. Jennifer Friedlander, *Real Deceptions: The Contemporary Reinvention of Realism* (New York: Oxford University Press, 2017), 12.

4. Friedlander, *Real Deceptions*, 12.

5. Hilary Neroni, *The Subject of Torture: Psychoanalysis and Biopolitics in Television and Film* (New York: Columbia University Press, 2015).

6. Alvin Toffler, *The Third Wave* (New York: Bantam, 1980).

7. Dallas Smythe, "Communications: Blindspot of Western Marxism." *Canadian Journal of Political and Social Theory* 1, no. 3 (1977): 1–27.

8. Christian Fuchs, *Digital Labor and Karl Marx* (New York: Routledge, 2014); see also Mark Andrejevic, "Estranged Free Labor." In Trebor Scholz, ed., *Digital Labor: The Internet as Playground and Factory* (New York: Routledge, 2013), 149–64; Nicole S. Cohen, "The Valorization of Surveillance: Towards a Political Economy of Facebook." *Democratic Communiqué* 22, no. 1 (2008): 5–22; Nick Dyer-Witheford, *Cyber-Marx: Cycles and Circuits of Struggle in High-Technology Capitalism* (Urbana, IL: University of Illinois Press, 1999); Vincent Manzerolle, "Mobilizing the Audience Commodity: Digital Labor in a Wireless World." *Ephemera* 10, no. 3–4 (2010): 455–69; and Vincent Mosco, *The Political Economy of Communication*, 2nd ed. (Thousand Oaks, CA: Sage, 2009).

9. Fuchs, *Digital Labor and Karl Marx*.

10. Alison Hearn, "Structuring Feeling: Web 2.0, Online Ranking and Rating, and the Digital 'Reputation' Economy." *Ephemera* 10, no. 3–4 (2010): 421–38.

11. Hearn, "Structuring Feeling," 427.

12. Hearn, "Structuring Feeling," 429.

13. Mary Madden and Aaron Smith, "Reputation Management and Social Media." *Pew Internet and American Life Project*, May 26, 2010.

14. See Bernie Hogan, "The Presentation of Self in the Age of Social Media: Distinguishing Performances and Exhibitions Online." *Bulletin of Science, Technology and Society* 30, no. 6 (2010): 377–86.

15. Michel Feher, "Self-Appreciation; or, The Aspirations of Human Capital," translated by Ivan Ascher. *Public Culture* 21, no. 1 (2009): 21–24.

16. Michel Foucault, *The Birth of Biopolitics: Lectures at the Collège de France, 1978–1979*, edited by Michel Senellart and translated by Graham Burchell (New York: Picador, 2008), 223, emphasis added.

17. Thomas Lemke, "Foucault, Governmentality, and Critique." *Rethinking Marxism* 14, no. 3 (2001): 51.

18. Andrew Dilts, "From 'Entrepreneur of the Self' to 'Care of the Self': Neoliberal Governmentality and Foucault's Ethics." *Foucault Studies* 12 (2011): 16.

19. Foucault, *The Birth of Biopolitics*, 224.

20. Feher, "Self-Appreciation," 30.

21. Jason Read, "A Genealogy of Homo-Economicus: Neoliberalism and the Production of Subjectivity." *Foucault Studies* 6 (2009): 28.

22. Read, "A Genealogy of Homo-Economicus," 28.

23. Read, "A Genealogy of Homo-Economicus," 28.

24. Maurizio Lazzarato, *The Making of Indebted Man*, translated by Joshua David Jordan (Los Angeles, CA: Semiotext(e), 2012), 91.

25. Read, "A Genealogy of Homo-Economicus," 30.

26. Fuchs, *Digital Labor and Karl Marx*.

27. Fuchs, *Digital Labor and Karl Marx*, 257.

28. Fuchs, *Digital Labor and Karl Marx*, 261.

29. Fuchs, *Digital Labor and Karl Marx*, 265.

30. Fuchs, *Digital Labor and Karl Marx*, 265.

31. Fuchs, *Digital Labor and Karl Marx*, 116.

32. Christian Fuchs, "Digital Prosumption Labor on Social Media in the Context of Capitalist Regimes of Time." *Time and Society*, October 7, 2013, DOI: 10.1177/0961463X13502117.

33. Daniel Trottier, *Identity Problems in the Facebook Era* (New York: Routledge, 2014), 14, emphasis added.

34. Geert Lovink, *Networks without a Cause: A Critique of Social Media* (Malden, MA: Polity, 2011), 41.

35. Lovink, *Networks without a Cause*, 40.

36. Lovink, *Networks without a Cause*, 40–41, emphasis added. Lovink also comments critically on a statement made by Facebook CEO, Mark Zuckerberg, "having two identities for yourself is an example of a lack of integrity" (cited in Lovink, *Networks without a Cause*, 41).

37. Lovink, *Networks without a Cause*, 41–43, emphasis added.

38. Lovink, *Networks without a Cause*, 42.

39. Jonathan Crary, *24/7: Late Capitalism and the Ends of Sleep* (New York: Verso, 2013), 9.

40. Crary, *Late Capitalism and the Ends of Sleep*, 10. The Marxist argument here should also note the extension of absolute surplus value as mechanisms emerge to draw out relative surplus value.

41. Crary, *Late Capitalism and the Ends of Sleep*, 30.

42. Crary, *Late Capitalism and the Ends of Sleep*, 62.

43. Crary, *Late Capitalism and the Ends of Sleep*, 72.

44. Crary, *Late Capitalism and the Ends of Sleep*, 98.

45. Crary, *Late Capitalism and the Ends of Sleep*, 99. The online application, twalue.com, measures the value of one's Twitter account. Users have the option of posting this to their Twitter feed. This can have the effect of either helping to sell the Self (that is, "this is what I'm worth"), or it can have the effect of encourag-

ing competition between users to amass more followers and to create more posts; all the while, the profit generated continues to be alienated from the prosumer.

46. Crary, *Late Capitalism and the Ends of Sleep*, 104.

47. "[T]he value of labor-power is the value of the means of subsistence necessary for the maintenance of its owner."Karl Marx, *Capital, Volume 1*, translated by Ben Fowkes (New York: Penguin, 1990), 274.

48. Therefore, as David Harvey explains, the laborer as subject of exchange still exists within the cycle, the cycle is that of C-M-C (commodity-money-commodity), whereas for the capitalist, the cycle is that of M-C-M (money-commodity-M'=M+ΔM, where ΔM is surplus value). David Harvey, *A Companion to Marx's Capital* (New York: Verso, 2010), 102.

49. Harvey notes, as well, the fact that "needs" are historical, dependent upon the history of class struggle. Harvey, *A Companion to Marx's Capital*, 103.

50. Silvia Federici, "From Commoning to Debt: Financialization, Microcredit, and the Changing Architecture of Capital Accumulation." *The South Atlantic Quarterly* 113, no. 2 (2014): 235.

51. Lazzarato, *The Making of the Indebted Man*, 94.

52. Lazzarato, *The Making of the Indebted Man*, 93.

53. Tiziana Terranova, *Network Culture: Politics for the Information Age* (Ann Arbor, MI: Pluto, 2004), 74.

54. Mark Fisher, *Capitalist Realism: Is There No Alternative?* (Winchester, UK: Zero Books, 2009).

55. Fisher, *Capitalist Realism*, 2.

56. Todd McGowan, *Out of Time: Desire in Atemporal Cinema* (Minneapolis, MN: University of Minnesota Press, 2011), 29.

57. Michel Foucault, *The History of Sexuality, Volume I: An Introduction*, translated by Robert Hurley (New York: Vintage, 1990), 95.

58. Todd McGowan, "Virtual Freedom: The Obfuscation and Elucidation of the Subject in Cyberspace." *Psychoanalysis, Culture and Society* 18, no. 1 (2013): 67.

59. Frank Smecker, *The Night of the World: Traversing the Ideology of Objectivity* (Winchester, UK: Zero Books, 2014).

Chapter 6

1. Renata Salecl, *The Tyranny of Choice* (London: Profile Books, 2011), 7.

2. On the politics of "witnessing," see for instance Giorgio Agamben, *Remnants of Auschwitz: The Witness and the Archive* (Brooklyn, NY: Zone Books, 1999).

3. Steven Shaviro, *The Universe of Things: On Speculative Realism* (Minneapolis, MN: University of Minnesota Press, 2015), 61.

4. Russell Sbriglia, "Object-Disoriented Ontology; or the Subject of *What Is Sex?*" *Continental Thought and Theory* 2, no. 2 (2018): 39.

5. Slavoj Žižek, *Disparities* (New York: Bloomsbury, 2016), 83.

6. Joan Copjec, *Read My Desire: Lacan against the Historicists* (Cambridge,

MA: MIT Press, 1994); Slavoj Žižek, *Tarrying with the Negative: Kant, Hegel, and the Critique of Ideology* (Durham, NC: Duke University Press, 1993).

7. Alenka Zupančič, *What Is Sex?* (Cambridge, MA: MIT Press, 2017), 37.

8. Interview of Alenka Zupančič by Agon Hamza and Frank Ruda, "Interview with Alenka Zupančič: Philosophy or Psychoanalysis? Yes, Please." *Crisis and Critique* 6, no. 1 (2019): 439.

9. Zupančič, *What Is Sex?*, 11.

10. Salecl, *The Tyranny of Choice*, 7–8.

11. Salecl, *The Tyranny of Choice*, 75.

12. Salecl, *The Tyranny of Choice*, 75.

13. Salecl, *The Tyranny of Choice*, 75.

14. Salecl, *The Tyranny of Choice*, 85.

15. Jacques Lacan, *The Ethics of Psychoanalysis: The Seminar of Jacques Lacan, Book VII*, edited by Jacques-Alain Miller and translated by Dennis Porter (New York: W.W. Norton and Co., 1997).

16. See Jonathan Crary, *24/7: Late Capitalism and the Ends of Sleep* (New York: Verso, 2013); Christian Fuchs, "Digital Prosumption Labor on Social Media in the Context of the Capitalist Regime of Time." *Time and Society* 23, no. 1 (2014): 97–123.

17. David Harvey, *The Condition of Postmodernity* (Oxford: Blackwell, 1989).

18. Gaby David and Carolina Cambre, "Screened Intimacies: Tinder and the Swipe Logic." *Social Media + Society* April/June (2016): 1–11.

19. David and Cambre, "Screened Intimacies," 7.

20. David and Cambre, "Screened Intimacies," 8.

21. Alex Abad-Santos, "In *Black Mirror*'s Bittersweet 'Hang the DJ', It's Technology versus Loneliness." *Vox*, December 29, 2017.

22. Jacques Lacan, *The Other Side of Psychoanalysis: The Seminar of Jacques Lacan, Book XVII*, edited by Jacques-Alain Miller and translated by Russell Grigg (New York: W.W. Norton and Co., 2007), 162.

23. Slavoj Žižek, *Incontinence of the Void: Economico-Philosophical Spandrels* (Cambridge, MA: MIT Press, 2017), 144.

24. Slavoj Žižek, "Sexuality in the Posthuman Age." *Stasis* 4, no. 1 (2016), 64.

25. Žižek, "Sexuality in the Posthuman Age," 64.

26. Frédéric Declercq, "Lacan on the Capitalist Discourse: Its Consequences for Libidinal Enjoyment and Social Bond." *Psychoanalysis, Culture and Society* 11 (2006): 74–83.

27. Declercq, "Lacan on the Capitalist Discourse," 75.

28. For a deeper analysis of *Her*, see Matthew Flisfeder and Clint Burnham, "Love and Sex in the Age of Capitalist Realism: On Spike Jonze's *Her*." *Cinema Journal* 57, no. 1 (2017): 25–45.

29. Kaitlyn Tiffany, "The Tinder Algorithm, Explained." *Vox*, March 18, 2019.

30. Slavoj Žižek, *For They Know Not What They Do: Enjoyment as a Political Factor*, 2nd ed. (New York: Verso, 2002), 21.

31. Roberto Simanowski, *Waste: A New Media Primer* (Cambridge, MA: MIT Press, 2018), 4.

32. Simanowski, *Waste*, 5.

33. John Cheney-Lippold, *We Are Data: Algorithms and the Making of Our Digital Selves* (New York: New York University Press, 2017).

34. Simanowski, *Waste*, 91.

35. Cheney-Lippold, *We Are Data*, 48.

36. Cheney-Lippold, *We Are Data*, 51.

37. Simanowski, *Waste*, 4.

38. Simanowski, *Waste*, 4.

39. Louis-Paul Willis, "'The Endless Space Between Words': Desire, Fantasy, and Interface in *Her*." In Cindy Zeiher and Todd McGowan, eds, *Can Philosophy Love? Reflections and Encounters* (Lanham, MD: Rowman and Littlefield, 2017), 245–46.

40. Zupančič, *What Is Sex?*, 11.

41. Zupančič, *What Is Sex?*, 16.

42. Clint Burnham, *Does the Internet Have an Unconscious? Slavoj Žižek and Digital Culture* (New York: Bloomsbury, 2018), 10.

43. Burnham, *Does the Internet Have an Unconscious?*, 12.

44. Burnham, *Does the Internet Have an Unconscious?*, 13.

45. Slavoj Žižek, *The Ticklish Subject: The Absent Centre of Political Ontology* (New York: Verso, 1999), 19.

46. Zupančič, *What Is Sex?*, 17.

47. Zupančič, *What Is Sex?*, 35.

48. Zupančič, *What Is Sex?*, 42.

49. Žižek, *Tarrying with the Negative*, 58–61.

50. Zupančič, *What Is Sex?*, 36.

51. Zupančič, *What Is Sex?*, 127.

52. Copjec, *Read My Desire*, 203.

53. Zupančič, *What Is Sex?*, 79.

54. Zupančič, *What Is Sex?*, 119.

55. Žižek, *For They Know Not What They Do*, 147.

56. Zupančič, *What Is Sex?*, 89.

57. Reza Negarestani, *Intelligence and Spirit* (New York: Urbanomic, 2018).

58. Or, as Terry Eagleton has argued, every rejection of a norm retroactively imposes a new one; and this is what we call history. Terry Eagleton, *After Theory* (London: Allen Lane, 2003).

59. Reza Negarestani, "The Labor of the Inhuman." In Robin MacKay and Armen Avanessian, eds, *#Accelerate: The Accelerationist Reader* (Windsor Quarry, UK: Urbanomic, 2014), 439.

60. Zupančič, *What Is Sex?*, 103.

61. Žižek, *The Ticklish Subject*, 299.

62. Slavoj Žižek, *Event* (New York: Penguin, 2014), 64.

63. Alain Badiou and Nicolas Truong, *In Praise of Love*, translated by Peter Bush (New York: Verso, 2012), 17.

64. Mladen Dolar, "Beyond Interpellation." *Qui parle* 6, no. 2 (1993), 81.

65. Zupančič, *What Is Sex?*, 119.

66. Jacques Lacan, *Transference: The Seminar of Jacques Lacan, Book VIII*, edited by Jacques-Alain Miller and translated by Bruce Fink (Malden, MA: Polity, 2015), 129.

67. Todd McGowan, *Emancipation after Hegel: Achieving a Contradictory Revolution* (New York: Columbia University Press, 2019), 99.

68. See for instance Levi R. Bryant, *Onto-Cartography: An Ontology of Machines and Media* (Edinburgh: Edinburgh University Press, 2014); Colin Cremin, *Exploring Videogames with Deleuze and Guattari: Towards an Affective Theory of Form* (New York: Routledge, 2016).

69. Zupančič, *What Is Sex?*, 122.

70. Slavoj Žižek, *Like a Thief in Broad Daylight* (London: Allen Lane, 2018), 144.

Conclusion

1. A fact I am reminded of every time I read the children's book *Olivia*, by Ian Falconer (New York: NY: Atheneum Books, 2004), with my kids.

2. I draw, here, on Todd McGowan's *Out of Time: Desire in Atemporal Cinema* (Minneapolis, MN: University of Minnesota Press, 2011).

3. Slavoj Žižek, *The Sublime Object of Ideology* (New York: Verso, 1989), 6.

4. Todd McGowan, *Emancipation after Hegel: Achieving a Contradictory Revolution* (New York: Columbia University Press, 2019).

5. Benjamin Noys, *The Persistence of the Negative: A Critique of Contemporary Continental Theory* (Edinburgh: Edinburgh University Press, 2010).

6. Slavoj Žižek, *Organs without Bodies: On Deleuze and Consequences* (New York: Routledge, 2004), 60.

7. Žižek, *Organs without Bodies*, 61.

8. Noys, *The Persistence of the Negative*, 13.

9. This includes the pioneering work of Jodi Dean, as well as newcomers to this field (some of whom who already have influential bodies of work) such as Clint Burnham, Svitlana Matviyenko, Jacob Johansen, Anna Kornbluh, and others. See, for instance, Clint Burnham, *Does the Internet Have an Unconscious? Slavoj Žižek and Digital Culture* (New York: Bloomsbury, 2018); Nick Dyer-Witheford and Svitlana Matviyenko, *Cyberwar and Revolution: Digital Subterfuge in Global Capitalism* (Minneapolis, MN: University of Minnesota Press, 2019); Jacob Johansen, *Psychoanalysis and Digital Culture: Audiences, Social Media, and Big Data* (New York: Routledge, 2019); and Anna Kornbluh, *The Order of Forms: Realism, Formalism, and Social Space* (Chicago, IL: University of Chicago Press, 2019).

10. Andrew Culp, *Dark Deleuze* (Minneapolis, MN: University of Minnesota Press, 2016), 48.

11. I owe this insight to Clint Burnham.

12. Michael Hardt and Antonio Negri, *Assembly* (Oxford: Oxford University

Press, 2018), 107. Subsequent references to Hardt and Negri in this chapter will be made using in-text citations.

13. Byung-Chul Han, *Psycho-Politics: Neoliberalism and New Technologies of Power*, translated by Erik Butler (New York: Verso, 2017), 5.

14. Han, *Psycho-Politics*, 5.

15. Bernard Stiegler, *The Automatic Society: The Future of Work*, translated by Daniel Ross (Cambridge, MA: Polity, 2017); Benjamin H. Bratton, *The Stack: On Software and Sovereignty* (Cambridge, MA: MIT Press, 2016).

16. Nina Power, "Digital Democracy?" In Leo Panitch and Greg Albo, eds, *Socialist Register 2018: Rethinking Democracy* (New York: Monthly Review Press, 2017), 175.

17. Power, "Digital Democracy?," 182–83.

18. Christian Fuchs, *OccupyMedia!: The Occupy Movement and Social Media in Crisis Capitalism* (Winchester, UK: Zero Books, 2014), 161.

19. Christian Fuchs, "Appropriation of Digital Machines and Appropriation of Fixed Capital as the Real Appropriation of Social Being: Reflections on Toni Negri's Chapter." In David Chandler and Christian Fuchs, eds, *Digital Objects, Digital Subjects: Interdisciplinary Perspectives on Capitalism, Labour and Politics in the Age of Big Data* (London: University of Westminster Press, 2019).

20. Louis Althusser, *On the Reproduction of Capitalism: Ideology and Ideological State Apparatuses*, translated by G.M. Goshgarian (New York: Verso, 2014), 59–68.

21. McGowan, *Emancipation after Hegel*.

Index

Page numbers in *italics* refer to figures.

YouTube, 145, 152

Zemeckis, Robert: *Back to the Future*
(film), 7
Žižek, Slavoj, 9–11, 25–33, 38, 54, 64–67,
94, 157, 163, 167, 171–77, 180–81,
185; on the class struggle, 29, 109; on
the crisis in interpretation of postmodernity, 87; on ideology, 29, 32,
70, 76–77, 118, 132; on the Lacanian
subject, 29; on the parallax gap, 111

WORKS: *First as Tragedy, Then as Farce*,
35, 37; *For They Know Not What They
Do*, 30–32, 172, 174; *Tarrying with the
Negative*, 172; *The Sublime Object of
Ideology*, 180–81; *The Ticklish Subject*,
31, 66
Zuckerberg, Mark, 57, 114, 129,
212n36
Zupančič, Alenka, 25, 28, 171–74, 176–
77, 180; *What Is Sex?*, 163